ROUTLEDGE LIBRARY EDITIONS:
CURRICULUM

Volume 32

THE ROLE OF EVALUATORS IN CURRICULUM DEVELOPMENT

THE ROLE OF EVALUATORS IN CURRICULUM DEVELOPMENT

Edited by
PINCHAS TAMIR

LONDON AND NEW YORK

First published in 1985 by Croom Helm

This edition first published in 2019
by Routledge
2 Park Square, Milton Park, Abingdon, Oxon OX14 4RN

and by Routledge
711 Third Avenue, New York, NY 10017

Routledge is an imprint of the Taylor & Francis Group, an informa business

British Library Cataloguing in Publication Data
A catalogue record for this book is available from the British Library

ISBN: 978-1-138-31956-1 (Set)
ISBN: 978-0-429-45387-8 (Set) (ebk)
ISBN: 978-1-138-31940-0 (Volume 32) (hbk)
ISBN: 978-1-138-32202-8 (Volume 32) (pbk)
ISBN: 978-0-429-45396-0 (Volume 32) (ebk)

THE ROLE OF EVALUATORS IN CURRICULUM DEVELOPMENT

EDITED BY PINCHAS TAMIR

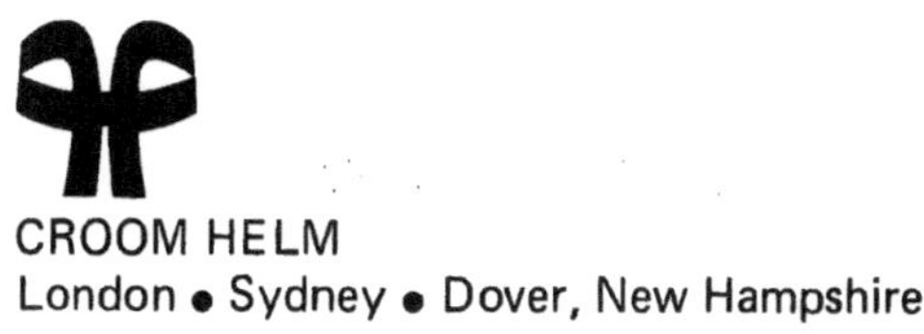

CROOM HELM
London • Sydney • Dover, New Hampshire

Croom Helm Ltd, Provident House, Burrell Row,
Beckenham, Kent BR3 1AT

Croom Helm Australia Pty Ltd, First Floor,
139 King Street, Sydney, NSW 2001, Australia

British Library Cataloguing in Publication Data

The Role of evaluators in curriculum development.
1. Science–Study and teaching
2. Curriculum evaluation
I. Tamir, Pinchas
507'.1 Q181

ISBN 0-7099-2470-4

Croom Helm, 51 Washington Street, Dover,
New Hampshire, 03820 USA

Library of Congress Cataloging in Publication Data

Main entry under title:

The Role of evaluators in curriculum development.

Includes index.
1. Curriculum planning – Addresses, essays, lectures.
2. Curriculum evaluation – Addresses, essays, lectures.
3. Curriculum consultants – Addresses, essays, lectures.
I. Tamir, Pinchas, 1928-
LB1570.R64 1984 375'.001 84-17610
ISBN 0-7099-2470-4

Printed and bound in Great Britain by
Biddles Ltd, Guildford and King's Lynn

CONTENTS

FIGURES AND TABLES

Figures

Tables

ACKNOWLEDGEMENTS

The organizing committee would like to acknowledge the support of the following:

Bar Ilan University, Ramat Gan
Ben Gurion University, Bee Sheva and Sdeh Boker
Haifa University
Hebrew University, Jerusalem
Israel Ministry of Education and Culture
Technion, Haifa
Weizmann Institute of Science, Rehovot

1. THE POTENTIAL AND ACTUAL ROLES OF EVALUATORS IN CURRICULUM DEVELOPMENT

P. Tamir

The Changing Role of Evaluation in Curriculum Development

When curriculum reform in science education was launched, together with Sputnik, in the late 1950s, the field of curriculum evaluation was practically non-existent. As observed by one evaluator at the time,

> Nearly all the science curriculum reform groups have faced the problem of evaluating student achievement. Most have turned to professional test development agencies for assistance. As might be expected, traditional achievement testing procedures were adapted to the new courses. [Yet] the problem of assessing student progress toward the distinctive goals of the new curricula is not a simple one (Heath, 1964).

This problem of matching evaluation of students' achievement to the objectives of the program had been recognized and dealt with much earlier by Tyler (1949) who had identified four major components in the curriculum development process. He presented these components in the form of 'four fundamental questions which must be answered in developing any curriculum and plan of instruction. These are:

> 1. What educational purposes should the school seek to attain?
> 2. What educational experiences can be provided that are likely to attain these purposes?
> 3. How can these educational experiences be effectively organized?
> 4. How can we determine whether these

purposes are being attained?'

Tyler's approach as described in his famous book Basic Principles of Curriculum and Instruction has become a model for curriculum development and evaluation even though the model was intended for a staff of a particular school who deliberate, plan, teach and evaluate their own courses.

The reform movement with its gigantic national dimensions, its 'center to circumference' mode of operation and its naïve assumptions about problems and issues related to the introduction of change in rather conservative educational systems, has not considered realistically the vast differences between its mission and that described by Tyler. It has taken years to develop and create modes of operation in terms of development, implementation and evaluation which would fit the needs of national curriculum projects. Early evaluation tended to concentrate on the measurement of outcomes and treated the classroom and the school as 'black boxes'. The realization that the process of implementation, namely the process of putting ideas and materials which embody these ideas into practice, may be the most crucial element in determining the success of curricular innovations, is reflected by a number of trends related to evaluation:

1. Increased emphasis on evaluatin of transactions to find what is actually going on in the classroom. Special classroom observation systems aimed at the assessment of classroom events and behaviours have been developed and used in thousands of studies.

2. Ethnographic methods have been borrowed from anthropology and used as a basis for new approaches known as 'responsive', 'illuminative' or 'case studies' which tend to be less limited, more open and more easily communicable than the more formal methods based on quantitative measurements of predetermined objectives.

3. It has become increasingly clear that successful implementation of a new curriculum depends, to a large extent, on better understanding of the potential and limitations inherent in the curriculum materials. Shulman and Tamir (1973) have alluded to this matter as follows:

> It is often taken for granted that a curriculum always teaches as advertised even if it does not attain all the results it may claim. When the publicity announces 'a ten transistor

> radio that reproduces sound like a Fisher receiver' we would at least expect to find the number of transistors as advertised, even if the sound fidelity falls somewhat short of the claims. Herron (and many others later on) has demonstrated that we had better count our curricular transistors.

Indeed the last decade has envisaged the development of materials or content analysis schemes aimed at finding out, on the one hand, to what extent do the materials reflect the declared intents, and on the other hand, perhaps even more importantly, what is the potential of the materials, what uses can be made of them, how they fit local needs, are they amenable to adaptation, etc?

4. While in the early 1960s the in-house evaluator was practically non-existent, more and more curriculum workers have become proponents of in-house evaluators who are regular or special members of the curriculum development teams. Their different roles will be discussed later.

5. Curriculum evaluation has become a respectable field of theory and action. Professional journals dealing either with evaluation or with curriculum regularly publish studies dealing with curriculum evaluation. A number of books dealing with evaluation devote considerable space to curriculum evaluation (e.g. Stenhouse, 1975; Lewy, 1977; Tamir _et al_.,1979; Lewy and Nvo,1981; Lewy and Kugelmas,1981).

One of these books deals with evaluation roles in education (Lewy and Nvo, 1981). Each chapter of the book is devoted to a particular role evaluation fulfils in various educational contexts. The following roles are included: diagnosis, selection, certifying, motivation, student assessment, improving teaching skills, assessing the learning process, educational accountability, measuring teacher performance, evaluating learning materials, implementation evaluation, increasing influence on decision making, school environment, evaluating the family, organizational climate, cost analysis and need assessment.

Certainly most, perhaps all, of the above can be related to curriculum evaluation. Yet curriculum evaluation has become a specialized field. The purpose of this chapter, as well as that of the rest of the book, is to focus on the inter-relationship between evaluation and curriculum development. It seeks to identify the roles that evaluators can play and have played in the context of curriculum development and their impact on the process of curriculum development.

Frameworks of Curriculum Development

Curriculum evaluation depends on the framework and context of curriculum development and implementation.

Six frameworks have been identified. The first five are presented in a historical-chronological order. The sixth has always been in existence, but has gained special importance more recently as national funding for curriculum development has been shrinking.

1. School-based curriculum development (e.g. Tyler, 1949).

2. Development by national curriculum study organizations such as the School Mathematics Study Group (SMSG), the Biological Science Curriculum Study (BSCS), the Physical Science Study Committee (PSSC), and the Chemistry Education Materials Study (CHEM Study) in the USA or the Nuffield Foundation science projects in the UK. This has been the dominant framework in the 1960s. Usually a project operates for several years (up to five) as a temporary independent organization and, having completed its mission, the project as such is abolished. Some of the projects were affiliated to universities (e.g. Harvard Project Physics at Harvard University) and others to organizations such as the Schools Council in the UK or the Curriculum Development Center (CDC) in Cambridge, Mass., USA.

3. Development within the framework of national curriculum development centres that operate as semi-independent organizations established as permanent organizations for continuous development, usually by ministries of education (e.g. the Curriculum Development Center in Israel, the Curriculum Development Center in Bangkok, or the Curriculum Development Centres in Scotland).

4. Development by teams operating in teaching centres located in universities (e.g. Learning Research and Development Center, the University of Pittsburgh or the Israel Science Teaching Center, Hebrew University, Jerusalem). Here too, as in item 3 above, the projects tend to be continuous and some have lasted for more than ten years.

5. Development by local regional teams consisting mainly of teachers but guided by curriculum development experts (e.g. Sabar and Shafriri, 1979).

6. Development with support of commercial

publishers who engage relatively small teams in curriculum development over many years (e.g. Space, Time, Earth and Matter (STEM) developed by Addison Wesley in the USA).

There are different alternatives for evaluation under each framework. Yet there are some differences between these frameworks which affect the problems and strategies of evaluation to be used to such an extent that it would be justified to discuss them separately.

Before dealing with each of the above frameworks we offer a general discussion on the relationship between curriculum development and evaluation.

Evaluation and Curriculum Development

We define evaluation as a systematic collection, analysis and reporting of information related to a specific programme or curricular innovation by structured and less structured approaches, using formal and informal means, for the purpose of facilitating decision making. In this chapter we intend to focus on decisions which affect curriculum development broadly conceived. This includes the following four stages: initiation, planning, materials development and implementation. The inter-relationships among these stages as well as relationships with evaluation and research are presented in Figure 1.1.*

As may be seen in the Figure, the starting point is a felt need and/or a sense of dissatisfaction. These feelings may accompany educators and teachers in their work or may represent outside criticism which reflects the socio-political context. Criticism of the curricula, especially of the learning material intended for the population of disadvantaged students is voiced, for example, mainly by the teachers who experience daily the difficulties of implementing it and have come to the realization that the existing material is inappropriate for their students. Criticism of the curricula in different sciences, on the other hand, often comes from scientists who perceive their obsolescence and incompatibility with scientific developments. The initial stage of curriculum development is also influenced by awareness of innovations introduced by outside forces, and, most significantly, by research and evaluation such as need assessment

* The model and many of the definitions that follow are based on Eden and Tamir, 1979.

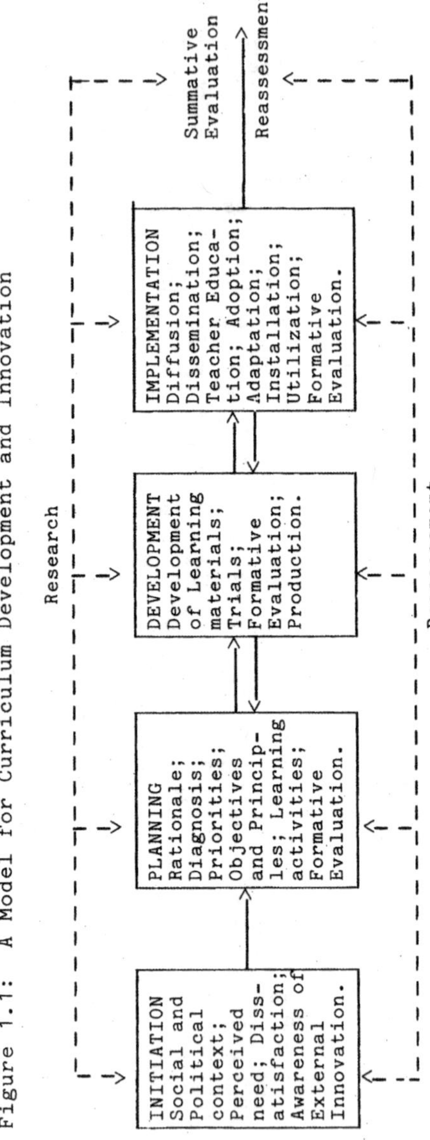

Figure 1.1: A Model for Curriculum Development and Innovation

or the results of national assessment or those of evaluation of currently used curricula.

The next stage is the planning of a curriculum, which includes the rationale, objectives, learning materials, and the relevant formative evaluation. The development of curriculum materials includes, in most cases, trials and formative evaluation and is performed by a team equipped with the necessary resources and skills. The final product of this stage is a package of instructional materials such as texts, guides and learning aids, which are now ready for implementation.

The components of implementation as presented in the model are defined below. Diffusion is the spread of information about an innovation mainly through existing networks of communication, while dissemination refers to planned strategies and actions to convey ideas and materials which embody them to the users. Teachers' education includes pre-service and in-service training of teachers, as well as the training of heads of departments and other kinds of educators who may be involved in implementation, for example, laboratory technicians. Adoption refers to the user's decision to use a particular innovation which is followed by the actual utilization of the materials in the classroom. Adaptation is the modification and adjustment of an innovation to meet the local needs of the students, teachers, school system and society. On the national level, adaptation refers to the selection and adjustment of a programme developed in one country by other countries; whereas on the classroom level it involves modifications guided by the specific needs of the students and their teachers. The scope of adaptation depends on the professional autonomy of the teacher: projects may prepare modular units which enable teachers to select materials and organize them into a programme suitable for the needs of their students. At a more advanced level, teachers may modify prepared materials and develop their own as part of the programme. Installation refers to the building of the framework and forming the conditions for the introduction of an innovation and its utilization in schools. On the local level, it includes the securing of learning materials and equipment, timetables, manpower, etc. On the central level, installation means the building of a support system. A support system is a centrally planned network to assist the user in utilization of an innovation by providing consultation, guidance, in-service training, opportunities for exchange of experiences, resources and supply centres. Utilization refers to the actual use of the innovation in the classroom. It embodies the interactions between students, teacher and materials and serves as the ultimate criterion of implementation. As suggested by Fullan and Pomfret (1977) two modes of utilization may be identified: fidelity and mutual adaptation. By fidelity we mean the use of a particular curriculum in a way which corresponds to the intentions of the developers; while mutual adaptation refers to the process of modifying and further developing the materials to meet local needs. It is important to note that no one best answer can be provided regarding the superiority of the fidelity or the adaptive mode. It may be useful to look upon these modes as extremes of a continuum. It is up to the teacher to decide which point on this continuum will best meet their particular needs and preferences. Usually less experienced teachers may profit by using a high level of fidelity. More experience and a higher level of self-confidence are often associated with more success in employing modifications. Recognition of this is especially important for evaluators who carry out formative evaluation, the aim of which is to improve implementation and to provide feedback relevant to the planning and development stages.

The cycle is concluded with summative evaluation by which the achievements of the new programme are examined and the groundwork is laid for re-assessment, which provides useful feedback relevant to each of the four major processes and which, eventually, may turn the whole wheel of curricular activity toward a 'second generation' curriculum. Overarching the entire mode, research is conceived as a key for creating new ideas, novel approaches, more efficient procedures and, most importantly, better and more profound understanding of the processes and the factors which influence them.

Evaluation in Different Development Frameworks

School-based curriculum development. As mentioned above, Tyler's model of curriculum development pertains to school-based development in which teachers initiate, plan, develop, implement and evaluate the programme. For the purpose of evaluation, teachers may benefit by seeking advice and assistance from evaluation specialists, especially in creating appropriate testing situations and in designing assessment instruments in a valid, reliable and readily usable form. Although best known for suggesting that evaluation is 'the process of determining to what extent the educational objectives are actually being realized by the program of curriculum and instruction' (Tyler, 1949, pp. 105-6), his conception of evaluation even 40 years ago has been much more comprehensive and certainly cannot be regarded in today's terminology just as summative evaluation.

Tyler suggests that evaluation and curriculum must be closely integrated in the continuous cycle of curriculum planning and development: 'as materials and procedures are developed, they are tried out, their results appraised, their inadequacies identified, suggested improvement indicated, there is replanning, redevelopment and then reappraisal' (ibid., p. 123). The procedures to be followed are clearly spelled out as follows:

1. Definition of objectives.
2. Creating situations which allow and encourage students to express the type of behaviour we are trying to appraise.
3. Selecting and/or designing appropriate evaluation instruments.
4. Collecting the pertinent evaluation data.
5. Analyzing and interpreting the results in terms of the stated objectives.
6. Formulating suggestions and recommendations based on the results.

While Tyler's model has obvious merits for school-based curriculum development, even there it suffers from serious weaknesses especially with regard to the appraisal of transactions, namely the interaction of materials, students and teachers at the classroom level. It focuses on the measurement of outcomes and does not pay enough attention to classroom and the school experiences. Even the learning materials are considered only in so far as they succeed or fail to bring about certain achievements, but there is no indication of direct appraisal of the materials as such by, for example, content analysis.

It may be seen that, even when the school is the unit of curriculum revision, the evaluation procedures suggested by Tyler are insufficient. It is certainly the case, when curriculum development on a regional or national level becomes our focus, and implementation, the interphase between development and usage, becomes crucial, that the deficiences of Tyler's model enlarge and become much more evident.

The need to employ multiple criteria has been convincingly argued by Scriven (1967), who points out that evaluation of any entity should be performed according to a weighted series of criteria, the weight of each being determined by the specific interests in the case. Stake (1967) has developed a useful framework which extends the role of programme evaluation beyond the measurement of outcomes to include antecedents and transactions and, most importantly, the various interactions which occur at each stage as well as interactions between the factors which operate at the different stages.

In the 1970s a revival of school-based development and evaluation was observed; this time, however, with a major focus on classroom transactions (Duckworth, 1970; Harlen _et al_., 1977). As classroom transactions are conceived as a major component of a curriculum, it should not be surprising that some evaluators see

> the collection of information about pupils' progress, or lack of it [as a means for] making decisions as to how to devise or adapt learning experiences to suit the pupils' needs. ... The kind of decision which will be affected by this information concerns the nature and degree of help to give individuals, the organization of the class and of the materials, the choice of materials and of examples, the feedback of the pupils, the interaction allowed between pupils and so on. These are all matters which the individual teacher has to decide for him or herself, whether or not other curriculum decisions are also made by the teacher (Harlen, 1981, p. 194).

One may observe that, while Tyler deals with a curriculum which has been entirely developed by the school staff, Harlen's suggestions are equally valid for teachers who teach a school-based curriculum as for those who teach a nationally developed curriculum, since in both cases the focus is on the curriculum at the classroom level. Since 'mutual adaptation' rather than 'fidelity' (Fullan and Pomfret, 1977) is the preferred mode of operation under most circumstances, the evaluation community has to face the responsibility of helping the teacher in conducting the kind of evaluation that will provide a sound basis for his/her adaptation decisions.

It may be appropriate to end this section by suggesting that one of the major roles of curriculum developers at any level (local, regional, national) is to take into account the role of teachers as evaluators and to consider the development of adequate assessment measures and procedures as their responsibility, much as they consider the development of any other component of the curriculum package.

National Curriculum Study Projects

In the early 1960s national curriculum study projects - such as the PSSC, CHEM Study and the BSCS at the senior high school level or Science A Process Approach (SAPA) and the Elementary Science Study (ESS) at the elementary school level - employed with some variations the evaluation model and procedures advocated by Tyler as described above. Gradually, however, it has been found that this model does not meet the demands of national projects such as those just mentioned. Grobman in Chapter 2 presents the evaluation story of the BSCS. Some projects, such as the PSSC or the CHEM Study,have devoted much less attention than the BSCS to evaluation. Quite extensive evaluation studies were carried out by some of the British projects such as the Nuffield High School Biology (e.g. Kelly, 1970) or Science 5-13 (Harlen, 1975). The Harvard Project Physics (HPP) in the USA which represents a second generation of curriculum development in that country, deserves special consideration with regard to its evaluation. Unlike the first generation high school science projects, HPP included evaluation right from its outset as an important component of the curriculum development process. It devoted a lot of expertise, time and effort to the design of innovative evaluation instruments; it succeeded in carrying out a controlled evaluation study employing a true experimental design (see, for example, Welch and Walberg, 1972).

Generally, evaluation projects located at universities, whether short-term or continuous, have tended to integrate research with evaluation. Rather than focusing on a series of small-scale evaluation activities following standard procedures, they have tended to employ innovative procedures, to deal with a variety of outcome variables in addition to cognitive achievement, and to develop innovative evaluation instruments.

Typically, the results of research-oriented evaluation studies were published in the professional literature and certainly added interesting and important dimensions to our knowledge about curriculum development and implementation. Unfortunately, the direct impact of these evaluations on decision making has not been documented. The writer suspects that in many cases there has been no such direct impact simply because most information became available too late.

The success of HPP in employing a true experimental design is the exception rather than the rule. It was possible to employ this design as well as a variety of comprehensive evaluation activities as a result of the great interest of the whole HPP team in research and evaluation. Recently the desirability of providing evaluators with the necessary conditions to carry out meaningful evaluation has been pushed to an extreme by Davis (1981), who suggests that the evaluator should actually 'run the show'. He developed a strategy called 'Standardised Evaluation' in which:

1. Programs with relatively clear-cut goals and operating procedures are selected for evaluation.
2. An evaluation expert is responsible for a research framework which includes both operation and evaluation of the program.
3. The program is implemented in a standard form. That is the field condition, the personnel and operation represent a reasonable approximation of optimal implementation according to the conception underlying the program.
4. Schools and classes are selected for participation in accordance with their willingness to comply with the demands of the research design.
5. The research design approximates laboratory models in terms of selection to treatment, monitoring of program implementation, repeated measurement of outcomes and control and monitoring of alternative treatments.
6. The results of the evaluation provide a standard for evaluating the program in normal field settings (ibid., p. 167).

It is interesting to note the enormous change

from the early 1960s, when evaluators hardly managed to gain any credibility among curriculum developers, to the early 1980s when some evaluators actually believe that they should be allowed to 'take over' the whole process. Davis' suggestion is a result of serious dissatisfaction with the quality and credibility of many evaluation studies, especially those pertaining to national educational projects, which do not deal directly with the regular school curriculum and for which norms and criteria of success or failure are often not available. It should be realized, however, that upon completion of such standardized evaluation, many problems of curriculum development and implementation will remain. In the case where the programme fails under the optimal conditions the verdict appears to be quite clear: either abandon or revise it. In the case of success, whether full or partial, the data would indicate that the programme may be worth trying on a larger scale, attempting to employ strategies and materials which were found promising in the standardized experiment. One should certainly be prepared to discover that many of the operations would not resemble those found in the early experiment. In other words, Davis' suggestion may be feasible and even desirable in certain cases, but at best should not be regarded as more than the first in a series of evaluation studies.

Davis has pointed out the crucial importance of implementation. This stage in curriculum development has received little attention in Tyler's model. Fullan (1981) and Tamir (1981) provide an overview of problems and issues concerning evaluation of curriculum implementation. Tamir (1981) suggests the following mapping sentence:

	A: <u>Components</u>
Implementation evaluation is a systematic collection, analysis and reporting of information related to a specific curriculum on	[Dissemination Diffusion Teacher education Adoption Adaptation Installation Utilization]

ROLES OF EVALUATORS IN CURRICULUM DEVELOPMENT

in relation to	B: Determinants		
	[Characteristics of the curriculum Strategies of implementation Characteristics of the adapters Characteristics of social, political, cultural context]		
from the point of view of	C: Levels of use	and	D: Degrees of use
	[Non-use Orientation Preparation Mechanical use Routine use Refinement Integration Renewal]		[Non-use Partial use Regular use Integrative use]
on the basis of	E: Data	by	F: Structure
	[Judgments Observations Questionnaires Interviews Examinations Other]		[Unstructured Partially-structured Structured]
mean	G: Mode of summary	for the	H: Role
summarized in	[Qualitative Quantitative]	purpose of making decisions about	[Selecting elements Modifying Qualifying the use]
of the programme when	I: Stages		
	[Implementation Planning Development]	is carried out.	

One may define a particular evaluation study by reflecting on a single line from the nine facets appearing in the mapping sentence. Whether single or multiple lines are chosen, it is always necessary to complement single line evaluations by the study of interactions.

Two other foci of curriculum evaluation of

national programmes are content analysis of curriculum materials and evaluation conducted specifically for the purpose of making decisions about adaptations. We have briefly discussed - under trends related to evaluation - the role of content analysis. Some of the approaches and strategies of content analysis are described by Ben Peretz (1977) and Tamir (1983). As to evaluation for the purpose of making decisions about adaptations, the reader is referred to Blum (1981) who presents a very useful checklist which covers most of the aspects that one has to consider in making decisions about the plausibility and desirability of adaptations.

Non University/National Curriculum Development Centres

Evaluation conducted under the auspices of national curriculum development centres resembles in many ways that described with regard to national curriculum projects. The two differ, however, in two significant aspects:

1. While national projects exist and are funded for 3-5 years, national curriculum centres are permanent organizations which are capable of developing long-term plans, employ standardized procedures and build continuously on their cumulative experience.

2. Curriculum centres are usually run by ministries of education and are not attached to universities. This results in a more practical and decision-oriented approach in curriculum centres, as opposed to a more theoretical and research-oriented approach in projects located in universities and run by university staff. The latter also tend to publish much more in professional educational journals.

Lewy's case study and the overview of his chapter present a comprehensive account of the potential and actual evaluation roles and procedures which have characterized evaluation in national curriculum development centres.

National Curriculum Development Centres in Universities

Examples of national curriculum development centres located in and affiliated to universities are the Learning Research and Development Center (LRDC) at the University of Pittsburgh, the Israel Science Teaching Center (ISTC) affiliated to The Hebrew

University of Jerusalem, the Weizmann Institute of Science, Rehovot and Tel Aviv University. These centres resemble non-university national curriculum centres in being permanent organizations which are capable of long-term planning, evaluation and research. They resemble other university-affiliated projects in their academic setting, in their greater dependence on the choices and expertise of available academic staff, as well as in their greater research and publishing orientation.

The essence of the LRDC strategy is to incorporate the work of individuals from diverse backgrounds who are working on problems in their own discipline areas (i.e. psychology, sociology, philosophy, anthropology) into an overall programme of evaluative research. This strategy is offered as an alternative to the traditional in-house one-shot studies conducted by a single team of evaluators. The emphasis in this strategy is for researchers to satisfy themselves with regard to the scientific excellence of their work and to seek answers to questions which they generate, rather than to attempt to second-guess the consumers' questions. Admittedly, there is no assurance that the answers to a collection of questions generated by different researchers will provide adequate information about the value of the programme. Nevertheless, Leinhardt presents convincing examples of studies conducted under this framework which provided useful information to consumers about the nature of the programme, the soundness of the formative evaluation (which was conducted mainly by the curriculum developers) and the effects of the programme on the learners and on the learning environment. Under this framework the role of the evaluator is to recruit researchers, to coordinate their work and to see that the results are presented in a usable form (Leinhardt, 1977).

The role of evaluators at the ISTC has been different from that of their colleagues in LRDC. Owing to the close relationship between developers and evaluators, the problems and issues selected for evaluation reflected real concerns evolving from the processes of development and implementation. The fact that ISTC has been operating in a university environment resulted in a continuous flow of evaluation studies which have actually helped in decision making but, at the same time, have become well known all over the world both for their methodology and for their findings. A detailed account of one ISTC project, namely the High School Biology

Project (IHBP) is presented elsewhere in this book (Chapter 8).

Regional Curriculum Development

Usually very little formal evaluation is conducted in the context of regional curriculum development, mainly because the teachers who take part are volunteers whose interests lie in curriculum development and implementation and who tend to shy away from evaluation. Even when guidance of experts is available many teachers feel threatened by or do not believe in evaluation (Leithwood, Wilson and Marshall, 1981).

These authors propose a series of strategies to promote evaluation within the context of the project which will involve the project team in a way which would enhance the use of evaluation data.

Sabar and Shafriri (1979) report on an informal formative evaluation. Dickman (1981) reports on an evaluation study related to regional curriculum development in which an eclectic use of quantitative as well as qualitative evaluation strategies was found to be useful in decision making and in the revision of materials. If the trend towards more regional curriculum development is to continue, more attention would have to be given to curriculum evaluation under these circumstances.

Commercial Publishers

Commercial publishers have not usually employed systematic evaluation studies as a means of guiding the development and implementation of curriculum materials. Nevertheless many commercial publishers do have evaluation activities linked to their market research. This kind of evaluation is based on the judgement of experts in the field. Once the textbooks are published, they also promote feedback from teachers and others, which influences their revised editions. Most publishers select their authors on the basis of their professional reputation and expertise. These authors are usually required to run in-service workshops for teachers either in teachers' conferences or in schools. These workshops provide important feedback. Data collected on the dissemination and adoption of curriculum materials are in themselves important means of evaluation which are carefully considered by most publishers.

ROLES OF EVALUATORS IN CURRICULUM DEVELOPMENT

The Evolving Roles of Evaluators - Overview of Case Studies

Review of the literature reveals a lot of curriculum evaluation studies but, by and large, the focus of these studies is on the information collected, its meaning and usefulness for clients and consumers (potential and/or actual) of the curriculum, as well as on research methodology. Very few studies focus on the evaluators; even those studies that deal with constraints related to the work of the evaluators do not deal systematically with the roles of evaluators in curriculum development.

The importance of the evaluators, their background, interests, ideology, experience and expertise on the nature of the evaluation studies they conduct has not received adequate attention. While a few evaluation studies have been constructed to provide answers to specific questions raised by the clients, in most cases evaluators are approached with a general request to evaluate a particular programme. It is usually assumed that the evaluators know how to do their job, and this includes the identification of problems as well as the choice of methodology. In some cases different evaluators, each known for his general preferences (e.g. experimental-quantitative as opposed to naturalistic-qualitative) are asked to evaluate a particular programme, so that results of different approaches may be available and operate as a triangulation, which supposedly provides richer information of a high explanatory power, on the basis of which sound decisions can be made.

In the case studies which follow in this book, a number of evaluators from different countries describe projects in which they were or have been involved, highlighting the points of view and the concerns of the evaluators. While each author tells the story in his/her own manner and style, all have had in front of them a request to relate to the following:

1. The structure of the project and the way evaluation was employed within that structure.
2. Personal characteristics of evaluators, their personal and formal relations with members of the curriculum development team, as related to the evaluation process.
3. Stages at which evaluation was conducted.

How were these stages determined?
4. Major problems and issues dealt with by the evaluation.
5. Target population and sample.
6. Methodology: experimental, naturalistic, action research, etc., nature of data, target population, methods of analysis, reporting.
7. The impact of evaluation on decision making regarding:
(a) curriculum development,
(b) curriculum implementation and
(c) other decisions - with concrete examples.
8. Political and social constraints and pressures in relation to the evaluation.
9. The extent to which evaluation moved on towards research (i.e. dealing with issues which did not bear directly on the programme under evaluation).
10. General conclusions and recommendations based on their experience.

The authors were not expected to discuss each of the ten aspects separately, but rather to bear them in mind without interrupting the natural flow of their individual stories. With the exception of _Lewy_ which presents a more general view, all chapters deal with the evaluation of science curricula.

Hulda Grobman, a professor of education, who happened to be married to the Director of the Biological Science Curriculum Study (BSCS), tells an interesting story which illustrates the problems she had to face being in a very delicate situation, both personally and professionally. Although the BSCS has been one of the leading national curriculum development projects in the USA, the entire story of its evaluation has not been told before, certainly not from the point of view of the person who was involved in the action and held the day-to-day responsibility in that area.

Fraser gives the hitherto unpublished account of the formative evaluation of the Australian Science Education Project (ASEP) which he considers to be 'among the most comprehensive employed in any Australian curriculum venture'. He presents useful concrete examples, indicates the potential benefits of the procedures employed, but, as well, uncovers the constraints and limitations.

Bond, _Dynan_, _Parker_ _and_ _Ryan_ describe an

evaluation study of an innovative Physical Science course in Western Australia. This is an example of a project which was supported by the Department of Education and the implications of this situation are highlighted.

The two chapters which deal with the Scottish Integrated Science program reflect two vastly different approaches. The fact that both chapters focus on the same curriculum helps to sharpen these fundamental differences. While Kellington and Mitchell have attempted to respond to the needs of the curriculum developers and sponsors - utilizing traditional evaluation strategies, Brown's chapter presents a relatively novel approach to evaluation in which the evaluator plays a much more sophisticated role - attempting to uncover the hidden agenda of curriculum development and implementation.

Elliott is focusing on a teacher education curriculum and tries to justify his approach by illustrating the importance of conceptualization for this kind of evaluation.

Tamir describes the evaluation of the Israeli High School Biology Project as an example of ongoing evaluation of a curriculum development project affiliated with a university.

Lastly Lewy's chapter, unlike the previous ones, does not deal with one particular project, but instead describes the mode of operation and the roles played by an evaluation unit which is responsible for evaluation of many projects in a national curriculum centre.

In the last chapter the Editor presents an overview of the case studies included in the book and attempts to identify the specific roles played by the evaluators in these studies. The result is a list of roles of curriculum evaluators which may be useful in illustrating the potential of evaluation in improving and in guiding curriculum development and evaluation.

REFERENCES

Ben Peretz, M. (1977) 'Comparative Analysis of Several Curricula in Biology Taught in Israeli High Schools: Theoretical and Practical Deliberations in Curriculum Planning.' Unpublished PhD Dissertation, Hebrew University, Jerusalem

Blum, A. (1981) 'Development of Integrated Science Curriculum Information Scheme', Science

Education, 5, 1-15
Davis, D.J. (1981) 'Standardized Evaluation of Educational Programs', in A. Lewy and S. Kugelmass, Decision Oriented Evaluation in Education, Philadelphia-Rehovot, International Science Services, pp. 155-68
Dickman, D. (1981) Initiation and Evaluation of Ideas: Decentralized Curriculum Development. Unpublished PhD Dissertation, Tel Aviv University
Duckworth, E. (1970) Evaluation of the African Primary Science Program, Educational Development Center, Newton, Mass
Eden, S. and Tamir, P. (1979) 'Curriculum Implementation - Retrospect and Prospect', in P. Tamir et al. (eds.), Curriculum Implementation and Its Relationship to Curriculum Development in Science, Israel Science Teaching Center, Hebrew University, Jerusalem, pp. 449-60
Fullan, M. (1981) 'The Relationship between Implementation and Evaluation', in A. Lewy and D. Nvo (eds.), Evaluation Roles in Education, Gordon and Breach, London, 309-40
Fullan, M. and Pomfret, A. (1977) 'Research in Curriculum and Instruction Implementation', Review of Educational Research, 47, 335-97
Harlen, W. (1975) Science 5/13 Formative Evaluation, Macmillan, London
Harlen, W., Darwin, A. and Murphy, M. (1977) Match and Mismatch, Oliver & Boyd, London
Harlen, W. (1981) 'The Role of Evaluation in Teaching', in A. Lewy and D. Nvo (eds.), Evaluation Roles in Education, Gordon and Breach, London, pp. 193-212
Heath, R.H. (1964) 'Curriculum Cognition and Educational Measurement'. Educational and Psychological Measurement, 24, 235-53
Kelly, P.J. (1970) 'Implications of Nuffield A Level Biological Science', School Science Review, 52, 272-85
Leinhardt, G. (1977) 'Outcomes of A Strategy for Program Evaluation', Science Education, 61, 1-17
Leithwood, K.A., Wilson, R. and Marshall, A.R. (1981) 'Increasing the Influence of Evaluation Studies on Program Decision Making', in A. Lewy and D. Nvo (eds.), Evaluation Roles in Education, Gordon and Breach, London, pp. 357-84
Lewy, A. and Nvo, D. (1981) Evaluation Roles in Education, Gordon and Breach, London
Lewy, A. and Kugelmass, S. (1981) Decision Oriented

Evaluation in Education, Philadelphia-Rehovot, International Science Services

Sabar, N. and Shafriri, N. (1979) 'Teachers as Curriculum Developers and Implementors', in P. Tamir et al. (eds.), Curriculum Implementation and Its Relationship to Curriculum Development in Science, Israel Science Teaching Center, Hebrew University, Jerusalem, pp. 207-9

Scriven, M. (1967) 'The Methodology of Evaluation', in R.W. Tyler (ed.), Perspectives of Curriculum Evaluation, Rand McNally, Chicago, pp. 39-83

Shulman, L. and Tamir, P. (1973) 'Research on Teaching in the Natural Sciences', in R.M.W. Travers (ed.), Second Handbook of Research on Teaching, Rand McNally, Chicago, pp. 1098-148

Stake, R.E. (1967) 'Countenance of Educational Evaluation', Teachers College Record, 68, 523-40

Stenhouse, L. (1975) An Introduction to Curriculum Research and Development, Heinemann, London

Tamir, P. (1983) Inquiry and the Science Teacher, Science Education, 67, 657-62

Tamir, P., Blum, A., Hofstein, A. and Sabar, N. (eds.), (1979) Curriculum Implementation and Its Relationship to Curriculum Development in Science, Israel Science Teaching Center, Hebrew University, Jerusalem

Tyler, R.W. (1949) Basic Principles of Curriculum and Instruction, University of Chicago Press, Chicago

Welch, W.W. and Walberg, H.J. (1972) 'A National Experiment in Curriculum Evaluation', American Educational Research Journal, 9, 373-83

2. EVALUATION IN THE BIOLOGICAL SCIENCES CURRICULUM STUDY 1958-65

H. Grobman

Introduction

With the assistance of a grant from the NSF, the BSCS was established in 1958 by the American Institute of Biological Sciences (AIBS) and opened offices in Boulder, Colorado in January, 1959 on the host campus, the University of Colorado. The stated purpose of the BSCS was the improvement of high school biology teaching and learning. For the period under consideration in this chapter, 1958-65, the sole funding source for the BSCS work in the United States was the NSF (1). In the United States, biology is usually taught at the tenth-grade level (senior high school - students aged 15-16) and it is taken by most students. Since the intent of the BSCS was to effect major change, the BSCS directed its initial efforts to the tenth-grade level and the initial materials were designed for the average student.

The BSCS did consider the preparation of a series of materials which teachers might use in the development of a course; however, after surveying high school biology teachers through their national professional organization, the decision was made to prepare complete course materials. Since the BSCS Steering Committee felt that there is no single valid approach to teaching biology, three parallel courses were to be prepared for experimental test, each with a different emphasis to determine whether any one was particularly appropriate for use in American schools (the _Blue_, _Green_, and _Yellow Versions_ of _BSCS High School Biology_). As parallel or subsequent projects, the BSCS prepared other materials for other needs; however, the concern of this chapter is with the evaluation of the _Blue_, _Green_, and _Yellow Versions_ of _BSCS High School_

Biology.

STRUCTURE OF THE BSCS AND ITS EVALUATION ACTIVITIES

The policy-making mechanism of the BSCS was a Steering Committee, including biologists and science educators, and during the later years an educational research specialist. Although initially this body was foreseen as an advisory group, it evolved into the policy-making and general oversight agent of the BSCS. The executive officer of the BSCS was the Director, who reported to the AIBS and to the BSCS Steering Committee and to its Chairman. The year-round work of the BSCS was carried on by a small headquarters staff, with additional specialized staff added during the summers, for the period during which intensive writing conferences were scheduled.

The experimental editions of BSCS materials were prepared by teams of writers assigned to each Version, with work on the Version coordinated by a Version Supervisor. The writers were brought together for 6-8 weeks during two successive summers for intensive writing sessions, followed by testing of these experimental editions in the school year following the summer writing session. During the summer writing periods, writers worked in couples, each team including a high school biology teacher and a college or university biologist. Following this two-year trial period, commercial editions were prepared by smaller teams of writers working at other locations for a six-month period.

The full time professional staff of the BSCS included the Director and Assistant Director (both biologists), a Fiscal Officer, a Director of Illustrations, an Editor, and several full time Consultants. The term Consultant was used for much of the professional staff, to obviate problems of relative status, particularly among those members who were on leave from high school and college teaching positions which carried widely varying levels of remuneration. Thus, the listing of much of the professional staff in the BSCS publications did not distinguish among the staff Consultants in any way, and there were no positions labelled Project Evaluator.

With one exception, the Consultants were invited to join the staff for a one-year period, to coordinate work on the trial use that year of BSCS course materials in the experimental classrooms. The remaining Consultant, the present author, was invited to join the permanent staff in 1960 in a public information capacity. During 1960-1, as the work of the BSCS test in the schools progressed, she became interested in the evaluation activities through reports submitted to the BSCS by the external evaluators of the project, Educational Testing Service (ETS). As BSCS field testing progressed, and the locus of the evaluation function shifted from external management of testing to internal control, the evaluation activities of this Consultant increased and she became closely identified with the evaluation programme. Though her evaluation concern was primarily with coordination of the testing programme, for purposes of clarity this Consultant will be referred to here as <u>Project Evaluator</u>, though this was neither her formal designation nor her full time assignment.

Thus the appointment of the coordinator of the testing programme was not the result of specific recruitment for the position but rather by gradual adoption of a role and the accompanying responsibilities; and the role was not a full time one. In today's context this may seem unusual. However, with the possible exception of the School Mathematics Study Group, the BSCS evaluation activities were more extensive than those of the then current NSF-funded projects, and the assignment of an educator to this role was the exception rather than the rule.

While most of the writing on the evaluation activities was done by the Project Evaluator, two or three other Consultants spent all their time on evaluation. Their function was to assist the teachers using materials experimentally, and to keep track of the progress of these teachers through reading their reports and through visits to their classrooms. For the purposes of this chapter, such Consultants will be called <u>Field-Test Consultants</u>.

The BSCS had many committees, some with a policy-making function, others responsible for actual preparation of materials. In 1961, as problems of communication with the external testing agency and questions concerning appropriate direction for the testing of the programme became matters of BSCS concern, a Committee on Evaluation was established, with the BSCS Chairman - an eminent biologist and a member of the writing team - becoming Chairman of the new Committee. This perhaps reflected a way of providing greater support for the Project Evaluator in her efforts in working with the testing agency. This Committee on Evaluation had three sub-committees; Test Construction Sub-Committee, Test Analysis Sub-Committee, and Laboratory Block Test Construction Sub-Committee (2). The appointment of these committees was the beginning of the effort to move the decision making on test policy to the BSCS, with technical assistance from the external testing agency. Thus, the BSCS took over test construction, with technical assistance of an external test agency, and became more self-directing in designing the testing aspects of the evaluation programme.

BACKGROUND OF THE EVALUATORS

At the time the role of Project Evaluator developed, the incumbent was the only member of the regular BSCS professional staff with a doctoral degree in education, and the only one with experience in education research. While her writing experience in professional journals as well as in journalism may have been influential in the initial consideration as Consultant with public information responsibilities, the doctoral degree was probably influential in this appointment since, as wife of the BSCS Director, her credentials had to be impeccable to preclude suggestion of nepotism. The Field-Test Consultants had strong high school biology teaching backgrounds, either through current high school teaching experience or teaching science education at the collegiate level.

All Consultants were participating members of a professional staff that shared in making many policy decisions and had input in virtually all such decisions. The Field-Test Consultants interacted more often and more directly with the experimental school teachers; the Project Evaluator, with the testing agency and the interested publics. All interacted with the writing teams, but the subject matter of those interactions were different. During the summer writing sessions on the student materials, the Field-Test Consultants were members of the writing teams and worked on a continuous basis with the writers. During the revision periods, as each part of the materials was considered, they provided information from the field tests as well as from the external reviewers. They also assisted in teacher training, again using feedback information to identify skills and knowledge needed for teaching BSCS Biology and potential problem areas in which teachers would need help. The rest of the year they visited testing programme schools, and resolved difficulties when these were reported or identified by schools, by test analyses, or in reviews of the materials received from professionals. The Project Evaluator maintained contact with the external testing agency. She kept track of the testing programme statistical data and participated in the analysis of test data. She worked with, and provided staff support to, the Evaluation Committee and its sub-committees. She also participated actively in the translation of data and test agency reports to the writing teams and to the public.

THE EVALUATION PROGRAMME

The evaluation was in four distinct phases: the pre-materials preparation (1959-60), the formative evaluation I (1960-2), the summative evaluation (1962-5) and formative evaluation II (1964-5). Aspects of the pre-materials preparation (which extended into the first year of formative evaluation) included: a survey to determine teacher needs; inquiries and discussions with other curriculum projects to explore options in organizing the curriculum development activities and in developing theories of curriculum; and two studies commissioned by the BSCS to prepare the groundwork for materials preparation.

The BSCS invited teacher comments through the *American Biology Teacher* to indicate the kinds of materials that would be most helpful to teachers in assisting them to improve their high school biology courses. A study was made of biology teaching 1890-1960, with an emphasis on organized efforts to improve the curriculum and the impact of such efforts (Hurd, 1962). A second study (Byers, 1961) attempted to identify characteristics of successful biology teachers that could be useful in teacher recruitment and training.

During the 1960-2 formative period, various types of evaluation were implemented. Reports were obtained from experimental classroom teachers, from students, and from test centres. Classrooms were observed by Field Test Consultants. Data were obtained on student performance on conventional and on specially constructed achievement tests, and significant variables related to performance were identified. Materials were reviewed by individual biologists, biology educators, and psychologists as well as by committees established for the purose by scientific and educational associations. The BSCS established a national system of volunteer, part-time *Field Consultants* who were college/university biologists or public school biology supervisors or biology teachers, to serve as information points for local inquiries about BSCS (3).

In the summative evaluation stage, tests for the 1963 commercially released edition were normed and comparisons were made with control groups, and significant variables were identified. In addition, two microevaluation studies were carried out by non-BSCS staff under BSCS sponsorship.

During the second formative evaluation, meetings were held with biology teachers and biologists in various parts of the country. Teachers using BSCS were invited to comment in letters or during visits of BSCS representatives to their schools.

THE 1960-1 EVALUATION (4)

The formative evaluation for the 1960 editions of BSCS Biology was focused on determining: feasibility of BSCS Biology; whether the materials could be used by tenth-grade biology students; for which students each Version was most appropriate; the significant variables in student achievement; and what modifications were needed in student laboratory, text and test materials, in teacher materials, and in teacher preparation to achieve an appropriate level of student learning.

The target population of BSCS High School Biology was tenth-grade students who take biology in schools in the United States. The test teachers were selected from volunteers located in geographic clusters, with 6-12 teachers in a cluster. (Thirteen teachers who had participated in the writing conference but were in areas without a cluster were also included in the initial trial group.) For 1960-1, there were 118 teachers with 14,000 students. Location of the clusters was determined by proximity to a collegiate institution with an experienced biologist who would assist teachers in preparing for use of the new materials; each such biologist had been a member of the 1960 summer writing team. Each cluster was coordinated by a Centre Leader, a high school biology teacher who had also been a member of the summer writing team.

Participating teachers agreed to teach all their tenth-grade biology sections with the experimental materials, and to use the BSCS materials as the sole teaching materials (rather than as supplementary to a conventional biology treatment). They also agreed to attend an end-of-summer Briefing Conference at BSCS headquarters in 1960 to become familiar with the materials; to write weekly feedback reports to the BSCS; and to attend weekly centre meetings designed both to provide group feedback reports to the BSCS, and to assist in the preparation for the following week's class work. The students of these teachers comprised the experimental students. With few exceptions, they were at the tenth-grade level and were divided relatively evenly among the Blue, Green, and Yellow Versions. All teachers at a centre used the same Version. Teachers were asked to indicate a preference among the Versions but the final assignment was made by the BSCS to provide rural-urban-suburban representation in the sample for each Version. Since this was primarily a feasibility study, no control group of teachers of non-BSCS Biology was included.

Tests administered to students in 1960-1 included a test of general ability, the School and College Aptitude Test - SCAT (1955); a newly constructed quarterly test for each Version, and a final Comprehensive Examination common to all Versions. Data from the achievement tests were examined in terms of Version, and of achievement by ability level of student (e.g. Can average students handle the material? Can below-average students handle the material? Is one version more suitable than another for a given ability level?). Item data were examined to determine mastery of concepts and of information.

At least equally important from the formative evaluation standpoint were the reports on the materials received from teachers. All teachers were given an extra set of the course materials so that they could write in the margin each week on the materials used that week, and send these pages to the Field-Test Consultants. In addition, after the weekly centre discussions, the centre leader prepared a centre report for the BSCS with criticism, suggestions, identification of problems and suggested solutions.

Reviews by biologists and biology educators were useful and used in detail. The reviews by psychologists and educators were uneven and on several occasions not constructive. For example, the sole, completely negative professional review of the materials was received not from any of the 18 professional scientific associations or 22 eminent biologists reviewing the materials during the two-year formative evaluation period, but from a psychologist who had been invited to review the Versions in terms of learning theory, but instead propounded his views on biology, and gave wide circulation to what had been invited as an in-house report with a different emphasis.

Serious problems of interpretation on the 1960-1 data were encountered because of the tardiness of receipt by the BSCS of reports on the data analyses and the incomplete or inappropriate sampling procedures used in data processing - problems that were resolved before the 1961-2 end-of-course data were processed. Despite these difficulties, several conclusions could be drawn from the testing as well as from other facets of the broad evaluation programme.

Findings, based on reports of teachers, centre leaders, Field-Test Consultants, the testing programme analyses and external reviewers include: students in the BSCS testing programme were slightly above the national level of all tenth-graders on aptitude, as measured by SCAT. (No comparison was made with all students taking biology in tenth-grade, but these doubtless were also somewhat above the average of all tenth-graders.) Average or above-average students were able to handle the materials without undue difficulty. Teachers who had special preparation and had a voice in selecting the _Version_ used, could handle the materials appropriately, though, as expected, the preparation time involved was greater than that for the traditional courses they had been accustomed to teaching. All versions appeared acceptable in terms of student achievement; however, after adjustment for ability level, _Green Version_ students scored significantly lower than _Blue_ and _Yellow Version_ students. (_Green Version_ students also scored somewhat lower on SCAT.) The tests and student materials were closely examined to determine whether remedial measures were needed for the _Green Version_. Based on an analysis in terms of a taxonomy of objectives for high school biology (adapted from Bloom, 1956, by Klinckmann, 1963), the tests reflected the BSCS objectives. The various statistical indices on the newly constructed tests indicated that these tests were at a reasonable level of technical quality. Reviews by biologists indicated that the materials were a valid reflection of modern biology knowledge and theory.

Visits to the test schools were useful sources of information, and provided a basis for interpretation of the teacher and centre reports, and the student scores. For example, students of one teacher were consistent over-achievers on the BSCS tests in terms of student ability levels as measured by

SCAT. The Project Evaluator was impressed with what appeared to be an unusual level of teaching and learning in the school, and mentioned this to a Field-Test Consultant. The latter was able to explain these unusual scores: she was a competent teacher, but the review sessions held by this teacher before exams were so closely focused on what would be asked in the test that one might well expect inflated test scores.

THE 1961-2 EVALUATION (5)

The activities of the 1961-2 evaluation closely paralleled those of the previous year, though using a larger sample, a control group comparison, several additional instruments, and a more detailed examination of significant variables. Tests used with the experimental group were the SCAT (1955) for a measurement of general ability, revised quarterly tests for each *Version*, a revised common Comprehensive Final, a new BSCS Impact Test to measure understanding of the processes of science, and the Cooperative Biology Test (1948). Also three attitude and opinion measures were administered at the end of the year. One was a selected set of 26 multiple-choice questions taken from the Test of Understanding Science - TOUS (Cooley and Klopfer, 1961); a second included items selected from an attitude scale developed at Purdue University; and a third was an adaptation of the semantic differential method. Control group students did not take the quarterly tests specific to the *Versions*. The analysis procedures used paralleled those of the 1960-1 evaluation. However, problems were encountered in analysis of semantic differential data, and because of lack of promised expert assistance in handling data for what was then a relatively new procedure for testing, the data were not analysed (see p. 39, Constraints).

The data analyses support a number of observations. Students were able to achieve desired skills to the satisfaction of the BSCS and of the teachers using the BSCS materials. Average and above-average students did well in all *Versions*. Tenth-grade BSCS students scored higher on the BSCS Comprehensive Exam than control group students; the latter scored higher on the conventional biology tests. Definitive differences were not observed on the Impact Test and the two attitude opinion measures. Student ability, student sex, and four variables which are themselves related - teacher salary, adequacy of laboratory, small class size (under 30), and proportion of school's graduates going on to college - account for about 75 per cent of the variance in student scores on the Comprehensive Finals. Variables not correlated significantly with achievement include: rural-urban-suburban school location, size of school, length of class period, number of periods per week, per pupil expenditure, and such teacher characteristics as age, years of experience, and number of undergraduate and graduate courses in biology for the sample population (6).

Students using a Laboratory Block tended to score slightly lower than non-Block students on the Comprehensive Final; this may reflect the omission of six weeks of instruction of Version content. Students achieving high scores on the Comprehensive Final tended to achieve high scores on the Impact Test and the conventional biology test. Above-average, ninth-grade students in situations with relatively good teacher preparation and good biology laboratories were able to handle the materials; but the higher correlation of BSCS test scores with ability at the ninth-grade level appears to indicate a higher premium on intelligence for mastery of the course materials.

THE 1962-3 EVALUATION (7)

1962-3 was a transition year. Teachers who had been in the testing programme were again given books (the 1961-2 edition) for their students, since the commercial editions were not yet available; of the three 1961-2 test centre teachers who remained in biology teaching, all but two continued to use BSCS materials in 1962-3. Other teachers with special BSCS training could purchase books for their students. A total of 950 teachers and their more than 85,000 students were using BSCS Biology Versions in 45 states, District of Columbia and Puerto Rico.

Evaluation emphases were: (1) on identifying techniques that are particularly useful in implementing BSCS Biology in the classroom; (2) on the further development of tests, so that adequate tests would be available to accompany the final editions of BSCS Biology, and (3) on obtaining more information on factors affecting successful implementation (e.g. are there any circumstances that promote more effective teaching of BSCS Biology?).

Data were obtained on 257 BSCS teachers (all of

whom had used BSCS materials in at least one previous year) and their 18,900 students, and on a control group of 100 teachers and their 5,400 students, selected by the external testing agency, the Psychological Corporation. Again, the BSCS sample was about evenly divided among the *Versions*, and about one-third of the students in each *Version* used a *Laboratory Block*. At the beginning of the year, all students took a general ability test, the Differential Aptitude Test - DAT (Bennett *et al.*,1958) and the BSCS Impact Test; at the end of the year they took the same form of the Impact Test and the BSCS Comprehensive Final. BSCS students also took the quarterly *Version* tests.

The results of the 1962-3 evaluation may be described briefly as follows. Student performance on the Comprehensive Final and Impact Test correlated highly with general ability. (Before further analysis, adjustment was made for general ability.) Boys generally out-performed girls on the Comprehensive Final; girls averaged slightly higher than boys on the pre-course administration of the Impact Test and held a small advantage on the post-course administration of the Impact Test, though the margin of difference had narrowed. Thus, as appropriate in further comparisons, an adjustment was made for sex of students. BSCS non-*Block* students out-performed control group students on the Comprehensive Final; the difference approached a full standard deviation. On the Impact Test, from pre-course to post-course, the BSCS non-*Block* students gained about double the points gained by control group students. Compared with non-*Block* students, *Block* students tended to score slightly lower on the Comprehensive Final and on the Impact Test; the differences on the Comprehensive Final are surprisingly small, given the six weeks that Block students stopped work on the regular course materials to work on the *Block*. Comparisons between non-*Block* students in each of the *Versions* indicate slight differences, some of which may reflect other school variables. The differences between BSCS and control groups on the Comprehensive Final and the Impact Tests were greater than in the 1961-2 testing.

Two observations are in order: first, this was the only year thus far in the BSCS evaluation where detailed reports were not published in the *Newsletter*. Publication of the 1962-3 evaluation report was not the top priority for the Project Evaluator/ Newsletter Editor, since the 1963 revision editions of *BSCS Biology* were already at the publishers and competing needs of other BSCS programmes utilized the same Project Evaluator. Further a turnover of BSCS personnel was imminent, as a result of problems in working with the funding agency (8). Thus the report was postponed several times, and after the Project Evaluator left the BSCS staff in the summer of 1965 it may have been shelved.

Second, and at least equally interesting, is the difference in student achievement during the second year a teacher used the BSCS materials. This statistical finding is confirmed by teacher reports on their second year of teaching BSCS: that they found pacing the material easier; preparations were less time-consuming and less frustrating since they knew the procedures and could order supplies in advance (which was not possible in previous years when the experimental texts were not available until weeks or even days before the material was to be taught); and they could anticipate teaching and learning difficulties and problems, based on the previous year's experience. A serious question raised by this finding, which was later replicated in the experience with other BSCS experimental classroom trials of materials as well as in other curriculum change projects, is that judgements about newly introduced materials are probably often being made prematurely, and the programme being evaluated may never have the second chance it deserves if the funder expects immediate, highly favourable results.

THE 1963-4, 1964-5 EVALUATIONS (9)

During 1964-5, BSCS test data were obtained for purposes of norming the tests, with over 11,000 students in tenth-grade biology classes and with teachers who had used BSCS Biology materials in at least one previous year. Although geographic distribution of the samples in each *Version* was not exactly balanced, there was a reasonable degree of similarity with regard to type of community, and type, size and facilities of schools.

The evaluation investigated performance on the BSCS Achievement Tests and the Comprehensive Final comparing the different forms of each test. Also administered were the Davis Reading Test (1961-2) and the Illinois Sciences Reading Comprehension Test (1961), selected by BSCS to be given to sample groups of students as pre- and post-tests in order to relate reading skills to BSCS achievement. Academic ability was measured by the DAT (Bennett *et al*., 1958).

The 1963-4 testing programme findings were not published by the BSCS. The report of the 1964-5 programme indicates the following. The results of the 1964-5 evaluation study are in general agreement with the results of the 1963-4 study. The groups of students for the two years were of about equal academic ability. The 1964-5 group had slightly higher means on the Comprehensive Final than the previous year's groups, but differences were generally smaller. The same trends of sex and Version differences appeared in both studies and the test correlational data were quite similar. The academic ability and the BSCS achievement tests were appropriate in difficulty for the groups. Males generally had higher test means than females on both ability and achievement tests. For the Version tests, for practical purposes the two forms of each test are equal in difficulty. Consistent differences appeared in ability and achievement among the students in the various Versions. Both reading tests were highly related to the academic ability test (DAT) and to the achievement tests.

In addition to the Version testing programmes, a study sponsored by BSCS was carried out at the University of Illinois concerning teacher variation in concept presentation using BSCS Biology [10].

During this time, many studies were done externally concerning use of BSCS Biology and, for some studies, comparing this with conventional biology. However, in reviewing these, often it is not possible to determine the limitations of a given study in terms of the adequacy of sample, the control of significant variables, the use of complete cases, the adequacy of training of the teachers, and the complete use of BSCS Biology or of a conventional biology text on which to base the treatment. And many studies reflect use of inappropriate criterion measures. Further, the problem of unintentional contamination of samples increased as publishers of other high school texts changed their editions to reflect some of the BSCS emphases to meet what they saw as strong competition from the BSCS books. Because of the limited nature of the BSCS summative evaluation efforts, the BSCS was often unable to produce its own data in support of its materials, and could not rely on external data with any degree of assurance of its validity. While some of these studies were exemplary, others were of questionable value, either because the validity of the data could not be assessed from the published report or because it was questionable.

Formative Evaluation II (1963-4)

A second formative evaluation (1963-4) was conducted in preparation for forthcoming revisions of the *Versions* (11). The reorganized *Version writing teams* held a series of meetings *in various* parts of the country with teachers in schools using the *Versions*. Teachers invited to these meetings *included* some who had taught with the experimental as well as with the 1963 editions, and others whose experience had been limited to the 1963 editions. In addition, the BSCS staff collected feedback from teachers, who had been encouraged in the teacher materials accompanying the *Versions* as well as in the *Newsletter* to provide *the BSCS* with their *reactions to t*he materials. The Area Consultant programme continued to be a source of evaluation information on problems and successes in school use of *BSCS Biology* materials.

Reporting

Throughout the 1958-65 period, an effort was made to make appropriate evaluation information widely available to the various BSCS publics, while still protecting the confidential nature of materials on individual schools and teachers. (During this period, no instance of a breach of this confidence was ever called to the attention of the BSCS.)

For the writing teams, the Field-Test Consultants coded material by teacher, chapter and version, and collated comments, carefully indicating the circumstances of that teacher/class/school in terms of what might prove to be significant variables, so that comments could be interpreted in an appropriate context. For example, a different interpretation is in order for comments of a teacher working in a school with 35-minute class periods and/or no running water in the laboratory who reports that a laboratory experiment is impractical, and a similar statement by a teacher whose laboratory periods are 120 minutes, and whose equipment is appropriate. The Field-Test Consultants made such reports available to the Version Supervisors and to the appropriate writers in a usable form. Reviews by specialists and associations were similarly circulated to the writers.

BSCS regular staff were kept up to date on all evaluation information gathered through formal reports at staff meetings and through informal input at staff meetings and conferences among various staff members. At each meeting of the Steering Committee, reports were presented by the Project Evaluator and by the Field-Test Consultants.

The statistical reports from the testing agency were put into context and summarized in layman's language by the Project Evaluator, and published on a regular basis in the BSCS Newsletter and in articles published in scientific and educational journals (12). The aim was to report fully and intelligibly. Staff and others involved with the programme as writers or as teachers and supervisors in the experimental schools were encouraged to write and speak about the programme and the evaluation findings.

Impact of evaluation on decision making

Evaluation had an impact on virtually all areas of decision making. There are probably several contributing factors. The evaluation was many faceted, and so could be useful in many areas. The permanent staff was small and was housed comfortably in its own wing of a building. The ambiance of the Project was not competitive. Everyone was genuinely busy and doing work perceived to be important. There was more work than could be accomplished, and sufficient recognition for all work; thus, a sense of genuine accomplishment could be felt without arguments over turf. Interaction among staff was frequent and cordial, and the decision-making process was an open one. Since input from evaluation was not dependent on periodic visits of an outside evaluation team, evaluation feedback could be introduced informally as relevant topics were under consideration. In the frequent meetings of the professional staff, it was possible to provide data on a timely basis, rather than through periodic reports which might arrive after decisions had to be made. Also it was possible for any staff members with evaluation information to contribute it, even when the situation had not been identified as one requiring a specific kind of evaluation input.

A few of the hundreds of instances of use of evaluation data in decision making are:

1. Based on input from the Hurd (1962) study and the survey of science teachers, the decision was made to prepare a complete package of student course materials accompanied by needed teacher materials.

2. Based on test results, the three *Versions* were continued, since all three were found to be usable by average and above-average tenth-grade students. Slower students often had difficulty. As a result, a later project focused on the slower learner.
3. While it had been felt by many writers and teachers that one of the *Versions* might be more difficult than others, and one more suitable to urban areas than others, the test and other feedback results did not support this hypothesis. And so it was suggested that, as far as possible, teachers be permitted to choose the *Version* they preferred, since, under evaluation conditions, this practice had resulted in successful use.
4. The testing programme findings concerning contribution of the laboratory to learning in *BSCS Biology* led to a strong emphasis by the BSCS on the importance of improving laboratories, an effort which was impressive in terms of changes made by school systems in their facilities.
5. Decisions concerning personnel for regular staff appointments and for summer writing conference participation in many instances directly reflected feedback through the Field-Test Consultants, concerning particularly effective teachers and supervisors.
6. Changes in office procedure for year-round operation as well as for the summer writing activity reflected evaluative feedback from participants and professional and support-staff members.
7. During the 1960-1 testing period, it was learned that teacher preparation materials were not adequate to meet teacher needs. For the next version, the teacher materials were restructured and made more detailed.
8. As a result of needs expressed by teachers, other student materials for classroom use were produced, including the *BSCS Single Concept Films*, the *BSCS Pamphlet Series*, and the *BSCS Second Course*.
9. Examination of teacher-made tests used in BSCS classrooms indicated that, for the

most part, these were not appropriate in cognitive level measured; virtually all items were unusable for inclusion in the BSCS-issued tests. Since the BSCS writers wanted tests to support rather than contradict the stated purposes of the course, books of test items were prepared for each Version and made available to teachers of that Version.

CONSTRAINTS, PRESSURES AND PROBLEMS CONCERNING THE EVALUATION

1. NSF exercised indirect veto power over various phases of the project including the evaluation, as line items were dropped from or added to the funding proposals. Though in theory the BSCS was independent, in fact it was clearly dependent on the good will of NSF as its sole funding source. The control strategy might be the mention, by an NSF staff member during an informal conversation, that the NSF would look with favour on a BSCS proposal were it not for a particular activity. For example, through such unofficial lines of communication, NSF personnel clearly indicated that they favoured external evaluation done by Educational Testing Service, which was also doing the evaluation for the NSF-funded chemistry and physics projects.

Large evaluation items in the budget were not looked on with favour. Fortunately, most of the evaluation activities were not so classified in the budget. For example, included under non-evaluation headings in the budget requests were funds for publication of experimental materials to be used for field testing, salaries and travel expenses of the Field-Test Consultants, and payment of small honoraria to participating teachers for providing feedback and to the college consultant who helped each of the teacher centres. (Of interest in this regard is the fact that the NSF did not appear to have any personnel trained in educational research on its staff or on its review panels at that time.)

Further, though the NSF supported curriculum revision, it did not wish to support what it termed educational research, viewing such support as infringing on the prerogatives of the US Office of Education (USOE). At the same time, the USOE was concerned about making grants to an NSF-supported project, since such grants might appear to be an infringement on NSF territory. Inter-agency efforts to resolve this impasse never got off the ground. This became a particularly delimiting problem during the summative evaluation period.

In the 1960s, in addition to the curriculum improvement projects, the NSF sponsored college and university institutes to upgrade science teacher preparation. Because the NSF did not wish to appear to be promoting a particular curriculum, after the first two years of the BSCS field testing (the formative evaluation period), NSF would not approve direct grants to the BSCS for teacher preparation either under its institute programme or in its curriculum improvement programme. If, in its grant proposals for teacher institutes, a college or university wished to focus on the BSCS materials - and many did - this was acceptable to NSF, but the BSCS could not itself sponsor such activities. At this time, the USOE was making grants to school systems for in-service teacher training, and some of these were directed towards preparation for introduction of _BSCS Biology_. This meant that the BSCS lost all control of teacher preparation for _BSCS Biology_ except through its published, teacher-oriented materials. And while many quality institutes focusing on use of BSCS materials were given, including some by BSCS writers and test centre teachers, in evaluation studies by BSCS or others after 1963 or 1964, there was generally no way of determining the kind of preparation - if any - of the BSCS teachers included in a given study sample.

2. The BSCS Steering Committee was comprised largely of biologists and biology educators who were not familiar with educational research or the use of such research in educational decision making. For several, test data were not viewed in the same light as data from experiments in science, even when the same statistical procedures were used. For example, on one occasion, a report indicated a numerical difference of 3 points (0.001 level of significance) between BSCS students and those in conventional biology courses on achievement tests. Such scientists could accept Field-Test Consultant non-quantitative feedback and place it in appropriate perspective; they had reservations about the significance of 3 points on an achievement test, statistical significance notwithstanding.

3. In the early 1960s, testing of students for the purpose of judging curriculum was expected to honour the conventions of educational and psychological testing, including use of control groups, existing standardized norm-referenced conventional

tests, differences in coverage and purposes notwithstanding. Any deviation from these was considered by much of the education establishment as ill-advised at best. Criticism from such influential educational sources disaffected several Steering Committee members from educators in general and from evaluation in particular.

4. Testing agencies were slow in adapting to the new needs of the curriculum studies and, particularly during the early formative evaluation period, such inflexibility created serious problems.

There were early differences between BSCS and ETS concerning appropriateness of certain types of tests, sampling techniques, and reporting methods, and of appropriate difficulty level of achievement tests. This led to a shift of locus of responsibility from the outside evaluators directing the test programme with BSCS in an advisory role, to direction of the testing programme and preparation of tests by the BSCS, with mechanics of test printing, distribution and data processing handled by the testing agency; it also led to the eventual change in contract for technical testing services to the Psychological Corporation.

One problem was the expected difficulty level of the achievement tests designed for the *BSCS Biology* materials. ETS insisted that the mean of a good achievement test should approximate 50 per cent. (This was the pre-mastery-testing era in academic subjects.) The BSCS countered that this was too difficult. This level would discourage teachers, students and parents, and also was too low to be a valid indicator of what students were learning. The BSCS intended to use the tests as a teaching/learning device in the classroom, as part of the BSCS student materials; it was concerned with the paucity of information gained concerning material learned on a 35-item or 50-item multiple-choice test with a difficulty level of about 50 per cent; and it was at least as concerned with the psychological impact of such test scores on the conventional student grading system. (At least one BSCS teacher overcame the psychological problem by automatically adding 20 points to each student's score when scoring tests for grading purposes.) While the initial BSCS achievement tests had a mean between 45 and 55 per cent, the problem was alleviated as the BSCS took on direction of tests construction and as the test writers became more experienced with test writing for the tenth-grade level.

Timing of evaluation reports presented a

serious difficulty and a point of conflict between BSCS and ETS. The urgency of the BSCS need for prompt reports on testing results and for detailed item data was not unusual practice at that time. Elegance of a report of test results received by the BSCS two months after the revision of materials to which the results applied, did not serve a useful formative evaluation purpose.

5. While the evaluation activities were on the cutting edge of a new profession, and the newness of the problems and the need for creating new ways of handling them were challenging, the situation presented difficulties. Not only were there no ready-made answers to be found in someone else's experience, there were few educators with sufficient breadth of vision with whom to discuss these problems.

Also, despite its location on a university campus, the BSCS maintained a high degree of independence from that university. This independence, while beneficial in many ways, did not provide the degree of collegial give-and-take for the Project Evaluator which would have been helpful as new areas were explored. There were no faculty members at the University of Colorado at that time engaged in similar activities, and the involvement by the BSCS with the university faculty was deliberately kept at a minimal level in order to project the image for the NBSCS of a national, representative group of scientists and science educators preparing curricula, rather than a group from a single university.

6. Because of the BSCS' success in keeping its publics well informed about materials and activities, it became increasingly difficult to carry out studies using comparisons with students using non-BSCS materials. Even before the 1963 editions became generally available, there was leakage through informal networks of _Version_ materials - in part or in whole - to schools, teachers and classes not in the official testing programme. Thus, comparisons with uncontaminated control groups became increasingly difficult. The problem was particularly troublesome after 1963, when many studies were done independently by outside investigators, and the reports of these studies frequently had insufficient information concerning samples to ensure that the control groups were not using any part of _BSCS Biology_.

7. One constraint - the hostility often found in curriculum-change activities to appropriate but critical evaluation information - was entirely

lacking. The receptivity of the *Version* supervisors and BSCS staff to evaluation *information* - to information about things that did not work or that had to be modified to make them work - made for a productive working environment. There was never any suggestion of the kill-the-messenger-who-brings-bad-news reaction faced in many curriculum evaluation situations. Evaluation feedback was eagerly sought provided it was constructive and specific - not feedback saying that 'it doesn't work', but rather 'step 3 of lab #27 doesn't work because ...'.

The writers and staff truly believed that curriculum experiments, like other true experiments, are just that - that, even with the best will, things may go wrong. And when something went wrong, there was an honest effort to make it work or to discard it. This attitude permitted an *esprit de corps* rare in modern organizations, and *produced* a *level* of productivity that was remarkable. Perhaps this kind of good will and commitment cannot continue indefinitely, but continue it did through these years of the BSCS.

8. The problem of external evaluators using conventional tests for purposes of evaluating students and schools, and for college admission was time-consuming and not readily resolved. Thus, for example, many hours were spent discussing with the College Entrance Examination Board (CEEB), the problems of *BSCS Biology* students in taking the CEEB Biology test *which reflected* traditional biology content. The CEEB rejected the role of curriculum innovator; its position was that it should reflect what is taught, not what should be taught.

After much discussion with BSCS of the problems faced by the BSCS students, CEEB changed its test to include items common to BSCS and conventional biology students and some unique to each. The BSCS took the position that this procedure penalized both student groups, since it did not validly reflect the achievement of either group, and the practice encouraged teachers of college-bound students to try to teach an eclectic course, including both conventional biology and *BSCS Biology*, thereby doing a disservice to both. *The problem* was not resolved in a satisfactory manner until, as the market for BSCS books expanded, coverage of what was actually taught became in fact primarily a coverage of *BSCS Biology*. During the same transition period the *New York State* Regents, after a discussion initiated by the BSCS, offered two separate tests in biology, one for students of conventional courses and the other for those in BSCS courses.

9. The plethora of data, particularly when the tests were expanded after the first year of field testing, became overwhelming. There was often more statistical information than could be handled by in-house staff with many conflicting demands on their time. Thus, some of the data may not have been fully analysed and integrated into the evaluation reports.

In the early 1960s computers had not reached today's level of sophistication, and access to computers was not as readily obtained. For example, the data on the semantic differential instrument administered as part of the 1963-4 evaluation were never analysed. The initial arrangements for analysis broke down because of the change in job location of the person initially accepting responsibility for this special data analysis. Similarly, perhaps some other data which could have been examined more closely were not, simply because of lack of staff time and the sheer mass of data. The staff time problem is another example of the indirect control by the funding agency.

As the _BSCS Second Course_ and _BSCS Special Materials_ moved into the formative evaluation phase, not only were evaluation funds for these new programmes limited but increased activities were added to the Project Evaluator's assignment with no increase in funding for Project Evaluator staffing.

GENERAL CONCLUSIONS

In many ways, the BSCS broke new ground in its evaluation processes. Since that time, curriculum evaluation activities have become more acceptable and the different approaches to evaluation developed in the 1960s and 1970s are becoming standard practice.

Some of the strengths of the BSCS evaluation were:

1. The variety of facets used in testing and in other approaches to data gathering.
2. The use of internal evaluators who had integrity, credibility and access to decision makers at the time decisions were being made.
3. The design of tests measuring cognitive levels beyond knowledge and application.
4. The openness of all BSCS operations, including the evaluation, which made the

end product, the BSCS Versions, more readily acceptable to the schools.
5. The broad involvement of people from different disciplines in various facets of the evaluation.
6. A valuable byproduct of the BSCS evaluation programme was the identification of a large number of excellent high school biology teachers who, through their involvement with the field testing, were encouraged to go on to further advanced degrees. An impressive number are now on collegiate faculties of science education.
7. High school biology laboratories were upgraded to a noteworthy degree and the fact that this resulted in considerable part from the BSCS materials' emphasis is reflected in the popularity of items listed in the BSCS Laboratory Checklist (Newsletter 9, September 1961). (During the formative evaluation, one school superintendent who was asked about the laboratories in his school reported the substantial improvement in the BSCS teacher's room. When asked if all the school's labs had been similarly improved he replied, 'No, because those teachers wouldn't know what to do with more equipment.')
8. The most impressive summative evaluation data were obtained through non-reactive measures: the well over 50 per cent of the high school biology textbook market held by BSCS Biology within a few years of its release for general use; the modifications made in the CEEB Biology Test within a few years, which reflected the major changes in content of high school biology courses; the changes in most non-BSCS texts to incorporate many of the new content emphases appearing in the BSCS books; the changes in college biology courses and texts in the mid- and late 1960s, reflecting the increasing sophistication of high school biology courses and new emphases; the virtual monopoly by persons connected with BSCS of the National Association of Biology Teachers (NABT), of the Outstanding Biology Teacher Awards, of the Presidency (starting

about 1963), and of the awards of honorary life membership by NABT to leaders of the BSCS.

Some less effective aspects of the evaluation include:

1. The use of inappropriate conventional tests by ETS as part of the evaluation, thereby wasting scarce resources and answering the question not relevant to the BSCS: how well do BSCS students do in areas of biology not considered appropriate by the BSCS writers?
2. Inappropriate reviews produced by some reviewers (i.e. reviews that did not bear on the speciality of the reviewer, and including areas such reviewers were not professionally competent to discuss) disaffected some of the Steering Committee, and may have reduced the level of evaluation activities such members were willing to support after 1962.
3. Hostility of some of the education research establishment to curriculum evaluation and evaluators as compared with research and researchers. The considerable success of _BSCS High School Biology_ in later years was in spite of, not because of, the education research establishment.

NOTES

1. For detailed descriptions of the structure and activities of the BSCS during this period, see A. Grobman (1969) and H. Grobman (1967, 1970). Lists of all BSCS publications are included in the _BSCS Newsletter_ Annual Report issued each year, and all publications through 1968 are included in A. Grobman (1969).

2. Concurrent with the development of the _Versions_, work was done at the University of Texas Science Education Center at Austin, Texas, developing a series of _Laboratory Blocks_ - intensive six-week, single theme, laboratory-oriented units for use in conjunction with the _BSCS Biology Versions_. Each _Block_ was developed by a single author who prepared materials on his home campus, with editing and initial testing at the Science Education Center, and then field testing, some of which was in conjunction with field testing of the _Versions_ by some of the

BSCS teachers.

3. This network was continued after the formative evaluation Phase I and remained a valuable source for feedback to the BSCS for the formative evaluation Phase II.

4. A detailed report of this evaluation is included in BSCS Newsletter 10 (November, 1961).

5. A detailed report of this evaluation is included in BSCS Newsletter 19 (September, 1963).

6. Some hypotheses concerning the lack of relation between each of these variables and student achievement are developed in BSCS Newsletter 19 (September, 1963).

7. Reported in summary in BSCS Newsletter 20 (February, 1964).

8. Reported in A. Grobman (1959), alsh (July, 1965) and the BSCS Newsletter 27 (October, 1965).

9. The 1964-5 evaluation is reported in BSCS Newsletter 30 (January, 1967), and details concerning the test standardization are in the Manual for the Comprehensive Final Examination (1966).

10. A detailed report of this study is included in BSCS Newsletter 30 (January, 1967).

11. Reported in BSCS Newsletter 27 (October, 1965).

12. The BSCS Newsletter distributed without charge on request was issued several times a year; circulation was over 30,000 copies. Bibliographies on the BSCS appear in the Annual Report issues of the BSCS Newsletter.

REFERENCES

Bennett, G., Seashore, H.G. and Wesman, A.G. (1958) Differential Aptitude Test (DAT), The Psychol-OGICAL Corporation, New York

Bloom, M.S. (ed)(1956) Taxonomy of Educational Objectives, the Classification of Education Goals. Handbook I, The Cognitive Domain, McKay Company, New York

BSCS Newsletter (1959-65) Biological Sciences Curriculum Study, 1959-65, Boulder, Colorado

Byers, F. (1961) Report to the BSCS Steering Committee, (unpublished), Boulder, Colorado

Cooley, W.W. and Klopfer, L.E. (1961) Test of Understanding Science (TOUS), Educational Testing Service, Princeton, New Jersey

Cooperative Biology Test, Form Y (1948) ETS, Princeton, New Jersey, Cooperative Test Division

Davis, F. and Davis, C.C. (1961-2) Davis Reading

Test, The Psychological Corporation, New York

Grobman, A.B. (1969) The Changing Classroom: The Role of the Biological Sciences Curriculum Study, Doubleday, New York

Grobman, H. (1967) Evaluation Activities of Curriculum Projects, American Educational Research Association monograph series on curriculum evaluation, no. 2, Rand McNally, Chicago

Grobman, H. (1970) Developmental Curriculum Projects, Decision Points and Processes, F.E. Peacock, Itasca, Illinois

Hurd, P. deH. (1962) Biological Education in American Secondary Schools, 1890-1960, BSCS bulletin series, no. 1, BSCS, Boulder, Colorado

Illinois Sciences Reading Comprehensive Test (1961) University of Illinois, School of Education, Urbana, Illinois

Klinckmann, E. (1963) 'The BSCS Grid for Test Analysis', BSCS Newsletter, 19, 17-21, Boulder, Colorado

School and College Ability Tests (SCAT) (1955) forms 3A and 3B, ETS, Cooperative Test Division, Princeton, New Jersey

Walsh, J. (1965) 'Curriculum Reform: Success Hasn't Spoiled NSF Program, but Biology Study's Status Reflects Problems', Science, 149, 280-2

3. THE FORMATIVE EVALUATION ACTIVITIES ASSOCIATED WITH AUSTRALIAN SCIENCE EDUCATION PROJECT

B.J. Fraser

In a recent book from the Stanford Evaluation Consortium, Cronbach and colleagues claim that

> Evaluators gain much experience in the course of designing and redesigning a study. Unfortunately, little of that experience is recorded for the benefit of the evaluation community ... Methods of evaluation would improve faster if evaluators more often wrote retrospective accounts ... (Cronbach *et al*., 1980, p. 214)

Moreover, Anderson and Ball (1978, p. 101) note that what exists in the literature in terms of reports of evaluation efforts almost exclusively focuses on summative evaluation, while reports of formative evaluation efforts are particularly scarce. One reason for this, of course, is that summative evaluation reports serve wider audiences, whereas formative evaluation reports are likely to be of interest predominantly to the curriculum developers themselves. Nevertheless, a portrayal of the formative evaluation procedures which were followed by a specific curriculum project could potentially provide valuable guidance to others embarking on formative evaluation initiatives.

The formative evaluation activities associated with the Australian Science Education Project (ASEP) are among the most comprehensive employed in any Australian curriculum venture. Despite this, information about the nature and effectiveness of ASEP's formative evaluation procedures has remained hitherto an unavailable source of potential insight for other people engaged in formative evaluation. Consequently, in an attempt to enlighten others involved in formative evaluation, this chapter aims to describe, illustrate with concrete examples, and draw implications from the formative evaluation activities associated with ASEP.

NATURE OF PROJECT AND ROLE OF EVALUATION

Between October 1969 and March 1974, ASEP developed materials suitable for the range of science courses and conditions at the junior high school level in all Australian states. ASEP materials published during 1974 included 41 units for student use, each occupying about a month's teaching time, and six service booklets and some audiovisual material for use with student units. For the development of ASEP, the sum of approximately 1.2 million dollars Australian was made available jointly by the Commonwealth Government and the six State Governments. Furthermore, the development of ASEP materials can be considered an important landmark in the history of Australian education because ASEP was its first national curriculum project in any subject area.

Descriptions of the historical beginnings of ASEP and the nature of ASEP's philosophy and materials are provided in detail elsewhere (Lucas, 1972; ASEP, 1974; Fraser, 1979a). In order to facilitate understanding of ASEP's formative evaluation activities, a few salient features of ASEP materials are noted here. First, ASEP materials are organized into a large number of relatively independent units so that the teacher has a degree of choice in which ASEP units to use and in what sequence. Second, ASEP materials cater for student individual differences by providing student options within each ASEP unit and by allowing students to proceed through the materials at their own rates. Third, ASEP materials are activity based and engage students in inquiry strategies.

Since ASEP's main charter was the development of materials, the primary goal of evaluation within ASEP was the formative one of guiding the ongoing development, revision and improvement of materials. The summative evaluation of individual or groups of units, therefore, was considered of relatively minor importance to internal project staff. It is noteworthy, however, that external evaluators or researchers have engaged in a number of interesting summative evaluation efforts in relation to ASEP and that these have formed the basis of a separate comprehensive review (Fraser, 1978a,b).

THE EVALUATORS

The people involved in formative evaluation were internal project staff who were designated as ASEP's 'Research Officers'. There was a close and cooperative relationship between curriculum developers and the Research Officers responsible for evaluation.

Although there were three or four full time Research Officers on average throughout the life of ASEP, it is important to appreciate that only part of their time could be devoted to curriculum evaluation initiatives. In particular, the writing of diagnostic tests for inclusion within ASEP units occupied a sizeable amount of the Research Officers' time and reduced their capacity to do curriculum evaluation work.

STAGES AT WHICH EVALUATION WAS CONDUCTED

Formative evaluation was conducted at each identifiable stage of ASEP's curriculum development process. Project staff determined the same stages at which all units were evaluated. In particular, prior to field testing, 'reflective' or 'armchair' evaluation was conducted to provide preliminary information to guide the development and modification of units. This involved a group of ASEP staff in scrutinizing each unit's first and second specification, and the presentation and approval of a first trial version, and later a second trial version, of materials to ASEP's academic and editorial staff. This reflective evaluation was found to provide a rather economical way of evaluating, eliminating and modifying units at an early stage prior to incurring the expenses of production and field trials.

The major formative evaluation efforts were associated with the field testing of prototypes of ASEP units. The majority of ASEP units underwent field testing twice. The first versions of ASEP units were subjected to local field trials in schools in Victoria, whereas the second versions underwent trials in a national sample of schools. However, there were a number of noteworthy exceptions to this pattern. First, as a few units were essentially adaptations of units developed previously overseas, these were subjected only to the second (national) field trials. Second, as time and funds ran out towards the end of the project, it proved necessary to exclude some units from the national trials.

SAMPLES

One major difference between the first and second trials was that the first trials involved a smaller number of classes (about eight) located in the Melbourne metropolitan area in close proximity to the ASEP headquarters, whereas the second trials involved a larger number of classes (over 20) drawn nationally from all Australian states. An important reason why the first trials were locally based was to enable close contact to be maintained between ASEP staff and trial schools. The restriction in the size and location of the sample for first trials also provided a relatively economical initial testing of materials. In contrast, the more comprehensive national trials were designed to determine the suitability of units in a wider variety of classrooms, to ascertain the specific needs of the various states, and to determine sources of equipment and aids for the units in various states.

RANGE OF METHODS OF FORMATIVE EVALUATION

The range of alternative evaluation techniques available for use in formative curriculum evaluation is quite broad (see Grobman, 1968; Baker and Alkin, 1973; Baker, 1974, 1978; Bloom, 1977; Champagne and Klopfer, 1974; Harlen, 1975; Krus *et al.*, 1975; Novick, 1976; Sanders and Cunningham, 1974; Steadman, 1976). It is noteworthy that ASEP's formative evaluation activities were also very broad in scope and encompassed numerous and varied approaches. A major purpose of this section is to provide concrete illustrations of each of the techniques followed by ASEP and record some tentative observations about their usefulness. Although there existed some differences in the evaluation procedures followed in the first and second trials, they were sufficiently similar in many respects to permit them to be treated together in this section.

Experts' Responses to Structured Questionnaire

The collection and collation of expert opinion was a major approach to the evaluation of the trial versions of ASEP units. For each ASEP unit, the same structured questionnaire was completed by a group of experts consisting of external consultants, teachers whose classes were involved in the classroom test of the unit, and members of State Advisory Committees (i.e. special groups of science educators and teachers organized by ASEP in each state to assist the Project). In particular, the State Advisory Committees paid special attention to any specific difficulties which were likely to arise in using the unit in their own state (e.g. because of special syllabus requirements).

In the case of the first trial of the unit Charge, a total of 39 experts provided responses to structured questionnaire items. The first group of experts consisted of four external consultants (mainly from colleges and universities) who were known for their special interest either in physics or physics education. The second group consisted of the eight teachers of the classes involved in testing the unit in schools in the metropolitan area of Melbourne. For this particular unit, three of the schools were coeducational government high schools, three were girls non-Catholic independent schools, one was a Catholic boys school and one was a non-Catholic independent boys school. The remaining group comprised 27 members of State Advisory Committees (five from South Australia, seven from Queensland, four from Western Australia, five from Victoria, three from Tasmania and three from New South Wales).

These experts were asked to provide their opinions about the 27 different aspects of the unit shown in Table 3.1 by responding on a five point scale ranging from 'very favourably impressed' to 'unsatisfactory'. It can be seen from Table 3.1 that the 27 individual items covered four areas, namely, ASEP philosophy, student materials, teachers' guide, and appearance and production. But, as people were allowed to omit a rating for any aspect about which they felt unable to comment, the frequencies of all ratings do not always sum to 39.

As different experts could have different perspectives, clearly the responses of each individual were important. But, at the same time, the total amount of information available tended to be unwieldy since the responses of 39 different experts to 27 different questions produced 1,053 different pieces of information. Also, the time pressures associated with ASEP's production schedule meant that the collation of feedback material and its use in revising units had to be completed within a fairly limited time period. Consequently, these time pressures led to some conflict between the need to pay careful attention to the differences in opinion expressed by each of the 39 experts, and the need to summarize the cumbersome set of data quickly in a manner which highlighted major trends. These considerations led to the practice of aggregating responses across the whole group of respondents as shown in Table 3.1. Although the curriculum developers had access to each expert's individual responses when rewriting the unit, a certain amount of time was saved by using summaries like that illustrated in Table 3.1 to identify general trends and specific areas for which the responses of individuals needed to be scrutinized more closely.

Table 3.1: Summary of Experts' Responses to Structured Questionnaire.

Items about the Unit Charge

	Aspects of Unit	Frequency of Rating				
		Very favourably impressed				Unsatisfactory
		1	2	3	4	5
1.	ASEP Philosophy					
1.1	Reflection of ASEP Objectives	17	18	1	-	-
1.2	Reflection of ASEP Content Themes	20	13	2	1	-
1.3	Adherence to ways of dealing with subject-matter according to Piagetian theory	11	13	8	1	-
1.4	Provisions for individual difference	16	12	9	1	-
1.5	Use of the enquiry approach	16	15	5	-	-
2.	Student Materials					
2.1	Authenticity of science content	22	11	5	-	1
2.2	Appropriateness for students' levels of development	11	19	6	1	-
2.3	Appropriateness for existing classroom conditions and resources	14	16	9	2	2

Table 3.1 (cont'd)

	Aspects of Unit	Frequency of Rating				
		Very favourably impressed				Unsatisfactory
		1	2	3	4	5
2.4	Organization and structure of learning experiences	15	16	6	2	-
2.5	Quality of tests	14	12	10	3	-
2.6	Suitability of students' recorded work	10	15	8	2	2
2.7	The name of the unit	18	8	2	-	-
2.8	The length of the unit	7	14	9	3	1
3.	Teachers' Guide					
3.1	Adequacy of information supplied	9	16	10	-	-
3.2	Adequacy of suggestions for classroom organization and procedures	11	12	6	2	1
3.3	Adequacy of lists of equipment required	17	13	4	2	-
3.4	Adequacy of lists of references and audiovisuals	2	6	12	7	-
3.5	Ease of use	10	16	5	3	1

Experts' Unstructured Comments

In addition to the structured questionnaire described above, each of the 39 experts were also asked to provide unstructured comments which were recorded either as responses to open-ended questionnaire items or which were recorded directly onto a copy of the unit itself. Also, some of these experts provided a covering letter which made additional general statements about a unit. In order to provide concrete illustration of the types of information obtained by these methods, Table 3.2 lists some typical examples of comments made by the same group of 39 experts who were involved in evaluating the first trial version of _Charge_.

Table 3.2: Unstructured Comments Made by Experts about the First Trial Version of _Charge_

External Consultants

This unit is brilliant in concept and execution.
Fine! The unit is experimentally based, interesting and relates to the environment.
The teachers' guide did not measure up.
Much improvement is needed in editing.

Teachers

I am afraid I could not justify the time involved in this unit.
The students became bored.
The unit achieves the goals of ASEP.
Although very enthusiastic at first, students lost interest towards the finish.
I feel the unit tried to cover too much territory.
I think it is an excellent unit and thoroughly enjoyed trialling it. Most of the trial class also enjoyed it and gained a lot from it.
A good unit which measures up well on most points.
When preparation time is taken into account, it would be unrealistic to think that it would be feasible to introduce ASEP into the schools unless laboratory assistance was assured.

State Advisory Committees

I tried the experiments myself and feel they would provide students with a good grasp of the concept of charge.
In general I thought the students' booklet showed a patronizing attitude to the teacher.
The teacher's guide is padded out with fairly useless photographs and diagrams.
The unit as a whole is excellent both in content and approach and provides a good set of graded options.
The standard of editing is incredibly low.
The layout needs improvement.
An excellent unit; the best I have seen to date.
The format of the teachers' guide is piecemeal.

Meetings of Trial Teachers and ASEP Staff

During the first field testing of each ASEP unit, trial teachers visited ASEP headquarters every two weeks to meet with the writers and other ASEP staff. At these meetings, ASEP staff could ask questions and teachers could report their experiences and problems. Teachers emphasized what students and teachers actually were doing in the classroom, and ASEP staff provided guidance about what future parts of the unit would involve. Also some audio- and videotapes were made of some lessons as a basis for discussion during these meetings. The national trials were not organized in a way which provided the opportunity for meetings between ASEP staff and trial teachers. Nevertheless, because of the value of this type of feedback, ASEP staff supplemented the list of national trial schools with several other local schools which could be visited by ASEP staff.

Trial Students' Responses to Structured Questionnaire Items

The evaluation of trial versions of units was based also on student responses to a short structured questionnaire. Table 3.3 shows six aspects of each unit which were rated by trial students using a five point scale ranging from 'liked very much' to 'disliked very much'. As there were relatively few items in this part of the questionnaire, it proved feasible to collate results separately for each individual class involved in the first trial. As a greater number of schools was involved in the national trial, results tended to be collated separately for the group of classes in each State. Table 3.3 presents data from two of the individual schools involved in the field testing of the first version of Charge. For economy, however, ASEP staff collated information for a random sample of only 15 students from each class instead of using all students. The bottom of Table 3.3 provides aggregated results for a sample of 105 students consisting of 15 students chosen randomly from the seven schools whose feedback had been received at the time of collation.

Table 3.3: Summary of Student Responses to Structured Questionnaire Items

School	Aspect of Unit	Frequency of Rating				
		Liked very much				Disliked very much
		1	2	3	4	5
School A (N=15)	Subject-matter	2	7	3	1	2
	Experiments	6	7	1	1	-
	Tests	-	5	6	1	3
	Photographs	1	7	6	-	1
	Diagrams and illustrations	4	3	3	2	3
	Reading level	1	6	4	2	2
School B (N=15)	Subject-matter	7	6	2	-	-
	Experiments	10	4	1	-	-
	Tests	3	7	2	3	-
	Photographs	7	3	2	1	2
	Diagrams and illustrations	11	1	-	-	3
	Reading level	5	4	4	2	-
Total for all Schools (N=105)	Subject-matter	24	49	15	11	4
	Experiments	53	33	8	9	2
	Tests	8	38	23	24	11
	Photographs	29	30	26	13	5
	Diagrams and illustrations	35	33	21	9	9
	Reading level	21	31	30	15	8

Trial Students' Responses to Unstructured Questionnaire Items

In addition to responses to the structured part of the student questionnaire, each student involved in the field testing of ASEP units responded to the unstructured part of the student questionnaire which included various open-ended questions. As this procedure led to the collection of sizeable amounts of information, ASEP staff involved in collation of feedback needed to establish some quick and convenient method of summarizing this information for use by the curriculum developers during rewriting. Table 3.4 illustrates how this was done by tabulating the frequency of common answers to each of six open-ended questions. The data in Table 3.4 are for the same sample of 105 students from seven classes involved in testing the first version of Charge.

Table 3.4: Summary of Frequent Student Answers to Open-Ended Questions

Question	Frequency	Answer
What did you like most about this unit?	29	Doing electroplating in Option 3.
	29	Doing experiments.
	15	Students work at their own pace.
	12	Reading about Benjamin Franklin in Option 6.
	8	Connecting circuits up.
	7	You can find things out for yourself.
	5	ASEP is informal.
What did you dislike most about this unit?	16	Writing down results of experiments.
	14	Giving verbal reports to the class.
	9	Not having enough equipment for the whole class.
	7	The fact that the class had already done some of the work earlier.
	7	Experiments on plastic strips that wouldn't work.
	5	The tests.
What did you find the most difficult?	24	Nothing.
	12	Getting some of the experiments to work.
	9	The work on insulators.
	6	Reading the booklets.
	5	The section on ions.
What can you do now that you couldn't do before?	52	Electroplating.
	23	Make a battery.
	14	Recharge a battery.
	8	Make a spark.
	5	Charge things electrically.
	3	Work with electricity safely without being frightened.

Table 3.4 (cont'd)

Question	Frequency	Answer
What do you know now that you didn't know before?	23	Electroplating.
	17	Batteries.
	12	History of Benjamin Franklin.
	6	To avoid standing near pointed objects when lightning strikes.
	5	Like charges repel but unlike charges attract.
	3	The finger is a conductor.
In what ways do you feel differently from before?	10	I'm not so scared of electricity now.
	5	I am beginning to like science more than I used to.
	4	I like to do science experiments at home.
	4	The importance of electricity in our lives.
	2	I'm sure I don't want to be a science teacher.
	2	If I was the seventeenth son of a soapmaker (like Franklin), I could still be famous.

Trial Students' General Comments

Trial students not only responded to the structured and open-ended questionnaire items discussed in the previous sections, but also were required to write down comments describing their general reactions to a unit as a whole. This information was collated by ASEP staff to produce a list of what were perceived to be the most salient comments made by students from each class involved in the field testing of a unit. In the case of the trial of the first version of Charge, some examples of the general comments made by students are summarized in Table 3.5.

Table 3.5: Sample of Students' General Comments

School 1

The funnys were unfunny.
The unit was good because it had a lot of practical work.
This approach is better than being taught off the blackboard by the teacher.
The unit was a waste of time except for the copper plating.
The core was boring.

School 2

I think the options are good ideas but I would rather be learning science from the teacher himself.
Most girls aren't interested in this unit; mostly boys like this sort of work.
I think in cases where you have to set up a complicated experiment or even simple experiments, more diagrams are needed than were in the booklets.
I wish we could do more of this.

School 3

I enjoyed the experiments.
It was boring in places.
It was confusing in places.

School 4

At the beginning I liked the unit because it was an entirely new subject. But towards the end, I felt bored.
I feel this unit was a good introductory unit to electricity, but I think it should have gone into the unit further and it should have been longer.
I would like some clearer explanations about ions.

School 5

I felt that the unit I did was too long but I enjoyed it.
I found the experiments much too long, especially in the first unit. At the end it was terribly boring.
There is too much reading to do.

School 6

In some parts of the book there are parts that are too hard to understand.
Some of the pictures are not clear enough.

Results of Student Achievement Tests

As use of student achievement tests was an important aspect in the formative evaluation of ASEP units, achievement data are illustrated below the second trial of Charge. Obtaining useful formative evaluative information from student achievement data, however, is not a simple matter. For example, the design of an appropriate and economical achievement test posed the difficulties described in Fraser (1973). Although some of the unit's important aims were effective and psychomotor, the need to use an economical paper-and-pencil instrument meant that it was easier to focus only to the unit's cognitive objectives. Furthermore, because ASEP units contain numerous sections of optional student material, it was necessary for a common achievement test to omit items measuring aims covered by optional sections and to restrict attention to objectives which were covered by the compulsory part of the unit or which were covered by several different options.

In an attempt to make interpretation of data more meaningful, use was made of a pre-test as well as a post-test and of a control group as well as the ASEP group. By administering the same test prior to and after completion of the unit, it was possible to gauge the changes in achievement which occurred during the time of studying Charge. The purpose of the control group was to prevent attribution of changes to the curriculum when they might have been attributable to other variables, such as the mere passage of time, current cultural events, or familiarity gained from taking the same test twice.

Altogether 22 classes, each from a different school, were involved in the testing of the second version of Charge in the six Australian states. Analyses were based, however, only on the 17 schools whose data had been returned in time for collation. Each of these schools provided two classes, one as an experimental class and one as a control class. This method of drawing two classes from the same school made the collection of control data easy to organize and quick, and also led to reasonable comparability between experimental and control groups. Of the 17 classes in each group, six were from New South Wales, five from Victoria, three from Queensland, two from South Australia and one from Tasmania; one class was at the Year 7 level, seven were at the Year 8 level and nine were at the Year 9 level; and ten classes were from government high schools, two from government technical schools, three from Catholic schools and two from independent non-Catholic schools. Also, in order to economize on testing time, a random sample of ten students who had completed both the pre-test and post-test were selected from each class for analysis. The total sample size was 170 for both the experimental and the control group.

Table 3.6 shows how achievement test data were collated (see Fraser, 1973). In particular, because of the need to obtain formative evaluative information to guide the rewriting of materials, students' total scores were not considered to be particularly relevant. Instead, student performance on individual items was examined in an attempt to identify specific objectives which were not being achieved well by students so that, in turn, material related to these aspects could be revised during the rewriting phase. The main descriptive information recorded in Table 3.6 is a statement of the objective measured by each item, together with the frequency of correct response shown separately for the experimental and control groups and for the pre-test and post-test.

Table 3.6: Differences Between Pre-test and Post-test in Achievement on Individual Items

Item	Objective	Group	Frequency of Correct Response		Significance Test[a]
			Pre	Post	
1	To recognize situations in the environment where electric charge arises	ASEP Control	110 110	132 119	3.17** 1.32
2	To understand how to earth charged objects in the environment	ASEP Control	35 22	32 33	-0.48 2.12
3	To understand that like charges repel	ASEP Control	71 65	108 86	4.52*** 3.00**
4	To understand that neutral bodies neither attract nor repel	ASEP Control	106 102	134 114	3.62** 1.81

Table 3.6 (cont'd)

Item	Objective	Group	Frequency of Correct Response		Significance Test[a]
			Pre	Post	
5.	To understand that unlike charges attract	ASEP	65	86	2.60**
		Control	59	64	0.63
6	To know how long ago Franklin worked with electricity	ASEP	93	109	2.03*
		Control	95	98	0.40
7	To explain an object's charge in terms of positive and negative charges	ASEP	67	100	4.16***
		Control	70	72	0.32
8	To understand that the sign of an object's charge depends on the material with which it is rubbed	ASEP	114	141	3.64***
		Control	118	115	-0.41
9	To understand that bodies rubbed together acquire equal and opposite charges	ASEP	30	40	1.48
		Control	34	41	1.07
10	To understand some attributes of a scientific model	ASEP	136	137	1.40
		Control	123	119	-0.53

a McNemar's z test
* Significant at the 0.05 level
** Significant at the 0.01 level
*** Significant at the 0.001 level

Despite the fact that pre-test and control data are available, the interpretation of the results in Table 3.6 is still far from simple. At minimum, the experimental group should have exhibited a greater pre-test/post-test improvement than the control group. For example, if statistical significance is taken as a guide, a minimum indication that the curriculum was somewhat effective in promoting a particular aim would be that the experimental group experienced a significant improvement in performance, whereas the control group did not. Table 3.6 shows that this minimal criterion, in fact, was met for six items (namely, items 1, 4, 5, 6, 7 and 8). On the other hand, this minimal criterion was not met for items 2, 3, 9 and 10, thus suggesting that the parts of the unit dealing with the objectives measured by these latter items were unsuccessful in promoting achievement of intended aims.

It is arguable whether the degree of change observed for the items with statistically significant results was large enough to suggest that the unit was sufficiently successful in promoting a certain aim and, therefore, needed no revision to further enhance achievement. For example, the data in Table 3.5 for item 1 showed that, among the ASEP group, the number of students correct increased from 110 to only 132 between pre-testing and post-testing. Therefore the data in Table 3.5 illustrate that, despite the fact that some ASEP staff were hopeful that 'hard data' about student achievement of intended aims might have provided a dependable foundation on which to base the rewriting of materials, the lack of clear criteria for interpreting such data made this ideal difficult to realize.

Visits to Trial Classes by ASEP Staff

Quite apart from the extensive written feedback obtained during formative evaluation from experts and students, substantial and useful evaluative information was obtained from classroom visits. In fact, during the field testing of the first trial version of each ASEP unit, numerous visits were made to trial schools by writers and other ASEP staff. During these visits, in-depth discussion with students and teachers, examination of written records of students' work, and informal observation provided valuable feedback information to complement and supplement that obtained using other methods. Close attention was paid to errors, inconsistencies and inadequacies in the materials as revealed by their use in the classroom.

ASEP's evaluation summary for the unit *Mice and Men* (ASEP, 1972a) lists some of the observations made by ASEP staff during the eight visits which were made to classes testing this unit. Examples of some of the observations which suggested areas likely to need attention during rewriting of materials were:

1. Many students did not read the whole activity before commencing the practical work.
2. The blank pages in the record book confused students.
3. The black and white photographs on display had been ignored.
4. Most students jumped sections of early work and moved into activities without properly reading instructions.

There are two noteworthy features of the use of classroom visits as a method of collecting formative evaluative information. First, observation and interview methods used during these visits were highly unstructured and spontaneous in comparison with much of the information collected through use of structured questionnaires. Second, as limited formal recording was done of information gleaned from these visits, there was less need to collate information than there was with other methods. Often curriculum developers would revise materials simply on their recollections of their own visits to school, or on the anecdotes and observations informally communicated to them by other ASEP staff who had made visits.

COLLATION AND USE OF EVALUATIVE INFORMATION

The collation of feedback information was an important part of formative evaluation procedures. Clerical assistants working in conjunction with ASEP's evaluation team were responsible for coordinating the final collation of all evaluation feedback into a form which was likely to be useful to the development team. During the national trials, however, part of the within-state collation of feedback was completed by coordinators of state trials before the information was returned to ASEP for overall collation.

Some data reduction was needed if the voluminous amount of information was to be reduced to a form which was manageable and useful when writers were revising their units. In particular, as the tables in this chapter illustrate, data from structured questionnaires were aggregated to highlight overall trends. This aggregation of student data was usually carried out across the total sample, although some national trial data were collated separately for each state. However, in contrast to the way that individual responses to structured questionnaires were aggregated, all open-ended comments made by experts (external consultants, trial teachers, State Advisory Committees) were included in the collation of information. That is, it was thought that the person responsible for rewriting a particular unit should take cognisance of all comments made instead of a somewhat arbitrary subset of comments chosen by the staff involved in the collation task.

The size of the summaries of evaluative information for each ASEP unit tended to be quite substantial. For example, the inclusion of questionnaire data aggregated nationally or within each State, together with a complete listing of all open-ended comments made by experts, resulted in an evaluation summary of 29 single-spaced pages for the ASEP unit *Pushes and Pulls* and of 18 pages for *Life in Freshwater*.

A notable feature of the evaluation summaries produced by ASEP staff for each unit was their inclusion of a comprehensive set of specific recommendations to be implemented when rewriting units. For example, the evaluation summary for the unit *Pushes and Pulls* (see ASEP, 1972b) included recommendations that:

1. The name of the unit be changed to *Forces*.
2. The amount of reading in the unit be reduced.
3. Summaries be included at the end of activities.
4. The calibration of the student force-measurer against a standard scale be deleted as an activity.
5. The photographs on pages 53 and 54 be interchanged.
6. More space for student responses be allowed in the record book.
7. The force-measurer be redesigned with a larger base to increase its stability.

UTILIZATION OF EVALUATION RESULTS

An important question involves the extent to which the recommendations made in evaluation summaries were acted upon in the actual rewriting of materials. Cohen (1973) has provided an informative table for the ASEP unit *Mice and Men* showing what action, if any, was taken to accommodate feedback information.

In fact, this table provides some good illustrations of ways in which information about specific weaknesses identified in materials through use of evaluation procedures influenced the rewriting of a unit. This table also shows that, for a variety of reasons, no action at all was taken during rewriting to cater for evaluative comments made.

It is difficult to comment either on the overall impact of ASEP's programme of formative evaluation activities or on the relative utility of the various sources of evaluative information. One impression gained from interviewing different writers within ASEP was that different people found different sources of evaluation feedback differentially useful. Whereas some placed greatest weight on numerical information based upon consensus of the opinions obtained from large numbers of students or teachers, other ASEP writers preferred more intuitive judgements gleaned from casual observation in trial classes or informal talking with teachers and students. Similarly, writers differed when rewriting materials in terms of the amount of weight they placed on information obtained from outside consultants, teachers, students and State Advisory Committees.

The direct usefulness of formative evaluation feedback when rewriting units often appeared to be related to its specificity. The big advantage of highly specific information was that it was clear to writers exactly where changes were needed within a unit. On the other hand, information on experts' views about some general characteristic of the materials (e.g. the overall organization of the unit) or data on student achievement of broad goals (e.g. comprehension of the concept of electric charge), did not pinpoint exactly what changes were needed to rectify a weakness. For example, one writer noted that feedback comments such as 'I didn't like this section' were not uncommon and did little to guide the rewriting of a unit. ASEP writers often felt that evaluation efforts had identified important weaknesses that should be overcome, but had not provided information about what changes would be needed to surmount the problems.

This simple point about specificity has important implications for the planning of future formative evaluations. Whenever evaluation resources for any evaluation are likely to be limited, it may be preferable to concentrate efforts on the collection of specific information which yields clear implications for rewriting, rather than attempting to pinpoint more general problems whose solutions are far from obvious to writers attempting to revise materials. It is possible, also, that differences in specificity might explain why several writers at ASEP found comments written directly onto inspection copies of units much more useful in guiding rewriting than the aggregated results from general questionnaires or tests of student achievement of fairly broad objectives. Based on her experiences in the formative evaluation of Science 5/13 in the UK, Harlen (1975) concluded that the results of children's achievement tests were of much less help in guiding the rewriting of materials than was information obtained from teacher questionnaires and classroom observation. In the case of the formative evaluation of ASEP, the specificity of items included in achievement tests often appeared to be a major determinant of their usefulness. That is, items testing specific achievement objectives tended to yield some information which was useful in guiding unit rewriting, whereas items assessing general achievement objectives usually failed to produce suggestions useful when revising materials.

In an attempt to obtain the specific feedback which would be useful when rewriting units, ASEP's later evaluation procedures involved asking trial teachers and State Advisory Committees the following direct question: 'If you were given the job of revising the unit, what changes would you make?' This question proved very successful because it elicited information directly relevant to the rewriting task at hand instead of general comments about strengths and weakness. Consequently, one simple but potentially useful inclusion in other future formative evaluations is a question which directly requests suggestions about desirable revisions.

The question of the effectiveness of different methods of formative evaluation cannot be divorced from questions of cost effectiveness. That is, others involved in designing formative evaluation procedures are likely to be interested in finding out, not only what methods used by ASEP might have been more useful than others, but also which methods were very expensive and time consuming and which were not. For example, in the case of ASEP, the use of student achievement testing proved sufficiently costly and time consuming (especially in terms of test development and data collation time) that this approach to evaluation was abandoned some time before all units had undergone a second trial. Although the collation of student questionnaire data was also time-consuming, considerable economy was achieved by restricting attention to a sample of only 10 or 15 students from each class. In contrast, the method of asking various experts to provide their reactions by writing on the unit itself provided a relatively inexpensive method for obtaining valuable information which could be used directly without collation when writers were revising materials. Similarly, through visits to trial classes, developers were able economically to gain first-hand insights which could be translated directly into action during the rewriting stage, without the need for other staff to be involved in collecting and collating information.

PROBLEMS AND CONSTRAINTS

The main problem associated with conducting formative evaluation of ASEP materials and utilizing evaluation results centred on shortages of time and funds. Since ASEP's main aim was to develop a certain number of units within a fixed budget, there were often difficulties in determining what proportion of the Project's total resources should be devoted to evaluation. For example, although it was the intention to subject units to two field trials, it proved necessary to exclude some from national trials towards the end of the Project when funds were running out. Also, since stringent production schedules had to be adhered to, there were problems in evolving methods which permitted evaluative feedback to be collected, collated and put to good use within tight rewriting deadlines. There is little doubt that time and financial stringencies meant that compromises had to be made in terms of the nature, amount and timing of the evaluation activities undertaken.

As ASEP's primary responsibility was the production of units within a fixed period, the time at which formative evaluative information became available was crucial. Clearly formative information could not guide rewriting unless it was available well before writing deadlines. In fact, these time stringencies led to the situation in which collation of information often had to be done before feedback had arrived from some trial schools and, in some instances towards the end of the Project, final rewriting was done without the benefit of any feedback information. Also, deadlines for revising units sometimes meant that the development team did not have sufficient time fully to utilize all the feedback information which was at their disposal. This experience highlighted the potential conflict that can arise between the need to satisfy production deadlines and to improve the educational merit of curriculum materials through making full use of all the formative evaluative information available.

Another problem which confronted curriculum writers was that feedback from different sources was sometimes inconsistent. For example, a unit might have appeared to be extremely well received in one state but not in another. Teachers could have been unhappy with a particular feature of a unit that was very popular with students. Also quite different reports were sometimes received from the teachers and students at different trial schools.

EXTERNAL EVALUATION

ASEP's formative evaluation efforts were conducted by internal Project staff and aimed to provide feedback useful in guiding the revision of curriculum materials. Consequently, this internal evaluation work tended not to move towards research. Nevertheless, external researchers and evaluators have completed an extensive body of research which is reviewed comprehensively by Fraser (1978a,b) and described briefly below.

Research into the impact of ASEP on a variety of student outcomes (e.g. inquiry skills, understanding of the nature of science, attitudes) suggested that students using ASEP materials performed neither better nor worse on most outcomes than students using alternative materials. For a measure of student enjoyment of science lessons, however, significant differences in favour of the ASEP group were observed (Fraser, 1979b; Fisher and Fraser, 1980a,b). Other research involving analyses of videotapes of science lessons has shown considerable similarity between the percentage of time spent on different activities in classrooms using different ASEP units, but marked differences between ASEP and conventional classrooms. For instance, the student was the source of activity for two-thirds of the time in ASEP classrooms compared with only one-fifth of the time in conventional classrooms. Also, when compared with conventional classrooms, ASEP classrooms were characterized by less fact-stating and a smaller proportion of lesson time spent with the whole class as the target of activity (Tisher and Power,1976; Power and Tisher, 1979). An extensive questionnaire survey has indicated that teachers consider that the major advantages associated with using ASEP materials include opportunities for student choice and differential rates of student working; while common problems include student reading difficulties, organization of equipment and assessment (Fraser and Northfield, 1981). Another series of studies involving students' perceptions of classroom climate has shown that, in comparison with students following conventional materials, students using ASEP materials perceived their classrooms as more individualized, more satisfying, and having better availability of resources (Fraser, 1979b).

It has been recognized that an important aspect of curriculum dissemination is the extent of purchase and use of curriculum materials (Welch, 1968). In fact, a recent major study by Owen (1978) has provided some interesting data about purchase and use of ASEP materials. For example, the amount of money spent by schools in purchasing ASEP materials between early 1974 and mid-1976 was found to be 1.4 million dollars Australian, an amount comparable to ASEP's total development budget. Furthermore, by the end of 1975, about two-thirds of all Australian schools owned at least some ASEP materials. The amount of purchase and use of ASEP materials, however, was found to vary markedly in different Australian states and at different grade levels in the junior high school. Also the amount of usage of ASEP materials increased with the existence of advisory personnel who advocated ASEP's use and increased when school syllabuses were fairly consistent with ASEP's philosophy. Another particularly interesting finding emerging from Owen's study was that previous participation of a school's head of science department in the field trials of prototypes of ASEP units was a major factor influencing the amount of use of ASEP materials in a school.

CONCLUSION

Because the literature contains few retrospective accounts of formative (as distinct from summative) curriculum evaluations, this chapter portrays the comprehensive and varied formative evaluation activities associated with the Australian Science Education Project (ASEP). It is hoped that this chapter will prove helpful to others embarking on formative evaluations through its provision of a detailed description of ASEP's evaluation approaches, its illustration of concrete examples of useful evaluation techniques and results, and its tentative conclusions about the relative usefulness of different techniques in guiding rewriting of materials.

Some specific but tentative conclusions based on experiences with ASEP's formative evaluation are summarized below:

1. Procedures of reflective evaluation involving a group of people vetting preliminary specifications and draft versions of curriculum materials are likely to lead to more economical use of resources by providing a basis for abandoning or improving materials prior to incurring the expense of production. and field trials.
2. As different writers found various sources of formative evaluation information differentially useful, it may be preferable in future projects to use evaluation resources to generate more than one type of evaluative information.
3. As the usefulness of formative evaluation feedback appeared to be related to its specificity, it may be more useful in future formative evaluations to concentrate efforts on collecting specific information, which yields clear guidance in rewriting, than to attempt to pinpoint more general problems whose solutions are far from obvious to writers.
4. Certain methods of collecting evaluative information (e.g. student achievement testing) are likely to be more costly than others (e.g. visiting trial classrooms or having experts write comments onto copies of materials). In particular, visits to trial classes by writers can be economic since they involve little recording and collation of information.
5. Data on student achievement on individual test items are likely to be more useful in guiding the revision of materials than results on total test scores.
6. Use of both structured and unstructured questionnaire items together is likely to produce information which is more useful than that obtained by either approach alone.
7. Because formative evaluations can generate large amounts of information, writers are likely

to find collated feedback results (e.g. frequencies of common responses to open-ended questions) more useful than raw data when rewriting materials.

8. A conflict can arise between the need to satisfy production deadlines and to improve the educational merit of curriculum materials through making full use of all formative evaluative information available.

ACKNOWLEDGEMENT

Parts of this chapter are based on a report of ASEP's curriculum development processes being prepared in collaboration with Dr David Cohen of Macquarie University.

REFERENCES

Anderson, S.B. and Ball, S. (1978) The Profession and Practice of Program Evaluation, Jossey-Bass, San Francisco

ASEP (1972a) 'Unit Evaluation Summary for National Trial of Mice and Men,' Unpublished paper, Australian Science Education Project

ASEP (1972b) 'Unit Evaluation Summary for National Trial of Pushes and Pulls, Unpublished paper, Australian Science Education Project

ASEP (1974) A Guide to ASEP, Victorian Government Printer, Melbourne

Baker, E.L. (1974) 'Formative Evaluation of Instruction', in W.J. Popham (ed), Evaluation in Education: Current Applications, McCutchan, Berkeley, California

Baker, E.L. (1978) 'Evaluation Dimensions for Program Development and Improvement', in S.B. Anderson and C.D. Coles (eds.), Exploring Purposes and Dimensions, New Directions for Program Evaluation, No. 1, Jossey-Bass, San Francisco

Baker, E.L. and Alkin, M.C. (1973) 'Formative Evaluation of Instructional Development', AV Communication Review, 21, 389-418

Bloom, B.S. (1977) 'Tryout and Revision of Educational Materials and Methods', in A. Lewy (ed.), Handbook of Curriculum Evaluation, Unesco, Paris

Champagne, A. and Klopfer, L.E. (1974) 'Formative Evaluation in Science Curriculum Development',

Journal of Research in Science Teaching, 11, 185-203

Cohen, D. (1973) 'Evaluation of Integrated Science Curricula', in P. Richmond (ed.), New Trends in Integrated Science Teaching, Vol. 2, Unesco, Paris

Cronbach, L.J. et al. (1980) Toward Reform of Program Evaluation: Aims, Methods, and Institutional Arrangements, Jossey-Bass, San Francisco

Fisher, D.L. and Fraser, B.J. (1980a) 'Evaluating the Impact of a National Curriculum Project on Content-free Cognitive Outcomes', European Journal of Science Education, 2, 45-59

Fisher, D.L. and Fraser, B.J. (1980b) 'A Replication of the Effects of Using ASEP Materials on Student Attitudes', Australian Science Teachers Journal, 26(2), 80-2

Fraser, B.J. (1973) 'Curriculum Evaluation Part II: An Illustration Using ASEP Trial data', Australian Science Teachers Journal, 19(2), 42-53

Fraser, B.J. (1978a) Review of Research on Australian Science Education Project, Curriculum Development Centre, Canberra

Fraser, B.J. (1978b) 'Australian Science Education Project: Overview of evaluation studies.' Science Education, 62, 417-26

Fraser, B.J. (1979a) 'Second Generation Curriculum Projects and Australian Science Education Project', School Science and Mathematics, 79, 507-12

Fraser, B.J. (1979b) 'Evaluation of a Science-based Curriculum', in H.J. Walberg (ed.), Educational Environments and Effects: Evaluation, Policy, and Productivity, McCuthchan, Berkeley, California

Fraser, B.J. and Northfield, J.R. (1981) A Study of ASEP in its First Year of Availability, Curriculum Development Centre, Canberra

Grobman, H. (1968) Evaluation Activities of Curriculum Projects, AERA Monograph Series on Curriculum Evaluation, No. 2, Rand McNally, Chicago

Harlen, W. (1975) 'A Critical Look at the Classical Strategy Applied to Formative Curriculum Evaluation', Studies in Educational Evaluation, 1, 37-53

Krus, P.H. et al. (1975) A Formative Evaluation Design for Assessing Instructional Materials, Studies in Educational Evaluation, 1, 131-7

Lucas, A.M. (1972) 'ASEP - A National Curriculum Development Project in Australia', Science

Education, 56, 443-51

Novick, S. (1976) 'The Use of Formative Evaluation Procedures for Improvement of a Socially-Oriented Course in Chemistry', Studies in Educational Evaluation, 2, 1-7

Owen, J.M. (1978) The Impact of the Australian Science Education Project on Schools, Curriculum Development Centre, Canberra

Power, C.N. and Tisher, R.P. (1979) 'A self-paced environment', in H.J. Walberg (ed.), Educational Environments and Effects: Evaluation, Policy, and Productivity, McCutchan, Berkeley, California

Sanders, J.R. and Cunningham, D.J. (1974) 'Techniques and Procedures for Formative Evaluation', Research, Evaluation, Development Paper Series, Northwest Regional Educational Laboratory, Portland

Steadman, S. (1976) 'Techniques of Evaluation', in D. Tawney (ed.), Curriculum Evaluation Today: Trends and Implications, Schools Council Research Studies, Macmillan, London

Tisher, R.P. and Power, C.N. (1976) 'Variations between ASEP and Conventional Learning Environments', Australian Science Teachers Journal, 22(3), 35-9

Welch, W.W. (1968) 'Impact of National Curriculum Projects: The Need for Assessment', School Science and Mathematics, 68, 225-34

4. THE PHYSICAL SCIENCE EVALUATION, WESTERN AUSTRALIA, 1978-79: AN APPLICATION OF THE ILLUMINATIVE MODEL*

D.J. Boud, M.B. Dynan, L.H. Parker and A.S. Ryan

THE CURRICULUM PROJECT

The Scenario

In Western Australia, the education system is structured so that, of a child's possible twelve years of formal schooling, seven are spent in the primary school and the remaining five in the secondary school. Approximately four-fifths of the state's 250,000 school-aged children are educated in government schools, administered, staffed and provisioned by the Education Department of Western Australia, centred in Perth, the state's capital city. The Education Department has developed extensive networks for, among its other functions, the development and dissemination of curriculum materials.

The Upper Secondary School Population - Changes and Options

In the early 1960s and before, a large proportion of children in the state terminated their education at the end of the tenth year (i.e. at age 15, which is the minimum legal school leaving age in Western Australia). Curricula offered in the remaining two years of secondary school (years 11 and 12) tended to be somewhat specialized, academic and oriented to

* This chapter describes an evaluation conducted in a style based on Parlett and Hamilton's (1972) model of illuminative evaluation. Problems and issues which were faced in attempting to implement the illuminative model are discussed by the authors, in a reporting style which itself aims to be 'illuminative'.

preparing students for tertiary studies. Retention patterns have changed, however. The proportion of students continuing their education past the compulsory years has increased steadily to the present level of approximately 60 per cent. This group now includes students with a wider range of aspirations, needs and abilities than it did in former years.

Students generally choose six subjects for study in years 11 and 12. At the conclusion of year 12, their performance in these subjects is assessed, both internally by the school, yielding a grade for their Certificate of Secondary Education, and externally by an examination known as the Tertiary Admissions Examination (TAE). Traditionally, the various tertiary institutions, in particular the universities, have had quite a strong influence on the upper-school (i.e. years 11, 12) curriculum, with respect to both the pattern of subjects chosen by students and the content of courses taught. In particular, four subjects have come to be considered by students and their teachers, as critically important for entry to certain prestigious professions such as medicine and engineering. These subjects - Chemistry, Physics, Mathematics 2 and Mathematics 3 - have become known colloquially as the 'big four' and currently attract a high proportion of the most able students. Given that English consumes another one-sixth of the students' 36-period academic timetable, there is clearly little time remaining for study of humanities or arts. Some observers and students regret this situation and refer to the 'stranglehold' of the big four on able students, only a small proportion of whom will proceed to tertiary studies in pure science. As one Education Department representative has expressed it:

> For years schools have been advising almost their entire complement of tertiary-bound students to do the big four. This is hard to justify since major decisions today are being made by economists, lawyers and such. So why channel many of our best people into science and maths?

There has also been, over the past few years, some disillusionment with the highly conceptual nature of the TAE Physics and Chemistry courses which were adopted in Western Australia during the 1960s, in accord with international trends. Some critics, both in Western Australia and elsewhere, have focused on lack of relevance to everyday life and lack of emphasis on technological and societal issues as major defects of these courses. In fact, the need for a less specialized, more practically oriented curriculum for the year 11 and 12 physical sciences was identified as far back as 1975, when the Education Department carried out a needs analysis.[1] The subsequent two years saw a continuing emphasis on this need, rationalized in terms of the increasingly changing nature of the upper school population of students. There was general agreement that these students required a new and different pattern of skills and knowledge, which could be provided in part by a broader, more practical focus and wider choice in their school subjects.

The Birth of Physical Science

Thus, following several years of activity within the Education Department including many formal and informal discussions among secondary, tertiary and Departmental representatives, agreement was reached in 1977 in regard to the offering of the new subject *Physical Science*. The latter was conceived as a single (i.e. six 40-minute periods per week) upper school subject, combining content from the disciplines of physics and chemistry, with an emphasis on associated technological and societal issues. Approval to offer the new subject for examination in the 1979 Tertiary Admissions Examination and for inclusion on the 1979 Certificate of Secondary Education was given by the appropriate authorities in Western Australia.

The Western Australian *Physical Science* course has three major aims[2], which are (1) understanding the physical world; (2) understanding science and the scientific process; and (3) developing attitudes about science and the community. It includes five core units and six optional units from which students were originally expected to choose at least three (later modified to two). The content of the course is related to three major conceptual areas - *materials*, *energy* and *change* - and three themes - *science*, *technology* and *society* - are developed throughout. Although *pure science* is the predominant theme, continuous emphasis is given to the supporting themes, by explanation and discussion on technological applications of science and their concomitant cultural impact. Although the course was designed on the basis that it should be as demanding conceptually as the existing TAE *Chemistry* and *Physics* courses, it was not intended to, and does not, have the same emphasis on quantitative treatment that these traditional physical science curricula have.

A decision was made to produce special course materials for *Physical Science*, to be written by a small team from the Curriculum Branch of the Education Department, using secondary and tertiary personnel as consultants. This was a decidedly innovative step to take for, although the Department had for many years been actively involved in the production of curricula for years 8-10 science courses, they had taken no previous initiative in curriculum development for TAE *Physics* and *Chemistry*.

For each core and optional unit of the course, a resource book was produced for student use. Associated with each of these was a teacher's guide which incorporated all the content of the student book together with guidance on resources, teaching suggestions and the outcomes expected for each section. Additionally, special case-study resource books dealing with particular industries were produced to assist classes with the industrial case-studies included in some sections of the course.

Schools were kept informed of developments about the new course and many expressed considerable interest in offering a course of this nature, pending the availability of appropriate numbers of interested students and staff. Toward the end of 1977, agreement was reached between the Department and 19 government schools[3] with respect to participation of the latter in an initial two-year trial of the course.

THE EVALUATION

Initial Negotiations

The origins of a research or evaluation project are often difficult to ascertain fully. Unlike the actual conduct of the evaluation, of which good records are kept, the progress of the initial, informal negotiations to establish a project are recalled more hazily. For one thing the establishment of a project is usually the result of discussions among many individuals with varying perspectives, and for another the reasons for evaluating are often not explicit. The beginnings of the *Physical Science* evaluation project are no exception to these general observations. It started through the conjunction of a perceived need (that of formally and independently evaluating the introduction of a major new course into the upper secondary school curriculum) with the availability and interest of a number of individuals. There also existed a desire on the part of the Education Department to develop cooperative ventures with local tertiary institutions.

The following are the recollections of the person (Dave Boud) originally approached by a representative of the body responsible for developing the Physical Science course, the Education Department of Western Australia.

> In the second part of 1977 I was employed as a Visiting Fellow in the School of Applied Science at the Western Australian Institute of Technology (WAIT). My role was to develop a new Graduate Diploma and Masters programme in Science Education for experienced science teachers and to conduct some of the core units. One of the students in the first (1977) intake to the course was a Superintendent of Science for Western Australia, who had been closely involved in the conception and development of the new Physical Science course. Part of my course was devoted to curriculum evaluation, and in particular to those 'new' approaches that I had been involved with in the United Kingdom prior to taking up the position at WAIT and naturally discussion centered on the applicability of the illuminative and other approaches to the evaluation of situations with which the students were familiar.
>
> From these tentative discussions about the scope and applicability of various approaches to evaluation there arose speculation about what might be the nature of an evaluation of a new curriculum. Having sounded me out about my interests, informal negotiations began between myself and the Science Superintendent in his role in the Education Department. Right from the start I enlisted the help of a colleague in the science education area in the School of Teacher Education, Muredach Dynan, who I knew was interested in both Physical Science and evaluation, but who at that time had no direct experience of some of the 'new' approaches which seemed appropriate to me.

As the discussions progressed it became necessary to formalise the situation with some kind of documented agreement between the bodies involved. By this stage those most directly involved (viz. the Superintendent, Muredach Dynan and myself) had agreed informally on the strategy and general aims of the evaluation. It was also agreed that the evaluation be conducted by a team from the Western Australian Institute of Technology drawn from the School of Applied Science and the School of Teacher Education, and that the evaluation should be seen to be independent of the Education Department and especially of the curriculum development team. A joint committee of senior officials from the Institute and Education Department and ourselves met to thrash out a formal agreement, which specified the aims, approach and responsibilities of the project.

Two themes became clear during these negotiations: those of credibility and control - the credibility of the evaluators and the control of the project. At first I had assumed that it was only necessary to demonstrate my experience and academic pedigree in evaluation to reassure the 'clients' that a competent job would be done, but I began to realise that this aspect, while important in getting the negotiations started, was not the most important one as far as the Education Department was concerned. They wanted evaluators who could demonstrate credibility to teachers and non-academics, people who understood enough about how schools worked and how teachers conducted themselves to be able to be accepted by the major participants in the trial of the course materials. For Muredach this was relatively easy as he had many years of experience as a science teacher and as a teacher trainer in Ireland, for myself with no teaching experience and no prior contact with high schools this came about through the way in which I was accepted by my students, all of whom were drawn from the population of teachers who might be implementing the *Physical Science* course.

The control of the project was a less easily

> resolved issue. It is one that involves compromise and the establishment of trust on both sides. To put it simply, perhaps too simply, in what was agreed to be an 'independent' evaluation, the evaluators wanted complete freedom to investigate whatever issues they wished and report on them to whichever parties they thought appropriate, whereas the Department wanted more restrictions on reporting and did not want to give carte blanche in advance of seeing the content of what was to be reported. Whilst the issue was never explicitly identified as one of trust, I believe in retrospect, that each party felt a real concern, in regard to what the other party might ultimately do. The concern was justifiable: the Department had had previous experience of being embarrassed by 'exposures' which they felt were unjustified from a research project mounted by another institution, and I had had the unforgettable experience of having a report censored by clients after open access had been negotiated.
>
> The control issue began to subside through further contact between the parties and the exercise of goodwill on both sides. It was finally agreed that a management group be established for the project with representatives from the two Schools of the Institute and the Education Department, that the project be jointly funded by the Department and the Institute and that the management committee be responsible for approving all reports, except those which were confidential and of limited circulation.

The point at which these early negotiations were completed coincided with the departure of Dave Boud from Western Australia. Tony Ryan (then of the Education Department's Research Branch, but shortly to become a Senior Lecturer in the School of Teacher Education at the WA Institute of Technology) joined Muredach Dynan as a Coordinator of the evaluation project. In addition, a full time Research Assistant's position was advertized, as a consequence of which Lesley Parker, experienced in science teaching and research in Western Australia and elsewhere, joined the evaluation team. Dave Boud's subsequent role in the evaluation was as an external consultant, and his regular comments on procedures and reports proved immensely valuable to the rest of the team.

The evaluation was thus set up as a cooperative but independently conducted venture, with the following general purposes:

1. To contribute to the refinement and validation of the materials produced by the project.
2. To obtain data on the effectiveness of the induction and continuing support provided to teachers introducing the course in the initial group of participating schools.
3. To provide potential later adopters with evaluative information concerning the philosophy, content and pedagogical features of the course, resources required to implement it, and its performance in the trial situations.
4. To provide, in conjunction with the course developers, a record of the background, conduct and outcomes of the project for the benefit of other teams and future curriculum work generally.

The Style of the Evaluation

From the beginning it was envisaged that the evaluation would not follow the traditional approaches to evaluation, in which the sponsors and evaluators specify items on what information will be sought, followed by the evaluators constructing or selecting test instruments to meet these requirements. Even the early informal discussions had revealed that the innovation involved several different interest groups, which seemed unlikely to be united by a common perspective on the course, its basic purposes and aims, or the significance of certain elements of content. Thus there was unlikely to be any real and valid consensus regarding what the evaluators could most usefully and appropriately do. The evaluators themselves held the view that their role was to assist each of the various interest groups (the senior officials of the Education Department, the course writers, teachers, students, tertiary personnel, etc.) to clarify its own perspective on the innovation and to be at least aware of the perspective of others - in other words, to give the participants a sound basis for making decisions and judgements. This view was reinforced by the interest of the Department's representatives in reactions which different groups were showing to the course. At the same time the evaluators saw as paramount the need to be sensitive to the innovation *in situ* and to be responsive to the unforeseen issues which arise during any innovation. Ultimately, in recognition of the above perceived roles and needs, the approach known as illuminative evaluation (Parlett and Hamilton, 1972) was proposed and accepted[4] in principle.

Many researchers (e.g. Parlett and Hamilton, 1972; Kemmis, 1978; House, 1978) contrast the illuminative and other similar styles of evaluation (e.g. Stake's 'responsive' and 'portrayal' approaches, 1972) with some of the more traditional positivist approaches to evaluation, particularly those which follow predetermined experimental designs, assume a basically detached role for the evaluator and concentrate on readily measurable outcomes of the innovation being studied. In comparison, evaluators adopting an illuminative style are likened to ethnographers, immersing themselves in the milieu of the innovation in order to identify significant issues and phenomena, and relating these to the expectations, perceptions and experiences of the various participants and other interested groups.

The above contrasts follow closely the polarization explicit in many debates on styles of research in general. The relative virtues of the positivist and interpretative research paradigms are frequently, and at times heatedly, expounded. Increasingly, the trend is less towards overpolarization of the differences between the positivist 'agricultural-botany' approach and the interpretative 'social anthropology' tradition and more towards approaches integrating elements of both paradigms, depending on the needs of the research situation. Nisbet (1974), for example, refers to a range of compatible research styles rather than a clash or confrontation between contrasting styles. He makes the point that 'spectrum', in fact, may be a better term to use than 'range', because:

> a spectrum has no sharp boundaries, and also (if it is not straining the metaphor) because you get white light by mixing all the different frequencies.

In this context it is interesting to note that, although it is firmly grounded in the interpretative, phenomenological tradition, with a heavy reliance on qualitative data, illuminative evaluation does not reject quantitative data. The methodology is in fact typically eclectic in that it can embrace a wide range of techniques including observation, interviewing and the collection and sophisticated analysis of questionnaire and test data. As has been pointed out elsewhere (Jenkins, 1976) 'illuminative evaluation is not a standard methodological package; the methods of investigation are themselves situational'.

Illuminative evaluation is thus best described as a process rather than a package. In general terms, an illuminative evaluator sets out first to identify major emerging issues as perceived by various participants in the innovation; second, to focus progressively on these selected issues by a combination of methods; and third, to induce and report on general principles and patterns within the operation of the programme. Reports on any or all of the three stages generally attempt to give an holistic picture of the innovation, representing faithfully the perspectives and special interests of all participants. Ideally, reporting is intended to be an open interactive process, with all key participants having equal access to information emerging from the evaluation. In presenting reports, illuminative evaluators generally try to avoid making judgements on the worth of the innovation, attempting rather to provide a comprehensive interpretation of the interacting elements that make up the reality of the innovation as it is experienced by each significant group.

The process attempts to illuminate rather than judge, to seek out issues rather than pre-select them, and to take account of the perspectives and interests of all legitimate audiences. Thus the illuminative evaluator attempts to inform those with an interest in the innovation and assist those who have a responsibility to make decisions about it. At the general level, Parlett and Hamilton suggest that there will ordinarily be three major audiences to be addressed. Translated to the case of the *Physical Science* evaluation, these three audience groups were: 1. *the project's participants*: teachers, students, school administrators, course developers, course consultants, tertiary personnel, the TAE Syllabus Committee; 2. *the project's sponsors*: the Education Department and the WA Institute of

Technology; and 3. interested outsiders, e.g. other researchers, curriculum planners, parents, potential adopters.

The above, of course, outlines an 'ideal type' illuminative approach. Some of the problems which arose in implementing this approach and some of the modifications subsequently made to the model are discussed in the following sections of this chapter.

THE PROCESS OF THE EVALUATION

Phase 1 - The Exploratory Process

In late 1977 and early 1978 we undertook the exploratory phase of the evaluation. In keeping with the illuminative model, we attempted in this phase to uncover key issues as perceived by the participants in the innovation. We conducted interviews and discussions with a wide range of people, including tertiary academic staff and Education Department representatives, as well as the principals, teachers and students of all 19 trial schools. There were 370 students involved initially in the trial and, rather than select a few of these students for in-depth study, we found it more useful and expedient at this stage to induce a number of group perspectives from among students. A good deal of observation of classroom processes was carried out, which was valuable in our attempts to understand the innovation from the students' and teachers' points of view.

During this phase it quickly became obvious that the perception of what constituted a key issue varied widely among groups. The task of deciding which issues to follow up in-depth was a difficult one and was made urgent by the fact that some issues required considerable data collection which would have to be commenced immediately. In the event, we took decisions in consultation with the management committee to commence data collection in relation to aspects of the evaluation which appeared to be of widest concern. A summary list of the major issues which emerged during the exploratory phase is shown below:

1. To what extent did the new course meet the needs which had originally led to the introduction of the new subject?
2. How well did the resource materials and teacher's guides meet the stated aims and objectives of the course?

3. What types of students were attracted by the Physical Science course and what aspirations did these students have?
4. How was the enrolment pattern in other school subjects likely to be affected by the introduction of the new subject?
5. What were the reactions/perceptions of potential consumers of the graduates of Physical Science, in particular the tertiary institutions? Had the perceptions of these institutions altered with the publication of course materials?
6. To what extent would the assessment procedures (both internal and external) match the objectives and content of the course?
7. How effective was the in-service programme proving to be in relation to the implementation of the course?

This list was not intended to be definitive and was considered subject to modification in the light of other issues which might emerge throughout the evaluation.

Two problems, related generally to the perspectives on research and evaluation held by us as individuals and by some of the participants and audiences of the evaluation, were evident during the exploratory phase of the evaluation. Firstly, of all the evaluators, Dave Boud, our now absent member, was the one with the strongest commitment to illuminative evaluation and with most experience in applying this approach. We remaining evaluators, partly because of our own personal backgrounds and training in science and research methodology, were initially less comfortable with the illuminative model. Although attracted by this novel and different approach, we were reluctant to eschew elements of the established, traditional positivist methodologies. We were also acutely conscious of the possible charge of subjectivity, which is frequently levelled at interpretative research and, from the very inception of the project, took a number of steps to counteract this possibility. We tended, for example to validate our impressions and observations by the collection of quantitative data if appropriate. We also rigorously adhered to certain elementary precautions - for example we adopted as standard practice, that visits to schools would be made on a rotational basis by each of us in turn, that major interviews would be undertaken by two of us together and that each of us would prepare detailed field notes of observations or interviews, so that recollections and perceptions could be cross-checked constantly. These data, together with tape-recorded interviews and key documents, were retained for future reference and further cross-checking if necessary.

The second problem, namely the expectations which others held of the evaluation, was not so readily resolved. In early interviews with tertiary personnel, teachers and others we found that many interviewees anticipated that the evaluation would make judgements about the course, the curriculum materials or even the teaching. In particular, there was the expectation that we would be measuring student achievement of the aims of the course. These misconceptions, understandable though they were, threatened to negate the whole illuminative process and to raise false hopes (or fears) about the nature of the emerging reports. We needed to constantly reiterate that, despite the connotations of 'curriculum evaluation', we were not going to pass any final judgements about the worth of Physical Science, nor were we going to measure any cognitive student outcomes. Above all we emphasized that the evaluation of teachers was not even remotely part of our brief.

Phases II and III - The Clarification and Reporting of Issues

Using the issues on the above list as starting points, we proceeded with the task of 'progressive focusing' on each issue. It is not the intention here to imply that each phase of the evaluation (i.e. exploring, progressive focusing and reporting) was distinct. In fact there was considerable overlap among phases, in that some issues (e.g. the effect of the introduction of Physical Science on enrolments in other school subjects) were only at the stage of being articulated by participants, at the same time that others (e.g. the characteristics of Physical Science students) were well on the way to being reported upon. This could be seen as typical of illuminative evaluation, in that the evaluators need continually take cognizance of emergent, as well as initial issues.

We were perhaps fortunate in that the first issue which we chose to pursue in depth and on which we considered it appropriate (given the demand from participants) to report widely, was not a particularly sensitive one. The issue concerned the academic and aspirational profile of students participating in Physical Science and their reasons for choosing the course. The data were gathered largely by means of a semi-structured questionnaire to students, with some back-up interviews. In regard to the presentation of findings, the only area which had to be handled carefully concerned the general perceptions of the difficulty of Physical Science and their implications. It was clear from the data obtained that there was a strong tendency both on the part of students and teachers to perceive Physical Science as an easier science course than either Chemistry or Physics - a situation not consistent with the intentions of the curriculum developers. Our data also indicated that the new subject had attracted a greater proportion of lower-ability students than Physics and Chemistry. In all, it was apparent that the Developer's intention to have Physical Science regarded as equal in status to Physics and Chemistry was not being fulfilled in the trial schools. This was a sensitive and complex area for discussion and, without our detailed statistical data, it is likely that the real situation in the schools would have been very difficult to present in a credible form.

Ultimately the brief report on this issue, entitled Characteristics of 1978 Physical Science Student Population, was cleared by the project's management committee for wide distribution. This report also incorporated a statement on enrolment patterns in other subjects. The latter, although potentially a sensitive issue, was in fact 'defused' by the finding that there was no particular universal trend in other subjects' enrolments following the introduction of Physical Science. The value of this report to various audiences was evidenced by the requests for us to obtain equivalent data on subsequent cohorts of Physical Science students.

From the preceding references to 'sensitive' issues, it is probably apparent to the reader that our interpretation of 'sensitivity' was influenced considerably by the attitudes of the Education Department. Rightly or wrongly, we were conscious, throughout the project, that the Department was the major sponsor of the study, contributing a considerable share of the necessary financial and other resources (e.g. time of its senior personnel) and facilitating easy access to documents, schools, classrooms, teachers and students. The needs of the Department were seen by us to be of paramount importance and, while other audiences were addressed at times throughout the project, the bulk of our written reporting was designed primarily for this major client. This situation may well be perceived by some as imposing undesirable bureaucractic constraints on the evaluation and thus compromising its independence. To us, however, it was a functional necessity.

As implied in the reminiscences above, it was clear from the beginning that at times there would be a need to reconcile some features of the illuminative approach (particularly in regard to reporting procedures), with the needs, customs and concerns of the Education Department. Like many government bodies, the Department was accustomed to more tightly defined, quantitative, positivist research designs. Moreover, the fundamental illuminative tenets regarding the active roles and the right to information of the various constituencies in the project were relatively novel and not altogether compatible with established, centralized, decision-making processes. It was both necessary and politic to make certain concessions, in particular to the Department's views regarding the need for confidentiality of some reports. Such concessions appeared to contribute significantly to the establishment of an atmosphere of trust between the Department and ourselves. It is interesting to note that, as the various reports of the Project emerged, the earlier concerns of the Education Department disappeared and open reporting became fully acceptable.

We also learned to take care to present our reports in such a fashion as to have appeal to, and be readily assimilated by particular audiences. A portrayal approach, the presentation of multiple realities and the use of what Stake (1972) has called a 'panoramic viewfinder' may be ideals to which illuminative evaluators aspire. However, in this case, such reports would have been of limited value to audiences conditioned to receive statements dominated by a more focused, statistical approach. Moreover, while it was an attractive idea to write a colourful report describing the way students and teachers perceived the course in action, there were two practical arguments against doing so. First, the time taken to do this would have precluded focusing and reporting on other issues of perceived importance. Second, such reporting was likely to place considerable emphasis on the perceptions of students. While students' views were obviously important to the Department personnel and others, more weight was likely to be given to the views of teachers, school administrators and tertiary academics in the decision-making processes.

We resolved this dilemma by producing a considerable variety of reports. Some reports addressed one or two issues only. Other reports focused totally on teachers' or students' perceptions of individual units. The two main reports of the project (Dynan *et al.*, 1979; Dynan and Ryan, 1981) were more holistic in style, addressing the main issues and incorporating description and interpretation of both statistical and qualitative data.

Other evaluators have also drawn attention to this need to tailor the format of reports to some extent to meet the expectations of the audience. House (1972) talking of 'the context of persuasion' points out that:

> the producers of the data *must* assume some burden in seeing their information is properly understood. Simply wrapping the baby up warmly and leaving him on the doorstep at midnight does not absolve one of responsibility.

Similarly, Walker (1980) in discussing descriptive accounts, comments that they 'may be accepted as true by the practitioners, but they are not likely to create appropriate bases for policy or decision making'.

The Role of the Illuminative Evaluator - Information Broker, Focus of Discontent or Tool of the Administration?

The clarification and reporting of two further issues will be discussed here to highlight certain key features of our experience with implementing the illuminative model. In regard to one of these issues - the attitudes of science experts in tertiary institutions towards *Physical Science* in the schools - we feel in retrospect that we read the overall situation correctly and indeed functioned as honest information brokers and facilitators of understanding. The other issue, however, a broad one incorporating several inter-related aspects of the implementation of *Physical Science* in the schools, held a number of surprises for us and caused us to reflect, more than at any other stage of the evaluation, on our own approach to the project. It was through the processes of clarifying and reporting this issue that we came to realize that the need for 'trust among participants' was a recurrent need, as well as a necessary pre-condition for a viable evaluation.

Firstly, to discuss the tertiary reactions to and perceptions of the new course. The involvement of tertiary personnel in the innovation had been quite widespread, both as honorary consultants in the writing of the course materials and earlier in the discussions of the course itself and its acceptance as sufficient preparation for tertiary studies. Although many tertiary personnel were disposed favourably towards the course and its written materials, others were suspicious of it for a number of reasons. For example, some perceived it as a possible threat to the viability of the established disciplines of Physics and Chemistry both at secondary and at tertiary levels. Moreover, they saw their own traditional control over upper secondary science curricula being eroded. In addition, an influential and articulate few were fiercely critical of the course's written materials produced by the Education Department.

It was our delicate task to represent the reality of these various, at times conflicting, tertiary points of view, ensuring that 'the silent majority' was not forgotten, and that the basis of certain fears and criticisms was understood. This we did in the form of a strictly confidential report to the Department, following which the Department, on its own initiative, took steps, in consultation with tertiary representatives, to alleviate the criticisms. Potential conflict was thus resolved. It is of interest to note that 18 months later, when the final evaluation report was published, it was possible to report widely and frankly on this issue of initial tertiary reactions to the new course. Thus, it would seem that a two-stage process of reporting (confidentiality being observed in the first stage) was effective and acceptable to everyone concerned.

It was during the pursuit of the second issue, relating to the implementation of Physical Science, that we came to appreciate in full the meaning of Parlett's (1975) statement that: 'the evaluation is in danger of being perceived as "a tool of the administration", "a focus of unrest" or both at the same time'. There were numerous reasons for pursuing the 'implementation' issue. In-depth knowledge of the implementation process was clearly necessary for achieving items (1) and (3) of the evaluator's original brief as well as impinging, to various extents, on all the issues identified in the exploratory phase. Although our continuing excellent relationships with senior Departmental personnel, teachers and students facilitated the gathering of such knowledge, there were some reactions from the actual curriculum developers which indicated clearly that in their view we did not understand and were not representing *their* perspective fairly and accurately in our reports.

The developers were basically experienced, confident science teachers, one of whom had nursed the *Physical Science* course from the time of the earliest discussions, through the trauma of birth and the subsequent stages of growth and development. Understandably they had a strong personal investment in the course and its written materials. Also understandably, they were ambivalent towards others collecting formative feedback about the course materials and perceived our feedback to be presented in a judgemental fashion, damaging to the infant course. This led to some tension between developers and evaluators until the matter was resolved in frank and open discussions between members of both teams. In retrospect it is clear that time for such dialogue should have been set aside earlier in the evaluation, in the interests of consolidation of trust between the developers and ourselves. However, pressures were such, in the initial stages of the project, that there was impatience on all sides for us to 'get on with the job' and produce something tangible. It is now apparent that the job cannot go on unless trust is first established.

The issue of whether or not detailed formative feedback on individual units of the course should have been collected is one which we still debate among ourselves. We three *in situ* evaluators considered that the collection of such feedback lent an essential focus to our 'in-school' activities. Moreover, the fact that summaries of the feedback could be provided regularly to the teachers, contributed to the latter group's perception of the evaluation as a worthwhile project and of the evaluators' 'in-school' activities as useful. We considered that such information was necessary in order for the evaluation project to maintain its independence of the curriculum developers, who otherwise would have been the sole authoritative source of formative feedback.

Dave Boud, however, viewed the act of feedback

collection as a major departure from the original illuminative model and a movement towards a bureaucratic model of evaluation. He considered that too much of the project's resources were devoted to pure curriculum development rather than to broader evaluative issues and those of long-term significance. He also saw a grave danger of the evaluation team being co-opted into the curriculum development in a quite inappropriate way. In his eyes, the performance of this particular formative function meant that the team was in danger of identifying too closely with the curriculum development and of having to evaluate in a context in which they were seen either to be supporting or challenging specific aspects of the curriculum material and the way in which the development team went about its work. This he saw as jeopardizing the independence of the evaluation, in that we could have been, at some later stage, evaluating what was implicitly our own contribution to the curriculum project. The problem raised for the independence of the evaluation project was indeed felt by all the evaluators. However, while independence needs to be guarded closely, it may be that some dilution of independence is inevitable, since evaluators are always a reactive, not an inert, element in the milieu of the innovation. In a sense their very existence is an important variable in the dynamic process of implementation. Thus, as was also implied in our earlier discussion of compromises made in regard to reporting procedures, absolute independence in such an evaluation project may be impossible.

IMPACT OF THE EVALUATION ON THE DEVELOPMENT AND IMPLEMENTATION PROCESSES

Evaluators like to believe that their reports are read (or listened to) by those involved or concerned with the particular innovation under study. They also hope that what they report is relevant and useful in terms of action undertaken and decisions made. Claims by evaluators for the effectiveness of their work in terms of impact on the overall developmental process are subject to the same dangers of bias as any other kind of self-reporting - the reader is duly warned! We have attempted to verify the accuracy of our comment in this regard by reference to statements made by developers, teachers and others involved in the innovation.

THE *PHYSICAL SCIENCE* EVALUATION, WESTERN AUSTRALIA

The most obvious ways in which this evaluation study affected the innovation processes were in relation firstly to the written course materials and secondly to the implementation of the course in the schools. At a more fundamental level, however, the very existence of the evaluation project had a subtly pervasive influence on the whole process. The presence of an independent team of evaluators, with high visibility at all in-service meetings and in the classrooms where the subject was being taught, was public evidence of the serious commitment of the Education Department to the success of the innovation. It enhanced the milieu of professionalism, expertise and enthusiasm for development surrounding the early phases of the implementation of the new course. All participants were encouraged to speak their minds with the understanding that views would be reported and, hopefully, acted upon. Increasingly, as data and reports emerged from the project, we were called upon, at conferences and elsewhere, to provide impartial findings of progress within the innovation.

In respect of formative influences on the development of the content and structure of the guides and resource books, on which students and teachers were dependent, there were two distinct stages at which observable effects were apparent. The first occurred early in the trial stage when, as alluded to earlier, feedback from some tertiary consultants and schools contained significant criticisms of some aspects of the content. While the Department did not totally share these misgivings it nonetheless responded by setting up consultative groups of academic specialists to review the core content of the resource books. This led to publication of a second 'trial edition' of the written materials and the consequent benefit of allaying many of the criticisms and anxieties expressed.

The second stage occurred after the first two-year 'trials' of the course. At that time, some key personnel in the Education Department felt that it might be possible to do a short, rapid review of the written materials, making sufficient modifications to permit early publication (either by the Department or an external publisher) of final versions of the guides and resource books. However, the detailed evaluation reports on the use of each unit and an interim summary of users' reactions to the content and style of the guides and resource books, were crucial factors in persuading the Department officers that it would be better to undertake a more comprehensive revision of the units. This was done, with the result that many of the modifications proposed by students, teachers and developers were incorporated in the new editions.

The evaluation project also played an important part in the early implementation processes. Reports of the teachers' perceptions of the in-service programme (which was the main strategy used to assist them) provided feedback to Education Department personnel. Data on student characteristics, enrolment patterns and initial perceptions of the course allowed teachers and developers to anticipate possible difficulties in respect of students' needs and competencies. Reports on issues which were raised by teachers often confirmed the direct feedback received by Department personnel.

There were, in addition, a number of issues where points were expressed more clearly (or forcibly) to us than to Department personnel. Hence it was possible to ensure that matters were fully aired. One example of this was the concern of teachers about the first Tertiary Admissions Examination. The course developers were unhappy with the emphasis given to examinations in the priorities of teachers and were not overly enthusiastic about the repeated feedback from us on this matter. However, action was taken to ensure good communication between the examination panel and the teachers and a 'mock' paper was developed and circulated by the panel. All those involved considered that the dialogue arising from this process was effective. Teacher concern was considerably abated and the first examination paper produced met with a wide consensus of approval.

Again, individual teachers sometimes held perceptions about aspects of the course which, though applicable in their own classes, were not in fact representative of the more general picture: it was not unusual for a few teachers to express surprise at the data and reported perceptions from their peers. Moreover, reported perceptions of students had a magnetic attraction for teachers, who often turned to the relevant sections of reports at the first opportunity.

At other levels too, the cumulative reporting from the evaluation study had important influences. Teachers and principals who were considering future adoption of the course were provided with written and sometimes verbal reports by us. Academic staff from local tertiary institutions were keen to have information about various aspects of the course's implementation - and there were more distant audiences too, particularly from other Australian states. As with all human activity, rumour diffused at a rate which appeared to be in inverse relationship to its veracity. It was not uncommon for evaluators to be given 'authentic' information - usually of disastrous import - about the innovation, which was quite at variance with the real situation. The evaluation reports thus served as an antidote to misinformation and a corrective influence on half-formed perspectives by participants and others. While not always leading to consensus of values or views, the overall effect of the reporting process was to provide the data for a more reasoned discussion of concerns and issues arising from the introduction of *Physical Science* into the schools.

RELATED RESEARCH ACTIVITIES

From time to time there is debate about whether the activities of 'evaluation' and 'research' are compatible. Some writers (e.g. Cooley and Lohnes, 1974) have taken the view that evaluation studies are essentially practical exercises in which consideration of research issues should be either deliberately avoided or placed second in importance. While it may be true that the purposes of evaluation are specific to the programme under study, the methodological issues faced in research and evaluation are often similar. Some of these common issues have been addressed by us elsewhere (Boud *et al*., 1979; Parker *et al*., 1979).

Also in relation to the compatibility of research and evaluation, other writers (e.g. Straton, 1977) consider that 'external constraints placed on evaluation studies' (e.g. time, resources, accessibility of subjects, political climate) preclude the conduct of true research. Again, while it is true that the evaluation project absorbed most of our available time and resources during its two-year life span, there were nevertheless some significant research studies associated with or derived from the project. Perhaps the major research task (in terms of time commitment) was that initiated by Muredach. This was planned to run concurrently with the evaluation procedures and involves a case-study analysis of the processes of development, diffusion and implementation of the new course in its first two years. Besides examining the strategies of dissemination, this research study seeks to explore the roles of teachers and others closely involved in the change process. The modes of implementation used by various teachers have also been examined within the context of the factors affecting teachers' decisions. At the time of writing this study is still in progress.

Another study was carried out by Lesley in association with David Andrich of the University of Western Australia, using evaluation data on students' initial and final perceptions of the difficulty of Physical Science relative to other science and mathematics subjects available in the schools (Andrich and Parker, 1980). The purpose of their analysis was to test the theory (Young, 1971) that curricula which place emphasis on relevant knowledge are likely to suffer a handicap in terms of their perceived status, when compared with more abstract curricula with less relevance to everyday life. They found some evidence supporting Young's theory and showed that, despite the efforts of the course developers and others involved in the dissemination of information about Physical Science, students persisted in their belief that the technologically and socially relevant Physical Science was 'easier', and consequently of lower status than the established, less immediately relevant, Chemistry and Physics courses.

Apart from the research studies described above, it was apparent throughout the evaluation that a number of other important research and evaluation questions were being raised. It is likely that other researchers will be encouraged by the publication of the evaluation reports to undertake further research studies in the near future in an attempt to provide answers to some of these questions.

REFLECTIONS ON THE EVALUATION

As this evaluation study drew to its close, we became increasingly interested in reflective discussions about the appropriateness (or otherwise) of the illuminative model with which we had commenced. We also wondered (ruefully at times) about the usefulness of the published results of the study. It may be worthwhile to touch briefly on these aspects at the conclusion of this chapter.

With regard to the model of evaluation, there is a unanimity of view among us about the advantages inherent in the general principles underlying the illuminative model. We did not attempt to apply all the guiding principles of this model and, as indicated by Dave Boud's criticisms, it can be argued that the actual process adopted bears little resemblance to the illuminative model in a number of important respects. Nevertheless, by seeking out and focusing on emerging issues and by reporting these in a manner which was non-judgemental and multi-dimensional, we felt that participants in the development and implementation of the innovation were enabled to see problems and perspectives in a broader fashion than would otherwise have been possible. While there were some early problems in clarifying the role of evaluators, all parties came increasingly to accept and understand the nature of our task and the consequent relationship between evaluators, developers and others involved.

This leads to the second aspect, namely the usefulness of the evaluation findings. Admittedly, there were occasions when we (and perhaps others) wondered whether the resources directed to the evaluation might not have been better directed towards, for instance, other services for the trial schools. However it is our view, in retrospect, that the evaluation study had a number of direct positive outcomes as well as a number of spin-off benefits. The direct benefits have been discussed earlier. In summary, these may be categorized into, first, those relating to the further development of the written guides and resource books and, second, those relating to the processes of implementation of the new course. In regard to the latter, the evaluation has had two distinctive roles. One relates to the immediate problems and issues of importance arising from the dissemination and implementation procedures adopted and the use of curriculum materials; the other has longer-term implications and relates to the broad principles and strategies which need to be adopted in bringing about major curriculum changes of any kind within school systems. It is our hope that, in respect of both these short-term and long-term goals, the outcomes of this evaluation will be positive.

Finally it is interesting to mention briefly some of the spin-off effects of the study. Perhaps the most significant is the growing acceptance of systematic evaluation as a necessary component of curriculum development and implementation. That is not to say that future curriculum developments in Western Australia will automatically involve 'outsiders' in the role of independent evaluators - though the practical and political advantages of doing so are unlikely to be overlooked by local decision makers. Associated with this trend is the awareness that curriculum innovation of this nature requires sophisticated competent professionals, together with the resources to support implementation in the schools. In this context, it may be relevant to note that, in another major curriculum innovation in Australia[5], those responsible have taken steps to have two evaluation studies carried out - one concerned with formative feedback from the use of trial materials; the other focusing directly on processes of development and early implementation.

A less obvious but equally promising development arising from the Physical Science evaluation project has been the strengthening of cooperation in the research and development field between the State Education Department and the local tertiary institutions. (The main evaluation reports form part of a growing series of cooperative research reports published by the Education Department.) Clearly such links between administrative bodies responsible for school curricula and tertiary institutions should, if managed with due regard to the respective interests and responsibilities of each, be beneficial in many ways.

The future of interpretative approaches to evaluation, like the illuminative model, would appear to us to be rosy. However, it is essential that these models be understood in terms both of their technical and human dimensions. With respect to the latter, the milieu of evaluations is characterized by many of the features of human group interactions and hence some knowledge of group processes is an essential prerequisite for illuminative evaluators. We found, for example, that the establishment and maintenance of trust among participants was a task pervading the evaluation, especially in the early phases. Once trust has been established it seems to be possible for the evaluation to proceed more autonomously (but never unilaterally) and the need for compromise and modification may be reduced. Illuminative evaluation advocates responsiveness to key issues as one of its operative guidelines. It is possible that the first key issue to be addressed is that of coming to terms with the values, expectations and priorities predominating in the milieu of the innovation.

NOTES

1. Survey of Upper Secondary Science Education

in Western Australia, (1975) Education Department, Perth.

2. It should be noted that these aims are identical to those of a course entitled Man and the Physical World, which was developed in 1976 as a physical science course in Victoria, another Australian state. The Western Australian Physical Science course can in many respects be regarded as a major adaptation and expansion of Man and the Physical World.

3. Non-government schools had also been invited to participate, and initially one school from this sector also took up the offer.

4. Parlett and Hamilton's 'illuminative' approach grew out of some research at MIT. (See Parlett, M. (1969) 'Undergraduate Teaching Observed', Nature, 223, 1102-4.) The term 'illuminative research' is drawn from Trow, M.A. (1970) 'Methodological Problems in the Evaluation of Innovation', in Wittrock, M.C. and Wiley, D.E. (eds.) The Evaluation of Instruction, pp. 289-305, Holt, Rinehart and Winston, New York.

5. The School Chemistry Project, sponsored by the Australian Academy of Science. The Formative Evaluation team comprises Ralph Straton and Renato Schibeci (Murdoch University). The Process Evaluation team comprises Tony Ryan and Muredach Dynan (WAIT).

REFERENCES

Andrich, D. and Parker, L.H. (1980) 'Evaluation of a New Physical Science Course: Students' Perception of Its Relative Difficulty', Proceedings of the Australian Association for Research in Education Conference, Sydney

Boud, D.J., Dynan, M.B., Parker, L.H. and Ryan, A.S. (1979) 'A Discussion of Issues Arising from the Physical Science Evaluation Project', Australian Science Teachers Journal, 25, 2

Cooley, W. and Lohnes, P.R. (1974) Evaluation Research in Education, John Wiley, New York

Dynan, M.B., Parker, L.H. and Ryan, A.S. (1979) Physical Science Evaluation 1978, Cooperative Research Series No. 3, Education Department, Perth

Dynan, M.B. and Ryan, A.S. (1981) Physical Science Evaluation 1979, Cooperative Research Series No. 6, Education Department, Perth

House, E.R. (1972) 'The Conscience of Educational Evaluation', Teachers College Record, 73, 3

House, E.R. (1978) 'Assumptions Underlying Evaluation Models', Educational Researcher, 7, 3

Jenkins, D. (1976) Curriculum Evaluation, The Open University Press, Walton Hall

Kemmis, S. (1978) 'Nomothetic and Idiographic Approaches to the Evaluation of Learning', Journal of Curriculum Studies, 10, 1

Nisbet, J. (1974) 'Educational Research: The State of the Art', Proceedings of the Inaugural Meeting of the British Educational Research Association, University of Birmingham

Parlett, M. and Hamilton, D. (1972) Evaluation as Illumination: A New Approach to the Study of Innovatory Programs, Occasional paper No. 9, Centre for Research in the Educational Sciences, University of Edinburgh

Parker, L.H., Dynan, M.B. and Ryan, A.S. (1979) Evolution of an Evaluation, Paper presented at Tenth Annual Conference of the Australian Science Education Research Association, Perth

Stake, R. (1972a) Analysis and Portrayal, Paper presented at AERA Annual Meeting

Stake, R. (1972b) Responsive Evaluation, Mimeographed Urbana-Champaign: Centre for Instructional Research and Curriculum Evaluation, University of Illinois

Straton, R. (1977) 'Research of the Evaluation Process: Current Status and Future Directions', Proceedings of the Australian Association for Research in Education Conference, Canberra

Walker, R. (1980) 'The Conduct of Educational Case Study: Ethics, Theory and Procedures', in Dockrell, W.B. and Hamilton, D. Rethinking Educational Research, Hodder and Stoughton, London

Western Australia, Education Department (1975), Survey of Upper Secondary Science Education in Western Australia, Perth

Young, M.F.D. (ed.) (1971) Knowledge and Control, Collier Macmillan, London

5. EVALUATION OF THE SCOTTISH INTEGRATED SCIENCE COURSE

S.H. Kellington and A.C. Mitchell

INTRODUCTION

The Scottish Integrated Science course was first proposed in 1969 and has been continuously developed since its introduction. This chapter is primarily concerned with a formative evaluation which took place during 1974-7. It is difficult to describe this evaluation in isolation from the development of the course and the influences on this development which have occurred since 1969. Consequently, the chapter begins with a brief review of the development of the course and includes a discussion of constraints on the development in so far as they have affected the role of the evaluation. Since any formal evaluation is context specific, the chapter does not include recommendations as a general model for evaluation but conclusions are drawn which may be helpful in the planning of future evaluations.

DEVELOPMENT OF THE SCOTTISH INTEGRATED SCIENCE COURSE

The Scottish Integrated Science course is designed for all pupils in the age range 12-14 years. The course was proposed in Curriculum Paper 7 (1969) following a review during 1964-9 of the provision of science education for the first two years in the secondary school.

To assist teachers in their presentation of the course, pupil worksheets were produced for each of the 15 syllabus sections. The main purpose of the worksheets was to provide support for discovery learning by supplying practical details and an outline within which pupils can operate through their own decisions and conclusions. Each worksheet contained activities arranged in a hierarchical order such that those demanding the greatest depth of understanding are placed at the end. It was envisaged that pupils, by being allowed to work at their own rate, would reach a level of understanding of each topic appropriate for their general abilities. It was hoped that the worksheets would be valuable in classes both streamed and unstreamed in ability.

By 1972, inadequacies had been found in the content and design of the worksheets and particular difficulties had arisen in teaching the course in unstreamed classes. Most of the problems were associated with the use of the course by pupils at both ends of the ability range. The less able pupils were finding some of the concepts to be very difficult and experiencing difficulties in reading the worksheets. On the other hand, the course was deemed to be insufficiently demanding for the most able pupils. As a result of these problems, a National Working Party was appointed by the Scottish Central Committee on Science in 1973 to structure the course so that aims and objectives appropriate for pupils of different abilities might be realized. The revised course was published in 1977 (New Science Worksheets, 1977).

Bearing in mind the problems which had occurred with a single set of activities and worksheets, the Working Party devised a branching structure of learning activities for pupils in three general ability groups. Pupils in about the lowest 20 per cent of the ability range were called the 'less able' and those in about the highest 10 per cent were called the 'most able'. Remaining pupils were called the 'average and more able'.

The following three sets of objectives are specified for each group of pupils:

Course objectives	-	for the whole course
Section objectives	-	for each section of the syllabus
Expected outcomes	-	for each pupil activity

Course objectives indicate the expected achievement of pupils by the end of the course in intellectual, practical and social skills and in the development of favourable attitudes. More specific 'section objectives' for each syllabus section are almost identical to the 'specific objectives' listed in Curriculum Paper 7 (1969), except that objectives for the less able pupils are listed separately and generally reduced in scope and depth from objectives for other pupils. The most detailed are 'expected outcomes' which relate to individual learning activities and, in contrast to the other sets of objectives, are expressed in behavioural form.

Pupil activities in a structured format are described in worksheets and in accompanying teachers' guides. 'Core' activities are considered appropriate for pupils of all abilities. 'Extension' activities labelled as a, b and c are provided for the less able, average and above average, and the most able pupils respectively. Extension a activities are intended to consolidate material in the core whilst extension b activities, together with those in the core, should enable pupils to cover the Integrated Science syllabus as stated in Curriculum Paper 7. Extension c activities are in the form of small projects and are intended for the most able pupils. The structure of a typical section of the syllabus is illustrated in Figure 5.1. All pupils are expected to undertake core activities but different pupils are expected to undertake different extension activities, according to their abilities. Teachers are offered guidance, in the accompanying guides, on ways of allocating extension activities and of organizing group teaching for unstreamed classes.

The following sections in this chapter are only concerned with the evaluation procedures which were carried out after the appointment of the National Working Party in 1973.

THE OUTLINE EVALUATION PROGRAMME

During 1974-7, three trials of course materials took place. The first trials were concerned with core and extension a materials and were limited to schools which had been involved in writing the materials.

The second trials were more extensive with 52 Scottish schools trying out the entire course and the whole range of materials. All schools used the materials with at least two classes in S1 and S2* but only approximately half of the schools were asked to carry out pupil assessments. During these trials, the major evaluation work was carried out and reports were prepared for members of the National Working Party to assist them in the editing of the materials.

The third trials were limited to materials for

*S1 = Secondary School Form 1 (7th grade); S2 = Secondary School Form 2 (8th grade).

Figure 5.1: The Basic Flow Diagram

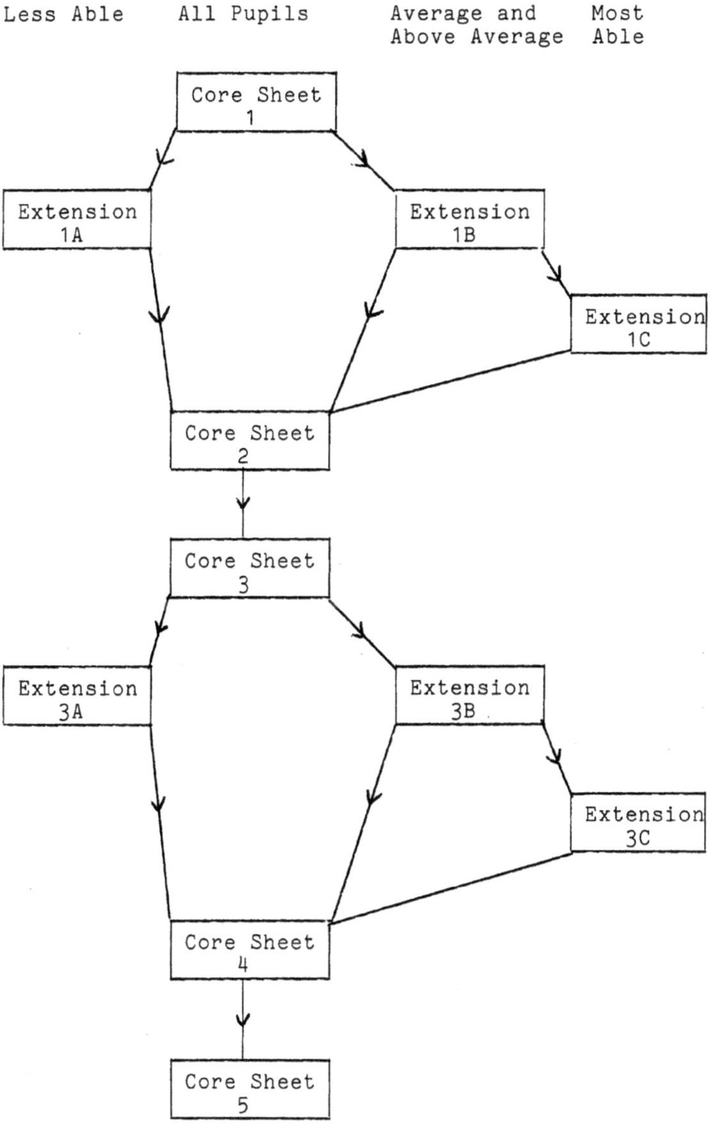

parts of two syllabus sections of the course, which had been substantially modified during editing after the second trials. The National Working Party was disbanded towards the end of the second trials and a sub-committee made final modifications to the materials prior to publication in 1977.

A summary of the course development and evaluation procedures is given by Kellington and Mitchell (1978a).

THE SCOPE OF THE EVALUATION

The National Working Party was formed initially to consider the educational needs of the less able pupils, to state appropriate aims and objectives of science education and to recommend a course which would enable these pupils to achieve these aims and objectives. At this time the Working Party had freedom of choice with respect to course structure and syllabus content. Shortly after its formation, however, the Working Party drew attention to the increasing tendency for pupils to be placed in classes unstreamed in ability, and concluded that the provision of science education for the less able should not be considered in isolation from that for pupils of higher ability. As a consequence, the Working Party was enlarged from eight to ten members in 1974 and extended its work to include the whole ability range. From this point it was charged with the responsibility of structuring the Integrated Science course, as described in Curriculum Paper 7, so that pupils in both streamed and unstreamed classes might achieve objectives appropriate to their ability.

The revised remit of the National Working Party placed severe restrictions on its operation and, consequently, on the questions open for investigation by the evaluators. The Working Party had to retain, for example, the philosophy and detailed recommendations in Curriculum Paper 7 and, except for the less able pupils, had to ensure that, as far as possible, all pupils would be enabled to achieve the stated objectives. Some freedom of choice was possible in respect of the way in which the Integrated Science course could be structured, but the main organizational decisions and decisions on the format of materials for pupils and teachers, which had already been made by the Working Party in the context of the provision for the less able pupils, were allowed to remain largely unchanged. These decisions constituted, therefore, self-imposed restrictions on the further activities of the Working Party.

Restrictions on the activities of working parties are not unusual in Scotland and in many other countries. It is common practice, moreover, to appoint working parties for a limited time to initiate change in only one or two aspects of a course. In this case, it was felt that a change in the underlying philosophy or syllabus of the Integrated Science course would be undesirable as the course had only been introduced some four years prior to the appointment of the Working Party. In addition, the implementation of new courses in science is very expensive and it was felt that the equipment purchased by schools should continue to be used in the revised course.

Owing to the restrictions imposed by its remit, the Working Party with the assistance of the evaluators was principally concerned with producing new course materials and advising on teaching methods. As a result, the evaluation focused on the materials and their use in the classroom and issues relating, for example, to the desirability of Integrated Science courses or of unstreamed classes were not open to the evaluators.

THE PURPOSE OF THE EVALUATION

The main purpose of the evaluation was to provide information about the achievement of pupils of different abilities as a result of using the new materials prepared by the Working Party. The information required was to be directed towards providing assistance in revision of course materials. In this respect, the evaluation can be described as 'formative evaluation'.

As well as providing materials for pupils, the Working Party also recommended methods for the organization and presentation of the course in the classroom. Accordingly, the evaluation programme monitored ways in which teachers implemented the course and noted difficulties which arose.

THE APPOINTMENT OF EVALUATORS

The Working Party appointed several consultants during the first two years of its existence. One of us (S.H.K.) was appointed as 'Consultant on Evaluation' approximately eight months after the first meeting of the Working Party. At the time, he was a lecturer in physics in a College of Education. The nature of the consultancy was initially imprecise but he attended all meetings of the Working Party and was invited to advise on matters relating to trials and evaluation and to carry out some evaluation studies during the first trials in 1974-5. Towards the end of these trials he was offered an appointment as evaluator but, owing to teaching commitments, sought funding for the appointment of a research assistant. He was deeply involved in the evaluation on a part-time basis whilst carrying out the normal duties of his post. The other of us (A.C.M.), a science teacher, was appointed initially for one year in the capacity of a full time research assistant immediately prior to the second trials but the appointment was extended for a further seven months. Additional assistance was available in 1974-5 from Mr T. Ralfe of the New Zealand Education Department on secondment in Scotland during this period. Mr Ralfe's primary role was in the editing of draft course materials but he was able to provide some assistance to trial schools in the carrying out of evaluation procedures.

THE ORGANIZATION OF TRIALS

The Working Party chose to limit the first trials in 1974-5 to schools which had been involved in writing the new materials because it was felt that teachers who had produced the materials should have an opportunity to try them out and to report on their success. It was hoped that the experience gained by the teachers through using the materials would be beneficial in the production of extension b and c materials. The first trials were regarded, therefore, as a preliminary exercise as far as evaluation was concerned. Nevertheless, an attempt was made to assess the achievement of pupils using the new materials and to compare their achievement with pupils in the same schools who were using the original materials.

The second trials were organized on a geographically representative basis and 52 schools were selected to try out the entire course and the whole range of materials with two classes in S1 and two classes in S2. A total of approximately 160 teachers and 4,200 pupils were involved in these trials. The main reason for selecting such a large sample was the desire of the Working Party to use the trials as part of the dissemination process. Evaluators were involved in the selection of the sample but several schools declined the invitation. The final sample of schools was reasonably representative of the Scottish Regions, contained a proportion of rural and urban schools similar to that occurring nationally, and contained schools with five distinctly different patterns of class organization in S1 and S2. In the majority of schools in the sample, science classes were unstreamed in both S1 and S2.

The third trials in 1976-7 were limited to syllabus Section 4 and selected parts of a few other syllabus sections. The evaluators selected twelve schools from those which had been involved in the second trials. Approximately 40 teachers and 1,000 pupils were involved in these trials.

EVALUATION PROCEDURES

As stated above, the main purpose of the evaluation was concerned with the assessment of pupil achievement of objectives and the improvement of materials for pupils and teachers. Table 5.1 indicates the procedures adopted in the investigation of various aspects of the course.

The procedures for assessing pupil achievement of objectives and for modifying materials are selected for further discussion not only because of their importance in the evaluation but also because they illustrate the most significant interactions between the evaluators and the Working Party.

The Working Party provided 183 syllabus section objectives and 414 expected outcomes. To provide information for course development it was considered necessary to provide some assessment for each syllabus section. It was accepted, at the outset, that it would not be possible to provide detailed information for all parts of the course but that results could form a basis for further, more detailed investigations by highlighting parts of the course which presented particular difficulties to pupils. The cautions by Harlen (1971) that formative evaluation has to keep pace with the trials and course development such that 'information has to be gathered economically' and that 'the luxury of tests which take a long time to administer, however thorough they may be, cannot be afforded' were also recognized by the evaluators. The following steps in formative evaluation as described by Harlen (1971) were followed in the evaluation.

1. Clarification of objectives and expression of them in behavioural terms.
2. Development of information-gathering

Table 5.1: Evaluation techniques and their relevance to aspects of the course (second trials)

Aspect of course	Questionnaires	Annotated materials	Assessment tests	Intelligence test	Pupil observation	Pupil progress cards
Course Structure	x					x
Course Objectives	x		x		x	
Section objectives and expected outcomes	x	x	x			
Pupil materials	x	x	x			x
Teachers' guide	x	x	x			
Assessment	x		x	x	x	
Departmental organization	x					
Class organization	x			x		x
Pupils			x	x	x	x
Teachers	x				x	x
Technicians	x					
Laboratories	x					
Resources	x	x				

procedures.

3. Collation of evidence and interpretation of results.

4. Use of results in revision of materials and future development.

The Working Party prepared objectives with the intention of describing what pupils should have achieved on completion of activities. These objectives were prepared to assist in course development and teaching rather than for evaluation purposes. The evaluators, consequently, found difficulty in using the objectives in the construction of achievement tests. Members of the Working Party assisted in clarifying the meaning of objectives but the lack of specificity, particularly in the depth of understanding or in the extent of skills envisaged, posed difficulties in assessing the validity of questions. It was unfortunate, therefore, that the evaluators were not more closely involved in the preparation of objectives during the production of the materials. As a result of these difficulties, the Working Party, on the advice of the evaluators, revised the presentation of the objectives for each activity which became known as 'expected outcomes' and described more clearly the expected behaviour of pupils on completion of activities. The requirements of the evaluation, therefore, focused attention on the need for greater clarity of stated objectives leading to a revised presentation which may be of assistance to teachers as well as to any subsequent evaluation.

Although the sample of schools in the trials was not the responsibility of the evaluators, the evaluators devised the information-gathering procedures. An important decision was concerned with the division of pupils in the trials into ability groups in response to the structure of the course for pupils in three broad ability groups as decided by the Working Party. Specific abilities of pupils in each group had been stated by the Working Party and also the proportion of the national population of school pupils which would comprise each group stated in terms of intelligence quotients. The evaluators were unable to select the first method on account of the difficulty of training teachers to consistently identify pupils in each group and identification of pupils by evaluators was considered impracticable. The second method using intelligence quotients was, therefore, adopted and the AH3 test of reasoning was employed (Heim et al., 1974). All results from assessment procedures were expressed in terms of groups identified on this basis.

Questions were constructed on the principles of criterion-referenced measurement such that, in particular, any pupil who has achieved the corresponding intended behaviour should be capable of answering a valid question correctly. In view of the wide range in ability of the pupils in the trials, questions were based closely on activities in the worksheets and language was simplified as much as objectives would allow. In addition, words used in worksheets were used in preference to other words which might be less familiar, the length and complexity of sentences were minimized, upper case letters and negative statements were avoided, many drawings and photographs were used to illustrate questions and, where necessary, questions were read out aloud by teachers from a script. The validation procedure for questions was similar to that recommended by Popham (1978), but the adequacy of the tests as a whole as a sample of behaviours was more difficult to ensure within the practical constraints of the evaluation. For example, testing was limited to one teaching period at the end of each syllabus section so as to minimize disruption of teaching, and each test contained several subtests each relating to objectives from the syllabus section. The number of questions within a sub-test, therefore, was limited and each objective could not be tested exhaustively. Owing to the large number of schools and the small evaluation staff, teachers administered tests. Uniformity in presentation was ensured, as far as was possible, through detailed sets of invigilators' instructions.

Results from assessment tests were analysed and interpreted by the evaluators in terms of the extent of achievement of objectives. Reports for each syllabus section were submitted to an editing subcommittee of the Working Party. Parallel reports containing collated information from teachers in the trials on the content and suitability of the materials were prepared by the evaluators and submitted at the same time as the reports on assessment. In determining acceptable levels of pupil performance and highlighting areas of concern to teachers in the materials, the judgement of the evaluators played an important part but the editing committee made final decisions about whether the recommendations should be accepted.

The timetable for revision of the materials was such that no time remained for further trials of the modified materials, except for two syllabus sections in which major revisions took place. There was, therefore, little opportunity for a continuing interaction between evaluation and course modification which is highly desirable in formative evaluation. In spite of the limited time available, significant changes in the course materials resulted from interaction between the evaluators and the Working Party. Examples of such changes were the introduction and subsequent modification of expected outcomes, the clarification of objectives, the matching of activities more closely to pupils' abilities, the simplification of language in worksheets, the introduction of summary statements on worksheets, substantial modifications to two syllabus sections and further trials, many minor modifications in pupil materials, and the introduction of guidance to teachers on assessment procedures.

THE ROLE OF THE EVALUATORS AND CONSTRAINTS ON THE EVALUATION

The role of the evaluators changed considerably during the duration of the project. As described above, one of us (S.H.K.) was appointed initially as a consultant with no specific brief. Through discussions in Working Party meetings, however, particularly in relation to objectives and their clarification, and through reports outlining possible evaluation procedures, the Working Party members recognized the potential value of evaluation to their work and proposed the appointment of an evaluator. This was an unusual step in curriculum development in science in Scotland.

Following the tentative early steps in introducing evaluation, the evaluation staff operated as objectively as possible in the gathering, analysis and interpretation of data. This role was often difficult to play. For example, several members of the Working Party had initiated the production of materials in teachers' groups, teachers in some trial schools had produced materials, and trial schools frequently sought the advice of the evaluators regarding the use of the materials. The perception of evaluators as advisers by teachers probably arose from the lack of a 'director' of the project or, indeed, of any other personnel specifically identified with the project. Although the relationships between teachers and evaluators were generally improved through this cause, the evaluators had to exercise care when offering advice not to influence teachers' opinions in such a way as to affect responses to questionnaires.

Towards the end of the evaluation procedures, the evaluators were far more familiar with the materials than any single member of the Working Party. Consequently, following decisions on recommendations made by the evaluators, the evaluators contributed considerably in the modification of materials and their preparation for publication. In addition, the evaluators prepared material on assessment for a general teachers' guide.

Subsequent to the disbanding of the Working Party, the evaluators became involved in the development of assessment procedures and are currently developing item banking procedures for the Integrated Science course and other courses (see Kellington, 1979; Kellington and Mitchell, 1981).

In certain aspects of their work, the evaluators were regarded as 'researchers'. Moreover, the funding of the evaluation was through a research grant awarded by the Research and Intelligence Unit of the Scottish Education Department. The limitations of evaluation procedures, when judged against research models, are well recognized and fully documented in the literature and many of these limitations were present in the evaluation. Nevertheless, the evaluators attempted, within the evaluation programme, to answer specific research questions concerning pupils' achievement of objectives and teachers' use of course materials (Kellington, 1978; Kellington and Mitchell, 1978b). But the conclusions reached, although limited in depth and scope, were found valuable by the Working Party and were placed on record as an encouragement to other investigators. Many research questions relating, for example, to the value of the objectives in teaching, the appropriateness of the course structure and the value of the guidelines for allocating activities to individual pupils, could not be answered during the evaluation programme. Other questions relating, for example, to the Integrated Science course itself and to the desirability of unstreamed classes were not appropriate in the context of the evaluation as explained above.

In general, the Working Party did not attempt to control the evaluators and relationships between the members and evaluators were cordial. The evaluators described the procedures which they intended to adopt and responded to recommendations from the Working Party. The strongest feelings of the Working Party on procedures were probably in respect of the use of tests, which were clearly felt by the Working Party to be required in order to provide tangible evidence on the value of the course materials being produced. Some members, for example, felt that a comparison between the original and new course materials through tests would be appropriate. The evaluators also wished tests to be used but felt that it was more important to investigate achievement of objectives by pupils rather than to attempt to provide results of general achievement. Proposals by the evaluators to adopt procedures of this kind were, however, readily accepted by the Working Party.

THE INFLUENCE OF THE EVALUATION ON CURRICULUM DEVELOPMENT

The evaluation programme influenced the development of the Integrated Science course in three main ways. Firstly, the members of the Working Party were led to question their strategies more closely through discussion with the evaluators. Secondly, the Working Party used results of the evaluation programme in their decision making in most aspects of the development. Thirdly, the evaluation programme brought the development to the attention of teachers through lectures, publications and visits to schools and so assisted in dissemination and implementation. This influence has extended beyond Scotland through international conferences, in-service courses, invited lecturers and publications.

It is difficult to assess the extent of the influence of the evaluation in other courses, but the following two cases give examples.

> Shortly after the completion of this evaluation, an evaluation programme using similar procedures and funded by the same method was established for a project concerned with developing materials for a technical education course in S1 and S2.
>
> More recently, the feasibility study of the Scottish Education Department on Foundation Level Science for S3 and S4 has drawn substantially on the style of objectives and assessment procedures which were developed for the Integrated Science course.

Although these two cases have been influenced by the evaluation, little formal contact was made with the evaluators, particularly in the first example, to ensure that members of the other projects were fully aware of the evaluators' views on the advantages and disadvantages of the evaluation techniques which had been employed in the Integrated Science course. It is still possible, however, for closer links to be established in the case of the Foundation Level Science course.

CONCLUSIONS AND RECOMMENDATIONS

An important decision to be taken when an evaluation is being planned is whether the evaluation is to contribute to the course development. If it is not, course development can proceed in isolation from evaluation procedures which will be mainly concerned with assessing the success of the development according to various criteria, such as the achievement of objectives, teacher satisfaction or satisfactory implementation. If the evaluation is to contribute to course development, then evaluation must become an integral part of the course development. Such an evaluation is usually described as formative evaluation.

The evaluation of the Scottish Integrated Science course was a formative evaluation. It was also an integral part of the course development. This integration was achieved through the attendance of the evaluators at Working Party meetings, during which discussion of evaluation procedures and conclusions took place, and the willingness of the curriculum developers and evaluators to work closely together in later stages of the project to fully utilize the information obtained by the evaluators in the improvement of the course materials was established. Good working relationships and a cordial atmosphere were vital in obtaining maximum benefit from the evaluation.

A programme of formative evaluation should commence at the beginning of course development. Adding an evaluation programme during course development can severely limit the scope and effectiveness of evaluation. It was unfortunate, for several reasons, that this evaluation programme was not planned at the beginning of course development. For example, discussion with the evaluators of appropriate forms of objectives at an early stage could have produced greater clarity for pupils and teachers in the specification of learning outcomes. In addition, the organization of the first trials could have been modified to the advantage of the evaluation programme and, perhaps, the trial by some very able pupils of materials intended for less able pupils could have been avoided.

The particular procedures selected for an evaluation and the way in which they are carried out are crucial in determining the nature and extent of conclusions which can be reached. Although the evaluators may be empowered to select and carry out procedures, the circumstances surrounding the evaluation may dictate aspects of an evaluation programme. The selection of procedures may be limited by, for example, the time, staffing and finance available. The way in which the procedures are carried out may be affected by restrictions in the facilities made available to the evaluator and by the extent to which trials are expected to contribute to the dissemination of new curriculum materials.

In this evaluation, the curriculum developers were very supportive of the evaluators in the procedures which they proposed to adopt. Although the evaluation was extensive and produced much information for the curriculum developers, it could have been more effective if greater resources had been available. A major problem was the restriction of the main trials to one school session for the extensive two-year course. This placed the evaluators under considerable pressure during the trials. An additional year would have enabled all the investigations and, in particular, the assessment of achievement of objectives by pupils to have been more thorough. An alternative strategy of restricting the length of the trials but supplementing evaluation staff might also have been beneficial. The number of staff concerned with evaluation, however, was very small and limited to one full time research assistant, one lecturer in a College of Education engaged part-time and an inspector on secondment from abroad giving a small amount of additional assistance. Compared with the size of the Working Party and the large number of schools, teachers and pupils in the trials, the evaluators were too few to take full advantage of the trials. It would also have been preferable to have nominated a project director to relieve the evaluators of the burden of providing schools with vital information on the course and materials.

The desire of course developers to use trials of new materials as part of the dissemination process can lead to the nomination of a large number of trial schools which can lead, in turn, to severe problems for a small evaluation team. Much effort is required, for example, in the production, distribution and analysis of tests, in visiting the schools to give instructions on evaluation procedures and in obtaining feedback from teachers and pupils. Limiting the number of trial schools and selecting schools in convenient locations can be advantageous to the evaluator.

In the main trials of this evaluation, 52 schools were involved. All schools received teaching and learning materials but only 22 schools were asked to carry out assessment tests. Even this reduced number was too large for the evaluation staff to use profitably. If a large number of trial schools is desired by curriculum developers for assistance in dissemination, it is essential that evaluators limit the schools in their investigations to a manageable number. It must be borne in mind, however, that cooperation from schools can vary enormously. It is wise, therefore, if selecting a small sample of schools, to ensure that all the schools included are keen to cooperate and sympathetic to the aims of the evaluation. Evaluators should of course, seek, objectivity in their investigations but random selection of trial schools can easily lead to the inclusion of several schools which are reluctant to submit responses.

The effectiveness of an evaluation is determined by a delicate balance between the questions which an evaluation is expected to answer and the practical constraints which are imposed on the evaluation. There is little doubt that effective formative evaluation is a lengthy process which requires much effort and expertise. Important decisions in curriculum development are often based upon information provided by an evaluation and it is not, therefore, to be embarked upon lightly. Unless a formative evaluation is planned carefully, funded generously and regarded as an integral part of curriculum development, then little valuable information may be obtained. Evaluation can easily become an empty, sterile exercise instead of making a valuable contribution to curriculum development.

REFERENCES

Curriculum Paper 7 (1969) Science for General Education, Consultative Committee on the Curriculum, Scottish Education Department, HMSO, Edinburgh

Harlen, W. (1971) 'Some Practical Points in Favour of Curriculum Evaluation', Journal of

Curriculum Studies, 3, 2, 128-34
Heim, A.W., Watts, K.P. and Simmonds, V. (1974) AH2/AH3 Manual, NFER Publishing, London
Kellington, S.H. (1978) 'The Achievement of Course Objectives by Pupils Following the New Materials for Scottish Integrated Science', Studies in Educational Evaluation 4, 2, 73-81
Kellington, S.H. (1979) Assessment Questions for Integrated Science, Teachers' Guide and Pupil Books 1 and 2, Heinemann, London
Kellington, S.H. and Mitchell, A.C. (1978a) An Evaluation of the New Science Worksheets for Scottish Integrated Science, Heinemann Educational, London
(See also 'Latest Developments in Scottish Integrated Science' by the same authors in School Science Review, June 1978)
Kellington, S.H. and Mitchell, A.C. (1978b) 'Implementation of the Scottish Integrated Science Course in Unstreamed classes', paper presented at the Bat-Sheva Seminar on Curriculum Implementation and its Relationship to Curriculum Development in Science, The Hebrew University of Jerusalem, 1978
Kellington, S.H. and Mitchell, A.C. (1981) 'School Based Assessment Using Item Banking', Information Papers 1 and 2 available from the authors
New Science Worksheets, Sections 1 to 8 (1977) New Science Worksheets, Sections 9 to 15; Extension C Workcards, Sections 1 to 8; Extension C Workcards, Sections 9 to 15; Teachers' Guide, Sections 1 to 8; Teachers' Guide, Sections 9 to 15, Heinemann Educational, London
Popham, W.J. (1978) Criterion Referenced Measurement, Prentice Hall, New Jersey

6. A RESEARCH APPROACH TO THE EVALUATION OF SCOTTISH INTEGRATED SCIENCE

S. Brown

INTRODUCTION

This case-study gives an account of a research approach to an evaluation of Scottish Integrated Science. The design of the study is different from much of conventional evaluation and puts its main emphasis on those issues that are of relevance to curriculum innovations _in general_ rather than being primarily concerned with the adequacy of _specific_ aspects of the integrated science course.

I shall describe the integrated science scheme and argue that a research approach to evaluation is suited to the evolutionary model of curriculum development that has been used in Scotland, although it does impose certain constraints on the findings. Exemplification of the way in which the research was able to generate hypotheses comes necessarily from only a limited set of the findings within the evaluation programme. One of the features of the work to which I shall pay particular attention relates to a source of tension that we encountered in trying to build a theoretical framework of hypotheses. Although we are independent university researchers and played no part in the development of the integrated science scheme, our work was sponsored by the Scottish Education Department under whose auspices the development was carried out and their concern was to identify ways in which teachers could be persuaded to effectively implement centrally planned innovations. To put it more bluntly, the Department wanted to know how to sell their products to teachers and we set out to develop some understanding of this through a study of one of those products and the responses of its potential customers. We had some difficulty, however, in maintaining this role since, from their own perspective, the science teachers were not first and foremost customers for other people's ideas. We were aware of the limitations of adopting a position in which we took the proposed innovations for granted and questioned the ways in which they were handled in schools, and increasingly the research came to be grounded in teachers' ways of thinking and to question the innovative proposals themselves rather than their implementation. Neither of these two stances corresponds to that of the outside, detached, objective evaluator nor to that of the evaluator who is a member of the development team.

SCOTTISH INTEGRATED SCIENCE

Scottish Integrated Science is not the outcome of a curriculum project that has produced a package of teaching material or of teaching methods for teachers to reject, accept, adopt or adapt. It has developed as a process of gradual curriculum reform in science within the relatively centralized system of education in Scotland. No one was employed as a curriculum developer to carry out the work; instead, over a period of five years a Working Party produced a syllabus and course outline which was then disseminated to teachers through the publication of *Curriculum Paper 7*: *Science for General Education* (Scottish Education Department, 1969).

On the one hand, the Working Party included Her Majesty's Inspectors, local authority advisers and college of education lecturers, all of whom have working conditions that are flexible enough to allow a substantial part-time commitment to such development work. On the other hand, there were teacher members for whom it was essentially a spare-time activity which they carried out in addition to their full time teaching jobs. The Scottish Education Department, through the Inspectorate, exerted an influence out of proportion to their representation in this group. This arose in part from curriculum development being seen as a justifiable component of the Inspectors' day-to-day work, but also because of the powerful patronage they can exercise in the recruitment of teachers to working parties and the control they are able to exert over the agendas for the meetings of such groups.

Although the curriculum is not legally controlled in Scotland, the development, dissemination and evaluation of courses, the organization of in-service work and the training of teachers is in the hands of a limited group of influential people. In one sense this has ensured that the course has been a remarkable example of success in curriculum development: it has been adopted by 80 per cent of secondary schools in Scotland (Brown, 1975; Brown, McIntyre, Drever and Davies, 1976), adapted for use in the Caribbean, Asia and Africa (Williams, 1979) and over 10,000 copies of Curriculum Paper 7 have been sold. However, the extent to which the intended classroom innovations have been implemented is rather less striking.

The new course, intended for pupils in the first two years of secondary school, was planned to be innovative in four broad areas. Firstly, it was to be a common course aimed at a new group of 'target' pupils, i.e. those in mixed ability classes in comprehensive schools. Secondly, the way in which the knowledge was organized was to be changed; science was to be presented in an integrated form. Thirdly, the use of guided-discovery was recommended as a change in teaching methods. Fourthly, the course was to be structured in relation to pupils' achievement of specified objectives. The Working Party provided only modest support for teachers in the way of guidance or curriculum materials in relation to these four innovations. A set of worksheets (Heinemann, 1969; 1974) were prepared with the intention of facilitating individualization of work in mixed ability groups, but their adequacy for that task and their appropriateness for the least able pupils was doubted by many teachers. This led to the establishment of a new Working Party with a remit to reformulate groups of objectives for each section of the course and to produce new worksheets, all of which were to take account of different levels of pupils' abilities (Scottish Central Committee on Science, 1977a-3).

What the Working Party meant by integrated science is not at all clear. The substance of the content appears (Jeffrey, 1977) to have been largely determined by the need to keep to a minimum the provision of new equipment for schools and by the demand that the course should be acceptable as a base for later Scottish Certificate of Education work in the separate sciences. In consequence, the integrated science syllabus corresponds very closely indeed to an aggregate of the alternative biology, chemistry and physics schemes for the first two years of Certificate work in those subjects.

The promotion of guided-discovery methods seems to have been a compromise reached by the Working

Party between the competing frameworks of learning by discovery and of programmed learning. Their prescription for a middle-of-the-road technique was not backed up by any declaration of an explicit conceptual basis, or general directions on how to go about its introduction, or advice about what factors should be taken into account in its implementation.

Curriculum Paper 7 implied a rational model of curriculum planning in terms of objectives, and it identified broad aims, general objectives (for knowledge and understanding, attitudes and practical skills) and specific objectives for each unit of content. However, the nature of the linkages between these various aspects of the course were not made explicit and Jeffrey (1977), a member of the Working Party, reports that the general objectives were developed *after* the content was selected. There is no obvious incentive or reward provided by the course to persuade teachers to abandon their traditional ways of thinking about their teaching, in terms of content covered or activities to be undertaken by themselves or their pupils and, instead, to adopt an approach that focuses on pupils' attainment of specified objectives.

It is unlikely that either the teachers or the other members of the Working Party had any experience of the practical problems of implementing the new ideas implied by the four innovations. Even if they were concerned about such problems, therefore, they would not be able to speak with any authority about them. Their practical trials were not trials of their innovative ideas but of the worksheets they had prepared over a number of years; indeed, their investment of time and energy in the preparation of these materials was such that they were understandably interested in the perfection of the sheets and not in questioning the ideas underlying them.

THE RESEARCH NATURE OF THE EVALUATION

Initially, the evaluation of the integrated science scheme in the familiar formative/summative mould was somewhat piecemeal; the various stages have been summarized by Jeffrey (1977). Prior to publication of *Curriculum Paper 7*, the Working Party appears to have used oral accounts from teachers in pilot schools and Inspectors as feedback on which to base the changes in the early materials. No details of their procedures have been published. They showed early concern for the development of test material for assessing pupils, and provided modest financial support to two research students for this purpose. These tests were administered to pupils of various levels of ability in both streamed and mixed ability classes (King, 1972, provides a description of the development, administration and results of half of these tests). A more substantial grant was provided for the evaluation of the very limited aspect of this curriculum, i.e. the attitude objectives (Brown, 1975, 1976, 1977) and, more recently, an evaluation of the 'new' worksheets has been carried out (Kellington and Mitchell, 1978).

The fragmentary nature of this evaluation programme probably reflects the unsuitability for developments of this sort of many of the evaluation models to which we are accustomed. Curriculum development *projects* can benefit in certain obvious ways from the systematic feedback of information from formative evaluation, and decisions can be made by users about the value of curriculum *packages* on the basis of judgements informed by summative evaluations. The Scottish Integrated Science scheme, however, with its pragmatically evolving development, but without any project or package, calls for a rather different treatment and the approach we have used has been at a general level of *research on innovation*, rather than a specific evaluation of the programme.

The research can be seen as having progressed through three stages. At the first stage the Scottish Integrated Science scheme was considered as a case study and evidence was collected to evaluate the implementation of the different innovative aspects of the course. Our plan was to explore the success of the implementation at three levels:

1. The extent to which teachers and administrators understood the various innovations and were willing to adopt them.
2. The extent to which the innovations were implemented in the classroom.
3. The extent to which implementation of the innovations led to the intended improvements in pupils' learning.

The evolving development model for the science curriculum in Scotland should be well suited to taking immediate account of findings from this sort of study, just as it can respond quickly to teachers' perceived problems by setting up working parties to deal with them.

With our <u>research</u> orientation, however, it was necessary to move on quickly from the first stage of evaluation of the case-study to a second stage that involved the formulation of hypotheses at a general level about the factors which influence the effectiveness of innovations. This second stage goal of generalizability clearly constrained the choice of what was to be evaluated at the preceding case-study stage, and the set of issues on which we focused were, therefore, of a rather different kind from those found in most reports of the evaluations of science curricula. It could be claimed that this constraint, imposed by the research model, affected the extent to which the evaluative findings from the first stage could have a direct impact and provide immediate practical benefits in helping to find solutions to problems encountered in the Integrated Science course.[1]

The third stage was concerned with an attempt to organize the general hypotheses into a summarizing framework that would help to explain teachers' responses to different sorts of innovation given the conditions under which proposals for change are introduced. The impact of this sort of theory-building research exercise on curriculum development is likely to be indirect in that it attempts to identify the issues that are salient in the planning of innovative strategies and to illuminate the debate and discussions about those strategies.

But what sort of theoretical framework were we looking for and what degree of generalizability can be expected of such a theory?

The research was sponsored by the Scottish Education Department and their concern was to find out how teachers can be persuaded to implement change in their classrooms. That implies that the teacher is seen as a 'consumer' and the research task may be seen as an analysis of the 'costs' and 'rewards' to the individual of 'buying' the innovation and as a search for a 'selling' strategy that maximizes the rewards and minimizes the costs. The

---

1 It is arguable whether <u>any</u> form of evaluation can realistically be expected to fulfil effectively this type of short-term function unless it is prepared to operate entirely within, and to sustain, the established system of values and practice; inevitably that form of operation would curtail the possibility of the evaluation exerting a reforming influence of any magnitude.

probability of being able to develop a comprehensive, generalizable theoretical framework for a strategy that innovators could use across different contexts and different innovations would seem to be very low. Theories are likely to be *ad hoc* in nature, context- and innovation-dependent, and only transferable to other contexts and innovations at the level of hypotheses to be tested and subsequently sustained or rejected.

We have found that the consumer model has something to offer as an appropriate way to summarize the arguments and hypotheses that have emerged from the evaluation of our case study, and I have discussed elsewhere (Brown, 1980a) the kinds of analyses that are involved in applying this theoretical framework to curriculum innovation. Nevertheless, there are severe limitations to the construing of the teacher as 'economic man/woman' and of innovations as 'profit and loss' accounts and this reflects a tension in our work which has not been fully resolved.

Our study of the implementation of the four innovations took place from 1974 to 1978, was multifaceted and was carried out in naturalistic settings in 76 schools. A survey component was carried out in 50 schools with about 500 teachers; a quasi-experimental study involved eight schools, 24 teachers intensively, a further 60 teachers more briefly and about 400 pupils; and the final action-research stage concentrated on nine teachers in two schools. The approaches we adopted included investigation of teachers' commentaries on their own teaching, pupils' attainments and attitudes, teachers' attitudes and understandings, classroom discourse, the effects of subject departments on implementation (including the influences that colleagues' attitudes have on individual teachers' attitudes to innovation) and the feasibility and effectiveness of outsiders' (ourselves) direct intervention in classrooms. It is not my intention to give a detailed account of the research methods that we used, except to say that they included numerous interviews (group and individual, structured and open-ended), extensive systematic classroom observation (about 200 hours), stimulated recall of lessons (using audio tapes), a variety of questionnaires, attitudes scales (teachers and pupils) and pupil attainment tests.

As researchers we had to treat the role we would adopt as problematic in the same way that an evaluator of a course has to address the issue of acting as an outsider or an insider with respect to the curriculum development team. In the first instance, we agreed to explore the factors influencing the effectiveness with which the innovations were implemented and, as that implies, our research questions were asked from the perspective of policy makers and curriculum planners who want to know how to be more effective in leading teachers to implement the changes that have been proposed. However, as our work progressed we found ourselves increasingly diverted from a position in which we took the proposed innovations for granted and examined the ways in which they were handled in schools, to one in which we tried to articulate teachers' perspectives and from that standpoint to criticize the innovative procedures and proposals and their underlying assumptions. This tension, to which I referred earlier, is apparent throughout our work.

The following three sections provide some exemplification of the ways in which we used our findings to generate hypotheses about strategies for effective innovation. They are concerned with teachers' involvement in planning, conceptual and procedural clarification, and the personalization of innovations.

TEACHERS' INVOLVEMENT IN CURRICULUM PLANNING

Teachers' evaluations of the worth of any proposal for change are likely to depend on the extent to which (1) the goals of the innovation reflect their own; (2) the proposal is seen as relating to the problems that are important for them; and (3) the implementation of the changes is perceived as straightforward or as difficult. To explore the congruence between teachers' concerns and those of the curriculum planners we conducted a series of group interviews with the science staffs of 50 secondary schools (Brown, McIntyre, Drever and Davies, 1976). Those interviews identified a sharp division between the concerns of the Working Party as presented in *Curriculum Paper 7* and those expressed by the science teachers.

In presenting their case for the innovations, the Working Party gave substantial attention, firstly to the demands that society makes of education for the provision of trained scientists, a political leadership that appreciates the capabilities and limitations of science and a scientifically informed lay population, and secondly to the implications of the nature of science for the teaching methods to be adopted and for the organization of the knowledge to be imparted. In stark contrast, the science teachers scarcely mentioned either society's concerns or the nature of science. Their attention was given primarily to questions of whether or not the innovations provided the opportunity and conditions for the teachers to do an effective and satisfying job, and of the extent to which the innovations would be constrained by the resources available. Neither of these issues were considered in any depth by Curriculum Paper 7.

Despite their contrasting priorities, however, both groups shared concern for establishing conditions that foster pupils' learning, feelings of security, interest and motivation, and also for the political or institutional constraints that are imposed by the Scottish educational system and, in particular, by the Scottish Certificate of Education. Unfortunately, within these areas, there was disagreement between the teachers and the planners. For example, the Working Party's arguments that guided-discovery methods would lead to effective acquisition of knowledge by pupils, and that the Integrated Science course would be an adequate preparation for the Certificate examinations in biology, chemistry and physics, appeared to be unacceptable to the teachers.

This identification of conflict over priorities is, of course, an element of the evaluation of this integrated science scheme, but within a research study of this type it is used to formulate more general hypotheses about the innovative process. In another publication (Brown and McIntyre, 1982) we use our evidence to explain why a Working Party with a substantial block of science teachers involved in the planning exercise should have produced a document for which the primary orientation is not that of the great majority of teachers. We identified several debilitating circumstances in the Working Party arrangement for curriculum development that could have led to this state of affairs, and we hypothesized the following as conditions under which substantial innovation could be achieved which takes into full account teachers' concerns:

1. Teachers should be the core members of the Working Party; Inspectors and other 'experts' should be consultants to, rather than members of, these groups, in order to avoid the paralysing effect that their presence has on teacher members.

2. Teachers should be given an opportunity to try out the innovative ideas (not just the curriculum materials) at an early stage in their development and before decisions are made to adopt the proposals.
3. Developments should be directed towards a number of alternative innovatory plans, thus avoiding the usual pattern of a single course plan and a uniform set of recommended innovations that denies teachers the opportunity to make judgements about the most appropriate programme for their own circumstances.

CONCEPTUAL AND PROCEDURAL CLARITY

Effective innovation is unlikely to occur unless teachers understand what changes are intended and how they are expected to achieve them. In our case the nature of the intended changes was far from clear. 'Integration', for example, was interpreted in different parts of *Curriculum Paper 7* as reflecting the unified nature of science, a pattern of inquiry common among the different sciences, interdisciplinary study, all knowledge seen as a unity and as an organizational arrangement where a given group of pupils receives all its science from one teacher. Only the last of these was made conceptually clear and this was the only interpretation that we were able to elicit from teachers during the interviews (Brown, McIntyre, Drever and Davies, 1976). The Working Party may have believed that the unifying features of integrated science were self-evident; we found no evidence that teachers understood, or were even aware of, those features.

In a similar way, there was considerable conceptual confusion on the issue of taking account of differences among pupils in mixed ability classes. The nature of the differences among pupils and of the tasks to be set in response to those differences were described in terms of five distinct conceptual schemes: Piagetian developmental stages, general intelligence test scores, behavioural objectives, Bloom's taxonomy and abstract/concrete materials (Scottish Central Committee on Science, 1977a-d). It appeared that the teachers were expected to articulate for themselves the connections among these schemes. The vast majority, however, retained their familiar practice of making intuitive judgements about pupils' 'ability' which they saw as a permanent and more-or-less unchangeable characteristic. The very small minority of teachers who made any attempt to differentiate the work allocated to pupils did so on the basis of pré-conceived notions of the individual as a 'more able' or 'less able' child (McIntyre and Brown, 1979).

Clarification of an innovation at a conceptual level may be a necessary prerequisite for its effective introduction, but for teachers to attain a full understanding it is likely that help with, and clarification of, appropriate classroom procedures for the implementation will also be needed. In the case of the 'guided-discovery' innovation in teaching methods, we assumed that the intention was that the teacher provide guidance that would be conducive to the pupils learning by discovery (this was, however, only one among several alternative interpretations in the document - none of which were elaborated). The suggestions about how a teacher might go about providing such guidance neither clarified the concept nor shed much light on how to manage the classroom activities. From teachers' commentaries on recordings of lessons they had taught (45 interviews analysing 225 relevant classroom events) we found no examples of guidance being used to aid pupils' independent thinking; the pattern was one of shepherding pupils through the 'right' experimental method to the 'correct' conclusion with the authority of the teacher's guidance acting as a constraint on, rather than as an encouragement to, a pupil's own discovery (McIntyre and Brown, 1979).

Our investigation of the innovation of 'teaching towards specified objectives' produced similar findings. Teachers' accounts (provided immediately after teaching a class) of how they planned and evaluated their lessons were unrelated to the rational 'objectives-lesson plan-evaluation' model that Curriculum Paper 7 had prescribed. This is not surprising since an examination shows that, although the document did identify objectives for the course at various levels, it provided no clarification on how the recommended classroom activities, specific objectives and general objectives were related to each other, and in most cases the specific objectives were not stated with sufficient precision for their attainment by pupils to be tested.

These and other findings in relation to the four innovations enabled us to assert with some confidence that, where adequate conceptual and procedural guidance has not been provided, effective innovation is unlikely to occur. But we were anxious to test the positive hypothesis that innovative ideas that are suitably clarified at both conceptual and procedural levels will have a greater chance of success. We explored this in relation to the innovation of taking account of differences among pupils in mixed ability classes. An action-research approach was adopted in which we used a mastery learning strategy that conceptualized differences among pupils and the associated differentiation of their work in terms of their performance on diagnostic tests. The teachers were provided with explicit statements describing the nature of the differences among the pupils and of the differentiated tasks, diagnostic tests, suggestions about how to cope with possible classroom management problems and opportunities to discuss and question the theoretical basis of the strategy and its implications for the classroom (Brown and McIntyre, 1981).

Our initiative had some success: differentiation of work occurred in 89 per cent of lessons in comparison with 37 per cent before our intervention, and those teachers who had previously expressed reservations about mixed ability teaching all displayed more favourable views after experience with our scheme. Our scheme, however, was 'personalized' for this group of teachers, in that we carried out an extensive study of their attitudes and teaching environment before designing the materials to suit the majority of the group. To the extent that we were unsuccessful, it was with two teachers who had distinctive ideologies that were in direct conflict with our ideas.

There was an obvious temptation to present the hypothesis that the probability of effective implementation of innovations is increased in circumstances where conceptual and procedural clarity are established by the curriculum planners.

That hypothesis, however, has to be qualified. The teachers we worked with rarely sought conceptual clarification of the complex and confused ideas underlying the innovations. We were led to conclude that the majority of teachers would only develop a concern for clarifying the concepts implicit in the proposals if they were to be responsible for making decisions about their own course structures, aims and materials, and if they were already convinced of the practicability of the changes to be made (by practicability, I mean that they must believe that they can cope with the changes, continue to meet the criteria for which they are accountable and retain enough energy to survive).

Detailed specification of the procedures to be used in an innovation might help to persuade teachers of its practicability, but that could lead to other problems since it would surely infringe on the teacher's role as decision maker and also on their classroom autonomy. Our interview findings certainly suggested that procedural clarification presented as a prescription about what teachers should do was resented as coercion; but those findings also sustained the hypothesis that, where knowledge or materials that suggest how one might go about the teaching tasks are provided in <u>response</u> to teachers' implicit or explicit requests for advice, they will be readily accepted (Brown, 1980b). This implies that very sensitive judgements will have to be made by outside innovators. On the one hand, it seems that procedural clarification <u>can</u> be presented by outsiders in a way that is acceptable to teachers, and that such provision is a necessary condition for the implementation of outsiders' innovations. On the other hand, detailed procedural schemes could be costly as well as supportive for teachers. Extrapolating from our observations of the use of standardized worksheets and packaged equipment, we suspect that procedural schemes, like these other support materials, could reduce the immediate pressures on teachers. However, they could also ensure that they show less initiative and flexibility and achieve less satisfaction from their work, as the planning and preparation is taken out of their hands leaving them to use routines that have been planned by other people.

PERSONALIZATION OF INNOVATIONS

Not only did our evaluation emphasize that it would be necessary for teachers to perceive the innovations as salient to their own aspirations and problems, if effective changes were to be introduced, but our action-research study confirmed that the information the teacher is looking for is of a <u>personal</u> type, that indicates what will be involved in implementing the change in his or her own circumstances. It is unrealistic, however, to expect that this sort of personal support for teachers could be provided by outsiders, such as ourselves in our action-research role, in anything but the tiniest minority of schools. In so far as the Integrated Science scheme addressed itself in any way to this problem, it appeared that the Working

Party assumed that the schools' science departments would be the source of such support and that the Head of Department would adopt a distinctly managerial role.

Our detailed evaluation of eight science departments (Brown, McIntyre and Impey, 1979) suggested that 'management' was an inappropriate concept for describing the ways in which they function. Heads of Departments' perceptions of their own roles, our observations of departmental characteristics and practices, the levels of consensus among staff and the relationships among the attitudes of individual teachers (Brown and McIntyre, in press) provided very little evidence of specific departmental policy-making, creative management and supervision or support for teachers in implementing the four innovations. In particular, it was not seen as appropriate for Heads of Departments to intervene in the individual teacher's methods of presenting the material, planning and evaluating lessons or dealing with the variety of pupils' learning characteristics in the privacy of his or her own classroom. Teachers are accountable to departments for covering the content of the course and keeping some discipline in their classes, but the ways in which they choose to work towards the goals of the course are seen as their own affair. This aspect of their autonomy is valued by teachers but it is maintained at the cost of the support and creative criticism of their colleagues.

In two of the eight schools we did find evidence of personal support for colleagues from teachers who had been given special responsibility for Integrated Science. We found that their efforts to operationalize the innovations and to provide guidance for their colleagues were associated with a number of characteristics that distinguished the teaching in these two schools from that in the others. Our classroom observation studies, for example, suggested that, when pupils are involved in practical work, most teachers move rapidly from one group to another making short and often superficial comments on the experiments; teachers in the two distinctive schools, however, were much more likely to become involved in substantial discussion, persuading pupils to think in more depth about what they were doing, rather than hustling everyone through the practical work, and to show an awareness of what they were trying to achieve.

We inferred from this evaluation of science departments a reluctance to emphasize the role of the Head of Department as that of manager - a role that would necessarily tend to set that individual apart from colleagues and to challenge some aspects of the other teachers' autonomy. That is not to say that we believe an innovation in management could never be achieved satisfactorily, but the introduction of a different balance of rewards would be necessary in a situation where the equilibrium of departments would be put at risk. Although the practices in the two distinctive schools sustained the idea that effective departmental support systems are possible, this was one area where we felt unable to proceed directly to hypotheses about how such initiatives might be planned and systematically tested in other schools. A necessary prerequisite to such hypotheses, we believe, would be research directed towards a greater understanding of the autonomy that teachers value, the sorts of intervention they find threatening and the kind of help for which they feel a need.

Even if we were to achieve a better understanding of teachers' autonomy, our findings suggest that hypotheses about departmental support systems would depend on the differences between schools in their physical environments and social relationships. These factors, we anticipate, will influence the nature of the support relating to innovations that it is appropriate to provide. But to what extent can we expect differences among individual teachers in the personalized information that is sought?

In our evaluation of Integrated Science we found only a minority of teachers whose ideological commitments on major educational issues substantially influenced their work in classrooms, and only rarely did we see what might claim to be a distinctive ideology of teaching reflected in a consistent classroom style adopted by a teacher. In the systematic classroom observation study, the uniformity of the strategies used by the teachers was remarkable and only two of the 24 had a style that was clearly distinguishable. For one of these, the innovation of teaching towards specified objectives was well suited to the emphasis he put on the consolidation of knowledge and probing questioning of his pupils; guided-discovery, on the other hand, was less easily related to his style. In contrast, the other teacher's constant encouragement of her pupils to find out and do things for themselves was far less conducive to the pursuance of specific predetermined objectives but fertile ground for guided-discovery.

There is nothing in these findings to suggest that the individual differences among science teachers, as reflected in the ways in which they go about their classroom teaching, would seriously undermine any generalized departmental support schemes, in the event that effective mechanisms with appropriate rewards could be found for the implementation of such schemes in schools. We would hesitate, however, to extend such a hypothesis to other subject areas. For the issues addressed in the earlier sections of this paper, such as conceptual clarity or teachers' involvement in decision making, there were no obviously subject-dependent relationships to be taken into account; but teachers with other subject specialisms might well not display a uniformity comparable to that among the science teachers.

SUMMARIZING THE OUTCOMES OF THE RESEARCH

It has been appropriate to summarize our evaluation of the innovations in Scottish Integrated Science in terms of a model of personal costs and rewards to teachers, because that model reflects the way in which the proposals were externally formulated and then offered to teachers. The evidence we have collected suggests that, in the past, innovations have largely tipped the balance on the costs side. For the teacher, the time and effort demanded, the loss of familiar and comfortable routines, the proposed adoption of other people's educational aims, the lack of involvement in decision making and the undermining of their role as an autonomous professional have been a high price to pay. In the examples I have discussed here I have tried to show that rewards in the form of the provision of clearly articulated ideas and procedural guidance that teachers can modify to suit their personal circumstances have been meagre. There is little indication that explicit account has been taken of teachers' immediate concerns and problems or that they have been encouraged to promote their own professional competence and creativity; and no attempt has been made to ensure that the circumstances in which departments can provide positive support systems for teachers will prevail.

Our 'market research' has indicated ways in which outside innovators can analyse the costs and rewards to teachers of implementing new ideas and can respond by modifying, concretizing, packaging and advertizing those ideas, and by planning an appropriate after-sales service; but the model was not designed to develop an understanding of how teachers could be helped to reflect on their own teaching, realize their own educational ideas and develop their own professional roles. In reporting our evidence to our sponsors we strongly supported the view that, in the long term, we have to move away from the 'teacher as customer' model if teachers are to receive full professional satisfaction from their work and schools are not to be deprived of their potential creative efforts.

It is not possible to ascribe a direct causal relationship between the findings of a research programme, such as I have described here, and national decisions on the curriculum. While we have provided evidence that no doubt has been taken into account in decision making, a complex network of influences arising from official reports and other people's research, thinking or reading precludes a simple analysis of the causes underlying decisions. However, it is certainly the case that new research and development has been initiated that seems to be consistent with our findings.

Our concern for conceptual and procedural clarification, particularly in the conceptualization and assessment of attainments (see McIntyre and Brown, 1978) is arguably reflected in the substantial group of studies that have been set up to conceptualize attainments and to explore diagnostic assessment and criterion-referenced reports of achievements in a whole variety of areas from oral competence in English to practical skills in science. On the other hand, there is no evidence of corresponding developments in the clarification of procedures for 'new' classroom teaching methods or in the development of ideas about how departments may be encouraged to adopt more effective roles in innovation.

There has been some change in the extent of teachers' participation in curriculum planning. The latest initiatives in science, mathematics, English and three multi-disciplinary courses, have been perceived and planned as school-based developments. Those developments, however, have been carried out within guidelines laid down by groups of Her Majesty's Inspectors who have found it difficult to relinquish their traditional control of curricular change. That is not to say that most of the work of the development that is involved in the collection of content and materials is not being done by the teachers, but their function has been that of a junior partner and essentially one of 'helping' the admittedly responsive, but nevertheless central, decision makers.

A COMMENT ON CURRICULUM EVALUATION, RESEARCH AND ACTION-RESEARCH

In an earlier section I argued for the adoption of a research approach to curriculum evaluation because of its suitability for the form of curriculum development that is used in Scotland. However, there is, I believe, a more general justification for using a research approach and our experience has led us to go further and conclude that action-research is the distinctively appropriate strategy for research on curriculum innovation.

Conventional curriculum evaluation is distinguished from research by its emphasis on the *immediate* concerns of, and the *specific* advantages to be gained from, the *particular* curriculum in mind. A wide variety of forms for such evaluation have developed but a problem common to all approaches has been that the evaluator has been expected to observe and comment in circumstances where curriculum developers (sometimes including the evaluator) are confident of, and committed to, the value of their new ideas. The developers, perhaps necessarily, tend to adopt *ad hoc* and opportunistic, rather than reflective and theory-based, strategies to get their innovations adopted and implemented. This undermines the extent to which the outcomes and processes of the curriculum and its implementation are open to systematic testing by the evaluator. In a situation where the developers' first priority has been to get their course implemented somehow (or even anyhow!), the evaluator's contribution to knowledge about innovation may inevitably be forced into a limited, idiosyncratic and speculative mould.

A research approach implies a strategy with a more *general* goal of acquiring new knowledge about curriculum innovation. Our early work concentrating on a passive analysis of the intentions and practice of Scottish Integrated Science was able to provide a good deal of information about the general factors that act as barriers to innovation. Although we believe this research approach to be more valuable than those of conventional evaluations of curricula, it did not yield positive theories about how effective innovation could be accomplished. That sort of constructive theorizing requires that the researcher hypothesize and test the action that may be expected to accomplish the desired innovation. It is this interventionist action-research stance that we now believe (see Brown and McIntyre, 1981; Brown, 1981) to be necessary if we are not only to identify what is and is not successful in our curricula but also to indicate the particular actions that are required to bring about desired improvements.

ACKNOWLEDGEMENTS

Much of the work reported in this case-study was carried out in collaboration with Donald McIntyre and Eric Drever, and any outcomes of value have arisen as much, if not more, from their ideas and efforts than from mine. All of us would like to express our thanks to the Scottish Education Department for the funding that they have provided for our research.

REFERENCES

Brown, S. (1975) Affective Objectives in an Integrated Science Curriculum, PhD thesis, University of Stirling

Brown, S. (1976) Attitude Goals in Secondary School Science, Stirling Educational Monographs No. 1, University of Stirling

Brown, S. (1977) 'Evaluation of Attitude Objectives: a Case Study', in Cohen, D. (ed.), New Trends in Integrated Science, volume 4, UNESCO, Paris

Brown, S. (1980a) 'Key Issues in the Implementation of Innovations in Schools', Curriculum, 1(1), 32-9

Brown, S. (1980b) Introducing Criterion-Referenced Assessment: Teachers' Views, Stirling Educational Monographs No. 7, University of Stirling

Brown, S. (1981) 'Curriculum Research, Curriculum Development and Innovation', paper presented to the SSRC Invitational Seminar on Curriculum Research: Agenda for the Eighties held at Birmingham University, January 1981

Brown, S. and McIntyre, D. (1981) 'An Action-research Approach to Innovation in Centralised Education Systems', European Journal of Science Education, 3(3), 243-58

Brown, S. and McIntyre, D. (1982) 'Costs and Rewards of Innovation: Teacher Perspectives', in Olson, J.K. (ed.), Innovation in the Science

Curriculum: View From the School, Croom Helm, London

Brown, S. and McIntyre, D. 'A Study of Scottish Integrated Science', Curriculum Inquiry, in press

Brown, S., McIntyre, D., Drever, E. and Davies, J.K. (1976) Innovations: Teachers' Views, Stirling Educational Monographs No. 2, University of Stirling

Brown, S., McIntyre, D. and Impey R. (1979) 'The Evaluation of School Science Departments', Studies in Educational Evaluation, 5(3), 175-86

Heinemann (1969/1974) Integrated Science Worksheets, Heinemann, London

Jeffrey, A.W. (1977) 'Case Study A: Evaluation of the Scottish Integrated Science Syllabus', in Cohen, D. (ed.), New Trends in Integrated Science, Volume 4, UNESCO, Paris

Kellington, S. and Mitchell, A. (1978) An Evaluation of New Science Worksheets for Scottish Integrated Science, Heinemann, London

King, D.J. (1972) Studies on Curriculum Paper 7: Science for General Education, MEd thesis, University of Glasgow

McIntyre, D. and Brown, S. (1978) 'The Conceptualisation of Attainment', British Educational Research Journal, 4(2), 41-50

McIntyre, D. and Brown, S. (1979) 'Science Teachers' Implementation of Two Intended Innovations', Scottish Educational Review, 11(1), 42-57

Scottish Central Committee on Science (1977a-d)
(a) New Science Worksheets: Sections 1 to 8
(b) Teachers' Guide: Sections 1 to 8
(c) New Science Worksheets: Sections 9 to 15
(d) Teachers' Guide: Sections 9 to 15

Scottish Education Department (1969) Curriculum Paper 7: Science for General Education, HMSO, Edinburgh

Williams, I. (1979) 'The Implementation of Curricula Adapted from Scottish Integrated Science', in Tamir, P., Blum, A., Hofstein, A., and Sabar, N. (eds.), Curriculum Implementation and its Relationship to Curriculum Development in Science, Israel Science Teaching Centre, Hebrew University, Jerusalem

7. SOME KEY CONCEPTS UNDERLYING TEACHERS' EVALUATIONS OF INNOVATIONS

J. Elliott

INTRODUCTION

For many disillusioned curriculum theorists and developers, the day of the national curriculum development project is over, or as good as. The curriculum development future for some now seems to lie in encouraging school-based curriculum development in the hope that it will be based on a more realistic understanding of the particular contingencies schools and teachers have to face in accomplishing change.

However, for many 'policy makers' outside the schools, school-based curriculum development will remain unsatisfactory as a response to the problems of change. For them the problem is not so much that of accomplishing change based on particular schools' perceptions of their needs, as that of accomplishing change in schools based on an assessment of the needs of the educational service as a whole. Thus, at the present time we find central and local government officials concerned about the formulation of recommendations with respect to the 'core curriculum', assessment procedures, record keeping, and school-based in-service training at the system level. For such people there can be no escape from the problem of how externally formulated change proposals can accomplish change in the schools, particularly since it is unlikely that they will want to enforce such proposals autocratically and thereby suppress the normal mechanisms of decision-making which prevail among teachers.

In my view 'policy makers' will only come to understand this problem better if they pay more attention than national curriculum projects did to the normal mechanisms of decision-making among teachers, and avoid the latter's mistake of formulating proposals for a type of person (we can call him 'the proposive-rational adopter') who does not in fact exist in the schools.

Fortunately, researchers in the field of innovation have begun to study the problems of change from the users' perspective (see Fullen, 1972). Research is in its infancy and at a highly speculative and exploratory stage. In my own attempts to study Junior and Middle School teachers' reactions to the Schools Council's Progress in Learning Science project (PLS) in its trial dissemination phase I found the work of Walter Doyle and Gerald A. Ponder (1976) on 'The Practicality Ethic in Teacher Decision-making' particularly helpful in interpreting data elicited in unstructured interviews with teachers from the schools involved.

In this paper I want to summarize Doyle and Ponder's account of 'the practicality ethic', and then, after giving a brief description of the project and the context in which it was disseminated, I shall try to show how this ethic operated in the judgements of the teachers we interviewed. In doing so I hope to contribute in a small way to our understanding of how teachers make decisions about change proposals.

THE PRACTICALITY ETHIC IN TEACHER DECISION-MAKING

Doyle and Ponder argue that, if we listen to the way teachers talk about change proposals, we will find that the term 'practical' is frequently and consistently used to label them and 'this labelling represents an evaluative process which is a central ingredient in the initial decision teachers make regarding the implementation of a proposed change in classroom procedure'.

Underlying change proposals are certain assumptions about their recipients. Doyle and Ponder pick out three which are represented in the 'change literature':

1. The rational adopter.
2. The stone-age obstructionist.
3. The pragmatic sceptic.

The most common image they believe to be that of 'the rational adopter'. He is a person who fits a highly formalized, rational model of how change ought to be accomplished. First, he clarifies his goals and the problems of achieving them. Secondly, he collects data about how the problems arise.

Thirdly, he deliberates about ways of resolving them. Fourthly, he implements his chosen means. Finally, he evaluates the success of his means in resolving the problems of achieving his ends. I shall indicate later how the PLS projects materials embodied this image of the teacher on the receiving end.

When the teachers on the receiving end fail to live up to this model in practice they often become 'stone-age obstructionists' in the eyes of the developers of the proposal. According to Doyle and Ponder it is this view of the teacher which has resulted in the development of 'teacher-proof' change proposals. Such proposals attempt to 'neutralize or bypass the teacher as an obstacle to educational advancement'.

They claim that the few descriptive studies which exist of teachers' reactions to change proposals suggest that such reactions do not in fact conform to either 'the rational adopter' or 'the stone-age obstructionist' image. Instead teachers react as 'pragmatic sceptics'. The pragmatic sceptic possesses the following inter-related characteristics. First, he describes his work in individualistic terms emphasizing the uniqueness of each classroom situation and the central role of personal preference in the choice of methods. Second, he expresses 'a concern for immediate contingencies and consequences', rather than long-term goals and outcomes. Third, he is orientated towards concrete procedures for dealing with classroom contingencies, rather than with abstract and general principles. These three features - <u>individualism</u>, <u>immediacy</u>, and <u>concreteness</u> - characterize the perspective from which the 'pragmatic sceptic' views change proposals. For Doyle and Ponder the origins of this perspective lay in the distinctive ecology of the classroom environment.

In his paper 'Learning the Classroom Environment' Doyle (1977) characterizes the most salient features of classroom environments in terms of their <u>multi-dimensionality</u>, <u>simultaneity</u>, and <u>unpredictability</u>. Classrooms are multi-dimensional in a number of respects. They contain large numbers of pupils with differing abilities, interests, and goals, who engage in a variety of activities and tasks. In addition, teachers have to perform a variety of different roles, e.g. processing subject matter, assessing pupil abilities, managing classroom behaviour, distributing resources. Multiple events can occur simultaneously and the teacher has to deal with them simultaneously, e.g. 'while giving assistance to an individual student during a seat work assignment, a teacher must also remember to scan the rest of the class ... or to acknowledge other students who are requesting assistance' (Doyle, 1977). The continuous possibility of 'the simultaneous occurrence of multiple dimensions' makes many classroom contingencies difficult to predict.

Although Doyle and Ponder do not explain in detail the relationship between 'the pragmatic sceptic' perspective and these features of the classroom environment it is not difficult to discern. The simultaneous occurrence of multiple dimensions explains their concern for 'immediate contingencies and consequences'. The unpredictability of many events explains their emphases on the particularity and uniqueness of each classroom situation. Given the complexity (multi-dimensionality and simultaneity) of classroom environments in which events are difficult to anticipate, teachers need to react quickly to events as they arise. And they can only do so if they already possess repertoires of conditional and concrete procedures, i.e. procedures which specify precisely what they ought to do <u>if</u> certain contingencies arise. Simply having abstract or general principles and goals in mind when entering classroom situations will not help them to meet environmental demands. Teachers do not have time 'within the situation' to translate principles and goals into concrete procedures for realizing them. Because classroom environments are complex and difficult to predict teachers tend to be orientated towards the concrete procedure rather than the procedural principle.

According to Doyle and Ponder, teachers who adopt 'the pragmatic sceptic' perspective evaluate change proposals in terms of their 'ecological validity'. They argue that the key concepts employed in such evaluations are those of <u>instrumentality</u>, <u>congruence</u> and <u>cost</u>.

A change proposal must contain <u>instrumental</u> content if it is to minimally qualify as practical. This means that it 'must describe a procedure in terms which depict classroom contingencies'. Change proposals which merely specify 'statements of principle or specifications of desired outcomes are not practical simply because they lack the necessary procedural referents'. Doyle and Ponder conclude that proposals which do not have procedural referents will seldom have any influence on classroom practice. They also argue that teachers' frequently voiced complaints that innovations are not clearly communicated to them can be 'directly related to the absence of procedural content'.

Instrumentality is not a sufficient condition of practicality. The extent to which the procedures specified in the proposal are congruent with the teacher's perceptions of his situation are also important. Doyle and Ponder claim that congruence has three apsects:

> 1. Does the procedure fit the way the teacher normally conducts classroom activities?
> 2. Has the procedure been demonstrated in settings which are congruent with the teacher's perceptions of his own, and does the spokesman for the proposal have practical experience of situations like the teachers'?
> 3. Is the procedure compatible with the professional self-image of the teacher, and in particular his view of his responsibilities towards his pupils?

The final criterion of practicality cited by Doyle and Ponder is that of cost which they conceptualize as 'a ratio between amount of return and amount of investment'. It refers 'to the ease with which a procedure can be implemented and the potential return for adopting an innovation'. 'Return' does not necessarily mean 'financial reward'; such factors as increased pupil satisfaction with lessons or increased recognition for the teacher's work are important returns.

THE 'PROGRESS IN LEARNING SCIENCE' PROJECT

The Schools Councils PLS project, directed by Wynne Harlen, began in April 1973. It was a new type of project in as much as its aim was not so much to provide teachers with suggestions for learning activities as with helping them to match activities more closely to individual pupil's levels of development (at the 5-13 age range). Wynne Harlen writes, 'We use the word matching to mean providing children with experiences which are comprehensible in terms of their past learning and present ideas but which also challenge these ideas and advance their learning.' (Harlen, 1976).

The project originated out of her work as the evaluator of the Schools Council's 'Science 5-13' project. Teachers involved in the project were perceived to have 'a problem of matching'. The main solution proposed by the PLS project was to help teachers base their classroom decisions on more systematic information about pupils' attributes. This information would be collected by teachers and based on their observations of individual pupils in the naturalistic setting of the classroom as they worked on normal classroom activities, responded to the teacher's questions, and participated in teacher-led discussions. As a guide to the observation and recording of pupil progress the project developed, with trial groups of junior school teachers, check-lists for earlier and later development. The items in the checklists are divided into attitudes (e.g. curiosity, cooperation, open-mindedness), enquiry skills (e.g. observing, finding patterns in observations, communicating), and concepts (e.g. time, length, life-cycle). For each attribute three statements are provided, each describing pupil behaviour at progressive levels of development in that attribute. The checklist for 'earlier development' contains 24 items and that for 'later development' 29 items.

Although the project emphasizes the use of the checklist as a basis for structured observation, it also encourages teachers to keep cumulative records of individual progress. However, its handbook for teachers stresses that, 'In the present context we are not concerned with gathering information in order to keep records, but only to keep records which help us make better use of the information gathered about children'.

Assistance in 'making and recording observations' is only one form of help provided by the project in its materials (published by Oliver and Boyd under the general title of Match and Mismatch). They also include topics around the themes of Children's Development and Learning and Making Decisions about the Learning Environment. The latter topics present ideas about the learning environment - what it consists of, what in it can be varied - and treats three main aspects; classroom organization, the selection of activities, and the role of the teacher.

I joined the project in January 1976 after the development stage was completed. My task was to evaluate its dissemination trials. Five LEAs were invited to participate in these trials. My job was to collect information about the problems of disseminating the project to, and within, these five LEAs in the hope that it would feed planning for the dissemination of the project in other areas of the country. LEAs were invited to send representatives to two dissemination conferences led by Wynne Harlen. They then had responsibility for planning their own local dissemination programmes. Four of the five LEAs chose to disseminate the project on a school-based pattern. In one LEA, teacher advisers, present at the 'representatives conferences', took responsibility for leading meetings in schools. In another, head teachers took this responsibility but did not attend the two conferences. Their initial information about the project was drawn from the materials and talks with the local teachers' centre warden who, having attended the conferences, acted as a co-ordinator. Two of the LEAs (referred to as areas A and C later) not only opted for a school-based pattern led by head teachers, but sent the head teachers to at least one of the conferences. Two junior schools in one LEA (A) and a first/middle school in the other (C) were involved. The views quoted in the next section are largely drawn from my interviews with heads and teachers (four per school) in these three schools. However, I also draw on material supplied by David Bridges and Clem Adelman from interviews they conducted in other areas.

My interviews took place in the schools after the series of meetings, held during the Christmas Term 1976, were over. I attended very few of the actual meetings; none in one school, one in another, and two in the third. Retrospectively, I am glad that neither I nor any members of the development team attended the meetings. Our presence may well have suppressed the sort of criticisms that were apparently expressed at these meetings. As Doyle and Ponder argue 'Innovation projects ... generate a set of control mechanisms which are typically absent from the normal teaching environment. Such mechanisms increase teacher passivity and suspend normal teacher reactions to improvement directives.' This is perhaps one of the reasons why 'the practicality ethic' is not easily discerned by curriculum developers and evaluators at the development phase. The school-based setting of these dissemination meetings isolated from much prior or ongoing contact with members of the project team allowed the normal processes of teacher decision-making to operate.

I think I managed to recapture the sort of evaluations teachers had been making at these meetings because by this time the head teachers had formed the impression, based on my study of the LEA representatives' conferences, that I was concerned to represent the practical teacher's point of view sympathetically to 'the theorists'. I know that in at least two of the three schools the heads had conveyed this impression to their staff before I went in to interview.

The projects materials had not been commercially published at the time the trial dissemination began in the LEAs. This meant duplicating sufficient copies for the trials. The scale of such an operation made it impossible to produce material covering all three themes of the project. A choice had to be made between different areas working on different themes or all areas working on a single theme. Wynne Harlen finally decided, let it be said in consultation with me, to limit the programme to the *Making and Recording Observations* theme plus two introductory topics.

All three schools in which I interviewed basically kept to the following sequence of topics outlined in the group leaders' guides and teachers' handbook for the *Making and Recording Observations* theme:

Introductory Topics	Topic 1 :	Introducing *Match and Mismatch*.
	Topic 2 :	Helping children learn by learning about children.
Making and Recording Observations	Topic 1 :	Finding out about children.
	Topic 2 :	What information is of most use?
	Topic 3 :	Recognizing the presence of various characteristics.
	Topic 4 :	Introduction to the checklist statements.
	Topic 5 :	Familiarization with the checklists.
	Topic 6 :	The value of making and recording observations.

The image of the teacher embodied in this sequence is very much that of 'the rational adopter'. The introductory topics deal with the project's view of the goal of teaching and the problem of implementing it, i.e. with matching. The next three topics invite the teacher to reflect about the principles which ought to govern observation and recording. It is only in the fifth topic that we find the instrumental content of the project being introduced in a concrete form. In practice this meant that teachers had to wait at least five weeks after the project was introduced for access to the checklist. It was, I believe, naturally assumed that the implementation phase would follow after teachers had become familiar with the checklist.

The director's response to the sort of criticisms reported in the next section has been to argue that we made a mistake in selecting the Making and Recording Observations theme as the sole way in with teachers. She feels retrospectively that an early consideration of some of the topics on Making Decisions about the Learning Environment would have resulted in less criticism being expressed with respect to the practicality of the project. She may well be right.

What follows should not be interpreted as an attempt on my part to actually assess the practicality of the project in the light of the concepts of the practicality ethic as they are described by Doyle and Ponder. Rather it should be interpreted as an illustration of the fact that these concepts do play a major role in teachers' evaluations of change proposals.

THE PRACTICALITY ETHIC IN ACTION

Teachers involved in the dissemination trials tended generally to perceive the project's in-service materials as spending too long on the underlying philosophy before getting to the 'meat' of the project; namely the checklist. In other words there was a lack of fit between the sequencing of topics suggested in the materials and the instrumental nature of teachers' concerns. The problem was first raised as an issue by the adviser, head and deputy from Area C at the second LEA representatives conference. On the first day Wynne had focused people's attention on the idea of 'matching' in a fairly abstract way. After tea the Area C representative re-opened the discussions by attempting to pin down the idea in the form of concrete procedures which are congruent with classroom conditions:

Adviser: If we have 30-40 children how can we match?

Wynne: Let's keep it to a small number of children before deciding how it can be extended.

Deputy: To what extent does the teacher intervene to give guidance?

Wynne: We do have cases of teachers giving guidance. I'm sure the teacher has a vital role here.

Deputy: Yes. The statement might arise 'How foolish to give the child that activity'. Whereas one might ask how the teacher can help the child perform the activity better.

Wynne: Handle in-service discussions how you like.

Deputy: The material is packed with information.

Adviser: The edited tapes give the impression of 'the match' from the end result.

Wynne: We have a good example of a teacher expecting children to have completed the set activity while she is away.

Head: Heads and deputies must think the in-service management through thoroughly. Otherwise staff will get frustrated and carry on just because the head says so.

It is clear that the head and his deputy are trying to think the thing through from the standpoint of the staff in their school; namely, from a practical 'frame of reference'. Wynne appears to be content to leave this to them while they want an opportunity to do it within the conference setting. The head's final comment is, in retrospect, highly significant because, as the meetings proceeded, in the majority of schools the teachers did indeed suffer from considerable frustration at not being able to get at the practical 'meat' of the project. In Area B a teacher adviser appears to have unwittingly perpetuated the frustration by withholding the checklist when teachers knew of its existence from the beginning. But, although the problem was especially highlighted here, it was a general one because most heads, albeit to varying degrees, followed the sequence outlined in the materials. Their reasons for doing this were understandable. They were involved in trials and partly saw themselves and their teachers as guinea pigs in the evaluation of an in-service programme. They therefore felt they ought to follow the sequence of the topics outlined for the sake of the evaluation. Whenever heads' anxieties about sticking to the programme were expressed to me I tried to reassure them by saying that they should do what they felt to be right for their teachers.

School in Area C

1st teacher

He (the group leader) keeps saying, 'We're coming to the meat, we're coming' you know and it's this great Armageddon more or less, 'the great judgement day is coming, we're coming to the meat'. Well, I've had enough thinking for a start; realizing my failures before I come to the meat.

2nd teacher:

I felt we were discouraged from reading on; that it would become a sort of discovery process through the discussion of tapes and slides ... 'If you have read ahead don't tell it to the others.' I felt that was the idea of the project. Take it week by week and stage by stage and wait until the materials were introduced to us and use the handbook very much as secondary.

3rd teacher:

And maybe it would have been less nebulous if we had read ahead.

4th teacher:

With the checklist I felt I'd got a peg to hang ... some ideas on.

School in Area A

Teacher:

No-one knew what it was leading up to or what it was about. I think that caused suspicion as well. The material is a classic case of giving people something to do when they didn't know what it was for ... You feel as if you're being given a little tit-bit on the side - 'And chew on that and if you're a good boy later on we'll give you a bone.' Just the way it was organized. The materials didn't explain what it was all about at the beginning. It was very late on when we started to criticize methods of recording, it was only then that I began to see what it was all about.

In their evaluations of the practicality of the project, teachers were not only concerned with the extent to which the materials described a concrete method but also with the extent to which they demonstrated the use of this method in situations which were similar to their own. In other words the description of a concrete method was necessary but not sufficient for a positive evaluation of the project. This also depended on the extent to which the method outlined was perceived to be congruent with the context in which the teachers were expected to use it.

For the majority of teachers the materials failed to demonstrate the feasibility of the checklist as a guide to the observation and recording of pupils' progress. The following propositions summarize some typical conclusions drawn.

1. Meeting the Demands of a Whole Class of Pupils is Incongruent with Looking at Individual Pupils in the Detail Required by the Project

> The videotapes (showing pupils working in pairs on activities and presented as examples of matches and mismatches) appeared contrived and we felt insulted, that's putting it too strongly, but we felt that it was unnecessary because it made the thing unreal ... I think we all thought 'yes, well, we've all seen these sort of things before but wouldn't it be nice to see those two children working and the teacher dealing with the other 33'. I think this is probably what we reacted against. Yes, we could all do all this with just those two children but you can't do that with two children when you've got 33 others who might be demanding your attention as well. If you want to do something with a couple of children, well there isn't any time really - the others are continually interrupting you ...

In real classroom situations teachers have to cope with events occurring simultaneously. An innovation is practical when it helps them to handle this level of complexity better, but not if it prevents them from doing so by isolating certain events for special attention to the neglect of others.

2. Meeting the Different Demands of the Variety of Tasks Teachers are Required to Perform is Incongruent with the Requirements of the Project

Teachers are required to pursue a range of purposes both inside and outside the classroom situation. One way of coping with this level of complexity was to involve pupils in activities which satisfy a range of criteria. An innovation would not be viewed as a practical one if it was perceived to involve setting up additional activities either for pupils or teacher. But there was certainly a tendency to perceive the project in this way in spite of the project's aspiration to help teachers satisfy the purposes of teaching and assessment through the same activities, and help them assess scientific progress on the same activities as they would assess other curriculum objectives.

> If you are going to achieve these things it would be marvellous for the child then other things are going to have to go because you can't always put them in the practical situations that these demand if you are going to cover the work that a school demands. I think initially when we discussed the various criteria in the list it did make us start looking at what we were doing and noticing children more, but then we came round to considering the practicalities of it and felt that as it was when we had spare time we didn't know whether to do preparation, marking or displays in the classroom; we only have so much spare time and always there is that problem. And we keep records anyway which we fill in incidentally when things arise and we felt that this would be yet another rod for our backs and when we'd filled it in or if we filled it in I think as a group we felt, I felt too, that there wouldn't really be much point in doing it because if we knew it we knew it, so why write it down and ... the chart that we had wouldn't really convey a great deal to the teacher who was taking the class over.

3. The Method of Recording Described in the Materials is Incongruent with the Teacher's need to Make Split-second Decisions in Response to Unpredictable Events in the Classroom

> You can get bogged down in writing things down. A lot of the classroom situation relies on you knowing by keeping things stored in your mind and then to have to make a split-second decision and if you want to record like the project suggests the only value it can have is for you to look back at the end and say 'Oh well, he made this progress in A.B.C.' but then it's too late. It's the end, unless these records are going to be passed on to somebody else which we were told wasn't the case.

Reporting on staff reactions in another school David Bridges reported a similar tension between the sort of information you need to carry in your head for purposes of classroom decision-making and the sort of information appropriate for reporting to others:

> The teachers had come to regard the Project's 'methods' (i.e. the checklist interpreted as a basis for ... record keeping) as unrealistic, clumsy and likely to elicit superficial judgements because of the number of headings under which entries had to be made. As far as I could interpret the present state of their thinking they seemed torn between, on the one hand, a conviction that information about and understanding of a child needs to be 'carried in one's head' if it is to inform day to day judgement and, on the other hand, a concern for its more systematic laying out in some form of record if it is to be communicated from one teacher to another. They were also anxious to find a form of record which was informative on crucial aspects of a child without becoming quite impractically large - from the point of view of either writer or reader.

Teachers tended to feel that the pay-off at the classroom level would not compensate them for the sacrifice in time and effort required to implement the innovation.

> Even when I first came I tried to do that, trying this individual thing, and it nearly killed me. Impossible. It lasted for about three weeks I think. I just couldn't do it. I just had to go back to 'lessons'.
>
> It's the terms that they use in the list. You've got to become familiar with them and it does take a long time to become familiar with them.
>
> Well yes, we came to the general conclusion that if this scheme was going to be carried out in school it would require a lot more time - and it would just be impossible to study every child so minutely as the outline and we didn't really see much point in it. We felt that if the checklist - or whatever you call it - came in filled in from another teacher - then just the ticked block on the chart would not convey to us a picture of the child. And if we already knew the child we didn't really see much point in putting down for our own information all the various points that arose. We felt that if we knew the child anyway if anything did arise we would jot it down in our notebooks.

The reaction 'we know our children anyway' was very common. Teachers often said this to justify their reluctance to use the checklist as a record-keeping instrument which feeds their own, rather than other people's, decisions. It would be easy to interpret this reaction as a defensive one against change. Some teachers were aware that their responses might be interpreted in this light. For example one commented:

> I detected a certain antipathy in the staff towards that method of recording. I think everybody feels 'What is the point because it isn't any better than what we're doing at the moment'. It could be interpreted as a defensive reaction because teachers are always being attacked and they also feel insecure as well as to whether they are achieving anything. But I don't think it was defensive. People were perhaps defensive at first on the course but ultimately when they saw what it was all about, No.

I think it is certainly true that the phrase 'we know our children already' is a defensive reaction. After all it is a defence against a perceived attack on the fundamental basis of professional self-esteem; namely, a teacher's understanding of his/her pupils. However, behind the defence we gathered evidence of the guilt the project generated in teachers. For example:

<u>Teacher A</u>:

> ... if you think beyond the course and what the course is trying to get at, you know 'match and mismatch'. O.K. you know a lot of your teaching is mismatching - some people felt that it was through mismatches that you learned more about the kids - but on the other hand this sort of thing can get you in a situation where you are very dissatisfied with what you are doing because, yes, you know what you should be doing, but you know you don't have time to cope with the situations perhaps you would ideally like to cope with. As you do more and more of PLS you realize that perhaps 'I should be improving A, B and C'. So perhaps in fact if we're speaking for the whole group, if we're really honest with ourselves and look beyond the level of the discussion that we've reached,

> we are inhibited by the fact that the head of our school is there. Because you do feel that the head has free time, that he can wander round, he can see what is happening ... It could be, I've been thinking about it, that O.K. we aren't inhibited but perhaps other people in the group felt inhibited, or perhaps if we really think about it we have been inhibited about some of the things we've said, because you know perhaps in your present situation, you can't see yourself carrying the ideas out.

Teacher B:

> I know exactly what A means because during our discussions it really makes me feel totally inadequate as a teacher. That child-study. You should be doing 31 of those perhaps. Sometimes you feel you can't talk because you know jolly well that you aren't putting it into practice. I think everyone would agree that children doing things in practice is the best method of learning. That's preaching to the converted here. But equally we know that we don't do that. We know, particularly in the middle school, that we haven't the time or there are organizational problems etc. ... It really is very difficult for teachers, and particularly me to come to terms with the fact that I'm failing hopelessly in many respects ... To me the conclusion even at the end of the second week was 'I'm just bashing my head against a brick wall really' in the light of the thing itself. It just seemed too ideal I'm afraid.

Teacher C:

> ... I think the project makes you feel that every minute of every day is valuable and one ought to be, certainly for one child, specifically meeting their needs, and I don't think I can do that and I certainly can't do it with every child in the class.

So, although the reaction is defensive, it is perhaps not always best interpreted as 'defence' or 'resistance' against change. Rather it is a defence against the demand to realize ideals to the full in what are perceived to be impossible circumstances. When teachers say 'we know our children already' I think they are claiming that, within the framework of the practical constraints which limit their freedom of action, they are doing their best and have made some progress towards knowing individual pupils, however imperfect that may be in the light of the demands of the project. Since many teachers felt that the implication behind the project was that they didn't know their pupils, they perceived it to be incongruent with their professional self-image.

Our interviews with heads and teachers left little doubt about the dominance of 'practicality' as a criterion for teachers' evaluations of the project. Other value criteria were used but not considered over-riding. The following was a fairly typical response:

> ... I think it was a good thing to do together. I certainly looked forward to the meetings just to exchange ideas because I did find that stimulating and it was nice to sit down and talk to colleagues without any pressure, the pressure of children knocking on the door, school dinners, or whatever it was, and I certainly think it made us look at some things with new eyes but I'm afraid I couldn't see from the practicalities of it. I couldn't see it being introduced into the school as a whole, that it was valid to our situation.

There was also little doubt that the concepts whose operation I have illustrated - those of instrumentality, congruence, and cost - are central to judgements of practicality. However, the data we gathered suggested that the conceptual framework described by Doyle and Ponder can be extended to include the concept of <u>built-in flexibility</u>. This concept underlay many of the views expressed by teachers. It refers to the extent to which possibilities for adaptation to particular circumstances are specified and built into a change proposal, and obviously originates in the perception of 'the pragmatic sceptic' of his situation as particular and unique. A change proposal which is perceived to specify possibilities for the legitimate adaptation of its instrumental content in particular circumstances stands a better chance of also being perceived to be congruent with the teacher's situation. With respect to the PLS project, teachers were by no means always clear about the extent to which the project sanctioned certain adaptations of its procedures to particular circumstances.

Area C

Deputy Head (Group Leader):

I think we're reaching the point now where our group may to some extent split away from the project, the project is supposed to be open to change, actually it isn't, because you have the list as specified there and there are certain assumptions made ... The checklist items in theory are not fundamental. In theory one can develop one's own criteria. I think that the way the project wants one to develop, they are fundamental. The fact that they make a checklist assumes that you are going to accept their list. I've come across it in quite a few projects. They say 'you can add to this list or take away from this list' but in actual fact it means 'please don't we've spent three years doing this. But we feel we've got to say it unless some clever bloke thinks of something we've missed out'. But the assumption is always there that we are going to accept their list. But the way we would like it to develop would be that the criteria would be ours as a group.

Area A

Teacher A:

... I found trying to fit this particular child into this checklist was useless because he just did not fit. He hadn't even reached the first stage in some things. Then what do you do? It doesn't allow for the bit before.

Teacher B:

Somebody had been talking about 'do we match the child to the activity or the activity to the child?' We in fact match the activity to the group but then match the child to the activity in the group. Flexibility is the name of the game and most of us are careful to do that.

IMPLICATIONS

If change proposals are to stand a chance of getting implemented under normal conditions of decision making in schools they should:

1. Specify concrete procedures for accomplishing change.

2. Provide examples of how these procedures might be implemented in typical classroom environments. A frequently expressed objection to the PLS videotapes depicting Matches and Mismatches was that the environment constructed for purposes of filming was an artificial one.
3. Specify ways in which procedures can be legitimately adapted and modified by teachers in the light of their own assessments of particular situations.
4. Provide examples of the sort of benefits teachers can expect in return for the effort they are expected to put into the implementation process.

The dominance of the 'practicality ethic' also has implications for the way change proposals are communicated. Instead of following the sequence implicit in 'the rational adopter' teacher image, the dissemination process should proceed from the concrete to the abstract, and from questions about practicality to questions about desirability. The process would look something like this:

1. Presentation of concrete procedure.
2. Demonstration of its practical feasibility in typical situations, e.g. using videotaped examples and case-study materials.
3. Teachers test its practicality in their situation by attempting to implement it.
4. Assessment of the desirability of the implemented procedure in the light of its underlying rationale: aims, purposes, principles.

The 'practicality ethic' does not preclude a consideration of underlying goals and principles. It simply assumes that the prior questions for consideration should be about the practicality of means rather than about the desirability of underlying goals and principles. Of course many 'pragmatic sceptics' may not want to go beyond the former. But not all of them simply want 'tips for teachers'. Some may reasonably assume that there is little point in busy teachers spending a lot of time discussing the goals and principles which underlie a change proposal if there is little chance of implementing it in their situation. So 'first things first'. The logic appears to me to be entirely functional for practitioners; in fact far more functional than that implicit in 'the rational adopter' image.

I have cited 'implementation' as stage 3 for two reasons. First, because I have found that, after exposure to a proposal, judgements about practicality tend to harden fast. One way of preventing this is to get the teacher to test the practicality of the proposal for himself. The second reason lies in the fact that many teachers only come to understand a change proposals, underlying goals and aims in any depth through trying to implement the concrete procedure it specifies. Understanding is *a posteriori* rather than *a priori*. This was argued by one of the head teachers involved in the PLS dissemination (see also Doyle and Ponder, 1976; Elliott, 1975).

Support for implementation should then be viewed as an integral part of the process of disseminating change proposals rather than an outcome.

REFERENCES

Doyle, W. (1977) 'Learning the Classroom Environment: An Ecological Analysis of Induction into Teaching', paper presented at the meeting of the American Educational Research Association, New York, April 4-8

Doyle, W. and Ponder, C.A. (1976) 'The Practicality Ethic in Teacher Decision-making', Mimeo, North Texas State University, Denton, Texas, USA

Elliott, J. (1975) 'Initiation into Classroom Discussion', in Elliott, J. and MacDonald, B. (eds.), *People in Classrooms*, Occasional Publications No. 2, C.A.R.E. University of East Anglia

Fullen, M. (1972) 'Overview of the Innovative Process and the User', *Interchange*, *3*, No. 2-3

Harlen, W. (1976) *Progress in Learning Science, Information Paper No. 6*, University of Reading School of Education

8. THE EVALUATION OF THE ISRAEL HIGH SCHOOL BIOLOGY PROJECT

P. Tamir

INTRODUCTION

In this chapter the writer intends to focus on evaluation as operated in relation to the Israel High School Biology Project (IHBP). This particular project was selected because of the special attention that has been paid by its staff to evaluation as well as the major role that evaluation has played in its day-to-day operation. As a member of the development team from 1964 to 1966 and as the director of the IHBP since 1968, the writer is also more familiar with events related to this project.

The IHBP is an example of a project located in a university and directed by university faculty. At the same time, however, it has maintained direct contacts with schools and the actual monitoring of instruction by establishing a variety of services such as supply centres, in-service training, and guidance in schools. Most importantly, it has maintained control over evaluation by undertaking the task of producing matriculation examinations. A brief account of the history of the IHBP will help in understanding the role that evaluation has played in its activities.

Curriculum Development and Implementation

In 1964 a group of selected Israeli high school biology teachers, under the direction of Professor A. Poljakoff-Mayber (a prominent plant physiologist deeply interested in education) undertook the task of producing a new high school curriculum in biology. The first matter to be resolved was whether to produce an original curriculum or to adapt one from abroad.

The decision to adapt was based on four

considerations. First, the need for curriculum reform was urgent, while expertise in curriculum development was scarce. Producing an original curriculum, although desirable, would take too long; adaptation promised a short cut. Second, Israel's financial resources are limited. The Israeli project could not have hoped to produce an original curriculum comparable in quality to those designed by the BSCS in the United States and the Nuffield project in England (1965a; 1965b), where huge expenditures had been required to secure the necessary time and expertise. Adaptation promised a better curriculum in the end. Third, the principles of biological inquiry are the same in Israel as in the United States and Britain. In 1964, the two main lines of revision in science curricula were teaching the structure of the discipline and promoting inquiry-oriented laboratory work. There seemed little to be gained from a reworking of the disciplinary content. Fourth, the approach of the BSCS and of Nuffield appeared sound, as did the materials they had developed. Adaptation of these programmes seemed worth trying. The BSCS was chosen over Nuffield because its materials were then at a much more advanced stage of development.

The BSCS programme is available in three versions (known as Blue, Green, and Yellow), each proceeding from a different point of view. The Blue Version (BSCS, 1963a), which employs biochemical concepts as a starting point, was judged too sophisticated for most high school students in Israel. Because of its ecological approach, the Green Version (BSCS, 1963b) employs a great many examples from North American environments; to adapt it would have required substituting plants and animals from Israeli environments. At the same time, the Yellow Version (BSCS, 1963c) offered two distinct advantages: 1. it was most like the conventional curriculum then in use, and so required the least extensive changes in teaching practices; it promised the least painful change over, and the most likely success; 2. the expertise of the project head was most relevant to the Yellow Version. Thus the Yellow Version was adopted.

The curriculum development group divided itself into pairs, each of which was assigned a chapter of the Yellow Version. A critical analysis was conducted of the content, examples, diagrams, laboratory exercises, and other features of the chapter. The analysis focused on two questions: to what extent were the various features of the chapter scientifically sound and up to date?; and to what extent were they suited to local conditions? The operation was not just an adoption but an adaptation, based on content analysis in the light of local needs and preferences.

Once every three weeks the whole group met. In each of these meetings one or two pairs of teachers presented their adapted chapters and a general deliberation took place. In most instances, biologists working on the topics under discussion were invited to participate, and they were the only professionals other than the teachers to enter these discussions. Consequently the decisions made were based to a large extent on the opinions of the scientists, whose competence was highly regarded and whose judgement was therefore usually accepted; the considerations of subject matter dominated the decisions. After these meetings the material was revised and handed to a professional writer to ensure stylistic coherence. The first two parts of the Yellow Version, *Unity* and *Diversity*, were prepared in this manner; the third part, *Continuity* was prepared in a later year.

Any adaptation of this kind involves a strong element of evaluation. The adaptors analyse the contents, review the pictures, consider the general layout, seek the views of experts and then, on the basis of their evaluation of the materials, deliberate and make decisions which guide the writing of the adapted version. Here is an example of evaluation built into the process of curriculum development right from its outset. The need of adaptors to decide which of the original materials can be used as it is and which requires modification forces them to evaluate and make judgements. In the 1960s this evaluation was done to a large extent intuitively. Today instruments which ensure more systematic evaluation of curriculum materials for the purpose of adaptation are available (e.g. Blum *et al*., 1981).

Important as this kind of evaluation is, it cannot substitute for a systematic evaluation of other aspects, such as the feasibility of the curriculum for local students and teachers, students' achievement, etc. This task was to be achieved by nominating an evaluator who had no responsibility for the actual development of materials but, nevertheless, participated in all the deliberations. However, as it happened, all the decisions described above about the selection of the BSCS Yellow Version for adaptation and the actual procedures of development which followed, including the determination of general aims, the planning and actual preparation of instructional materials (i.e. the two first stages of curriculum development described by Lewy, 1977) were not based on either the formal or informal evaluation of the nominated evaluator. These decisions were based primarily on the assumption that a programme which had been found to be feasible in the USA had high probability of being feasible in Israeli schools. Other decisions concerning the selection of programme components, modification of programme elements and the specification of minimal conditions for usage (such as minimal laboratory facilities) were made by the development team based on deliberations and expert judgement.

At the same time the evaluator occupied himself with designing a formal evaluation scheme which was aimed mainly at assessing students' achievement in the following areas:

Cognitive achievement in biology.
Understanding the nature of science and its processes.
Ability to analyse and comprehend biological research.
Inquiry skills (such as formulating hypotheses and designing controlled experiments).
Attitudes toward science and nature.

A considerable amount of effort went into the selection and design of evaluation instruments. Some available instruments were translated into Hebrew with some modification (e.g. the 'Test on Understanding Science' - TOUS); some made use of test items taken from tests designed by the BSCS in the USA and some were designed by the evaluator with the consent of the project team.

The American BSCS Project conducted large-scale evaluation studies until 1963. The conclusions of these studies were based mainly on teachers' reports, staff visits to classrooms, and the results of paper-and-pencil multiple-choice tests given to students. A limited budget had been allotted to evaluation, and it proved rather difficult to obtain the cooperation of professional evaluators (Grobman, 1969). Consequently, there has been no systematic evaluation of the BSCS programme since 1963 (Grobman, 1970).*

* For more details on the evaluation of the BSCS in the USA see Chapter 2 in this volume.

Although this evaluation yielded data on limited aspects, it was sufficient to show that the BSCS programme could be used successfully in many American classrooms. This evidence has certainly affected favourably the Israeli development team in the decision to embark on the project: 'If the Americans can use it successfully, there is no reason why the programme wouldn't work in Israel as well, provided we do it right.'

In many ways evaluation in the Israeli High School Adaptation Project followed the lead of the BSCS in the USA. Nevertheless, the different conditions which raised the need for curriculum adaptation required modifications of the evaluation as well.

As early as 1965 it had been decided to conduct a follow-up study that would take four years and include three groups of students in grades 9 and 10, representing the three types of schools in the country. Based on a battery of tests of cognitive and affective outcomes, this study was finished in 1969. The follow-up of those students who had participated in this study, and who had then continued their study of biology in grades 11 and 12 (as biology majors), was continued through 1971. The results of these studies have been published (see Jungwirth, 1969, 1970, 1971, 1972; Tamir, 1972; Tamir and Jungwirth, 1975).

Along with the formal evaluation study just described, informal evaluation took place based on visits to schools, discussions with teachers and other sources. A special characteristic of the IHBP was its step-by-step publication of materials, which extended over five years. This continuous process had its drawbacks. For example, in several instances a class completed the published materials before the next unit was available and the teacher had to continue even though the students had no textbook.

In retrospect, though, the step-by-step Israeli process has had certain advantages, prime among them the opportunity to learn from mistakes. Feedback collected on the early chapters assisted the team in making decisions with regard to the writing of the next ones. The extended period of development also gave teachers and schools the opportunity to try some of the materials before committing themselves and their students to the new programme. This process of consumer evaluation has received little attention by the evaluation experts, yet it may be a decisive factor as far as programme adoption is concerned.

By consumer evaluation we refer here to a process whereby teachers and schools utilize samples of curriculum materials as a means for deciding whether or not to use a programme, and in what ways to use it with different students and by different teachers. This is an informal evaluation process which takes advantage of the wisdom and judgement of practising teachers rather than that of learned evaluators.

Diffusion Implementation and Evaluation

One of the criteria used to judge the success of a programme is the rate of its adoption by the schools (Welch, 1968). In spite of the existence of a centralized educational system in Israel, the project team decided, in cooperation with the Ministry of Education, that adoption of the programme would be purely voluntary on the part of teachers and schools. In the first years, books and materials were made available only to teachers who had participated in a special in-service training course and only to schools which had an adequately equipped laboratory. This evaluation of antecedants was helpful to the teachers and to the individual schools, and at the same time increased the probability of successful implementation of the programme.

Naturally, those teachers who participated in the writing group taught the first twelve classes, comprising 300 students, in the year 1965. Of these, four classes were in kibbutz schools, one class in an agricultural secondary school, and the rest in city academic schools in various parts of the country. The number of classes and students increased rather slowly in 1966 (550 students) and 1967 (1,000 students). Many teachers were suspicious and chose to wait and see what would happen. Apparently, by 1968, the feedback coming from the trial schools was favourable enough to start a wave of adoption (4,000 students in 1968, 8,000 in 1969, 40,000 in 1974). It is interesting to note the characteristics of the teachers and schools that first chose to follow the new programme. In 1969, of about 100 teachers, 70 had teaching experience of less than three years. In that year about half of the kibbutz schools, 20 per cent of the academic city schools, and 5 per cent of the agricultural schools used the programme. Most of the prestigious city academic schools had not yet adopted it. These were anxious about the new matriculation examination that was to be introduced, and were still waiting for the results of the evaluation study which had begun in 1966. Then, too, some teachers were afraid of the extra work and of the new competencies required to teach the new programme adequately.

Later on, after the first two groups of biology majors had taken the matriculation examination and had proved that they could meet its rather ambitious requirements with no damage to their grades, more and more schools joined the new programme, with 80 per cent of the schools using it in the year 1975, and most schools in the year 1980.

Unlike curriculum projects which have conceived their primary function to be the design and development of curriculum materials, the Israeli Biology Project has placed at least equal emphasis on providing the necessary conditions for adequate implementation and for assessment and evaluation. In each of these phases the Project team has made a point of cooperating with various departments and key persons in the Ministry of Education, as well as with other persons and organizations related to biological education. Such cooperation has proved to be instrumental both in implementation and in evaluation. In a country with a centralized education system, such as Israel, a policy of involving the system will yield better results than one which attempts to fight it.

How does one go about involving the system? The approach used was to identify key persons, such as the Chief Inspector and the Head of the Examination Department, and to secure their interest and sympathy on the one hand, and to seek their advice and opinions on a regular basis on the other. Moreover, where and when necessary, the IHBP has been ready to assist these government officials in various matters and to respond positively to their ideas and suggestions. These personal relations led to full cooperation and assisted with evaluation in many ways.

The Utilization of Evaluation Findings

There were eight major findings of the evaluation described above. 1. Students studying the new programme achieved more than did their controls (who studied the conventional programme) on paper-and-pencil tests that assessed functional knowledge in biology, comprehension, application, analysis of research, and the design of experiments.

2. Students of the new programme achieved considerably more than did their controls in open-ended laboratory experiments. 3. Students in the new and the traditional programmes did not differ significantly in their understanding of science (as measured by the TOUS - Test on Understanding Science), or in their general attitude toward biology. But students in the new programme performed better than their controls in the SPI (Welch Science Process Inventory). 4. The new programme was found to be better adapted to city and kibbutz schools than to agricultural schools. In fact, students of similar IQ who studied in agricultural schools achieved consistently less than equally able students in city and kibbutz schools. 5. The new programme was found inadequate for a large portion of the lower IQ students whose parents had emigrated from Asian and North African countries. 6. Performance in biology was found to be multi-dimensional. By that we mean that different measures, such as paper-and-pencil tests and practical laboratory tests, yielded different results. A given student might reach different levels of achievement on different measures. Hence a comprehensive and valid evaluation would require a variety of measures, representing different formats of tests as well as different types of tasks (a practice not employed in other countries such as the USA). 7. External examinations may be profitably used to direct the implementation of a new programme and promote practices congruent with those of the programme's designers. 8. In principle, it is possible to obtain respectable achievements while studying a curriculum designed in one country and adapted by another, provided that local constraints receive the attention and treatment they deserve.

The evaluation in the first five years was designed to obtain information regarding the achievements and attitudes of the different types of students who studied the new programme, thereby giving teachers and schools firm data as a basis for their decisions regarding adoption of the new curriculum. Yet, as with any research, the findings raised questions. As a result, a second generation of studies emerged.

It is often argued that evaluation studies have very little effect on the actual development and implementation of curricula, either because the results are published too late or because curriculum developers are reluctant to rely on the results and tend to follow their personal impressions instead.

This was not the case in the Israeli project. Table 8.1 offers several examples of how evaluation results have been used in curriculum improvement.

Table 8.1: The Effect of Evaluation Findings on the Development and Implementation of the Biology Programme

Finding	Consequent Action
There was low interest in the study of botany (Tamir and Jungwirth, 1974).	Integrating the study of topics common to both botany and zoology (e.g. regulation, reproduction).
Teachers tended to teach about the same organisms that they studied in college (Tamir, 1976b).	Attending to the balance of topics presented in college biology courses for prospective teachers.
Students had trouble applying statistics in biology (Jungwirth and Dreyfus, 1972).	Preparing special exercises involving the use of statistics and holding special in-service activities.
Culturally deprived students whose families came from Asian and North African countries achieved poorly (Tamir and Jungwirth, 1972).	Preparing a Hebrew version of the BSCS slow learners' text and designing supplementary modules; in-service courses for teachers.
Students completing grade 10 achieved poorly in inquiry skills; by the end of grade 12, most students reached a satisfactory level (Jungwirth, 1970; Tamir and Jungwirth, 1975).	Preparing instructional materials to promote inquiry skills; reducing the expectations for grade 10 students, allowing inquiry skills to develop gradually. Promoting use of <u>Invitations to Inquiry</u>.
Students showed poor understanding of some aspects of the nature of science (Jungwirth, 1972).	Informing teachers of this finding; incorporating the history and philosophy of science in teacher training.
It was impossible to cover all the topics in <u>Diversity</u> in grade 10.	Designating some topics as core and the rest as electives.

Table 8.1 (cont'd)

Finding	Consequent Action
Students had more trouble interpreting tables than graphs, and distinguished poorly between descriptions and interpretations (Jungwirth and Dreyfus, 1972; Tamir and Jungwirth, 1975).	Including in the matriculation examinations some problem situations, presented in tables, that required distinguishing between descriptions and interpretations.
Achievement scores on different tasks and from different test formats showed low correlations (Tamir, 1974a).	Varying the tasks and test formats that constituted the matriculation examination, and urging teachers to use similar variety in their classroom evaluation.
Students of the new programme achieved better than controls both on inquiry tasks and on knowledge of content (Jungwirth, 1970, 1971; Tamir, 1975a).	Acceptance of the new programme by content-oriented teachers, and of the new matriculation examination as the national standard for biology majors.
Teachers used the matriculation examinations to guide their teaching (Tamir and Jungwirth, 1975; Ben-Gal, 1973).	Allocating funds and efforts in designing a better matriculation examination.

It may be useful to discuss some of the consequent actions in more detail. The finding that students in agricultural schools as well as those whose parents had immigrated to Israel from Asian and North African countries performed more poorly, resulted in the establishment of three new curriculum development teams. One team developed special modules for agricultural schools which included topics of special interest to these schools, such as the mineral requirements of plants or the special nutritional problems of farm animals. In addition, many more examples of the application of biological principles in agriculture were included. Moreover, a special biology matriculation examination which addresses various agricultural aspects and applications was designed to match the objectives and subject matter of the agriculturally-oriented biology curriculum.

As to the slow learner, two separate teams developed two different curricula, one aimed at the lowest 15 per cent of the school population and the other at the intermediate level, namely those who are below-average but above the lowest 15 per cent. High school biology teachers are now in a position to select from a variety of instructional materials which differ in their level of sophistication, in their cognitive demands and even in specific topics. Yet, in all of them, students are expected to be actively involved in investigations in the laboratory, in outdoor studies and in problem solving.

A special feature of the Israeli biology curriculum is the emphasis on inquiry. Various curriculum materials, such as inquiry-oriented laboratory investigations, invitations to inquiry, single topic films and television lessons, have been developed or adapted from abroad. It is now possible for a teacher to use these materials to gradually develop inquiry skills in the students without pushing too hard too soon. For example, a student at the end of the 10th grade may not be required to design his own experiment but, at the 11th and 12th grades, students are expected to design their own experiments and to actually work according to their own design. This emphasis on inquiry led to the design and employment of original evaluation measures and procedures (see below). It also resulted in a general acceptance of the inquiry approach by teachers (Dreyfus, Jungwirth and Tamir, 1982).

Communicating Results

The IHBP evaluation results have been communicated to a variety of audiences. Local reports were aimed primarily at teachers, administrators and curriculum developers. In addition a great number of studies were published in the professional educational literature in countries such as the USA, UK, Canada and Australia. In Israel, evaluation reports were published in teacher journals (*Maalot*), nature journals (*Teva Vaaretz*), curriculum literature (*Theory and Practice*, *The Curriculum Center*, the *Ministry of Education and Culture*), methods literature (*Methodica*, Tel Aviv University Publications) and quite frequently in the popular *Biology Teacher's Bulletin*, which has been published 6-8 times yearly since 1968. The aim of this bulletin has been to present current information about various biological topics, to offer practical suggestions and classroom ideas, to provide teachers with a vehicle for presenting their own ideas, criticism and queries, and to present the results of studies and surveys concerning the development and implementation of the IHBP.

Following is a sample of titles related to curriculum evaluation which were published in the Biology Teacher's Bulletin in the years 1968-80:

Suggested changes in the matriculation examination.
How suitable is the syllabus at the 3 point level?
Assessing individual projects.
Participation of teachers in designing the matriculation examination.
The role and structure of the oral examination.
The importance of evaluation for teachers.
A good word for the anathemic doctrine: teach for the test.
Examiners: examine yourselves.
The oral examination as a means for individualizing instruction.
The relationship between attitudes and nature field-work.

Since 1970 about 50 evaluation studies related to IHBP have been published, in the USA (24), UK (16) and other countries (10). Of these about half deal with students' achievements, a quarter with implementation and classroom utilization and the rest with teachers' perceptions and behaviours. That these studies were welcomed by close to 20 respectable journals all over the world may be partly a result of the fact that the BSCS has been widely used in the USA and in many other countries. At the same time, however, it may be an indication of the wide interest in these evaluation studies, as well, perhaps, as their cumulative nature, something rarely found in other places.

Evaluation papers related to IHBP have been presented in a number of professional conferences organized by associations such as the Asian Association of Biological Education, the American Association of Research in Science Teaching, the American Educational Research Association, the Australian Science Educational Association, the Israel Educational Research Association, the Bat Sheva International Conference and the International

Conference on World Trends in Science Education. Thus, the impact of evaluation of the IHBP has been significant and broad. Several evaluation instruments which were developed under the framework of the IHBP have been used in other countries (e.g. inquiry-oriented laboratory tests, cognitive preference inventories). As in other curriculum development projects located at universities (e.g. Individualized Science at the University of Pittsburgh, Project Physics at Harvard, and the Humanities Project at the University of East Anglia) a number of evaluation studies led to more general research dealing with problems such as misconceptions, logical errors, quantitative understanding, modes of performance, cognitive preferences, attitudes of students towards the use of animals in learning biology, the interests of students in different biological topics, the role of the laboratory in instruction and the effect of the school environment on students' learning.

Recently a new evaluation strategy - retrospective curriculum evaluation - was developed for assessing the long-term effects of the IHBP, which has shown, for example, that 11 per cent of the variance in students' achievement in biology in their first year at the university can be accounted for by the nature of their high school curriculum (Tamir and Amir, 1981).

Lastly, an important feature of evaluation operating as part of a long-term curriculum project is the establishment of permanent facilities such as a test item bank; standard computer programs as well as advanced planning of computer analysis; a pre-arranged sample plan, with indices of stratification; existence of a full list of subjects included in the target population; existence of contacts and liaison personnel in schools, different departments of the Office of Education, universities and other interested institutions. During the years the entire project team became involved in various aspects of evaluation through the involvement of the team in the construction of the matriculation examinations which provide feedback on a regular basis.

THE IMPACT OF ASSESSMENT ON IMPLEMENTATION

Assessment and evaluation are extremely powerful means of affecting what is taught in schools and how it is taught. Following are examples of such effects brought about by the evaluation of the IHBP, especially by the changes in the matriculation examinations. In this way evaluators have direct influence on the instructional process. This rather unusual argument may be clarified by a brief description of the matriculation examination:

> A theoretical test (paper-and-pencil) accounts for 60 per cent of the total examination score, and is structured as follows:
>
> Part A:
>
> 30-35 multiple-choice items test for functional knowledge and comprehension.
>
> Part B:
>
> Several problem situations are presented either verbally or, more frequently, in a table or graph. Students are required to describe the phenomena represented by the data, and to make inferences based on the data as well as on their ability to apply general biological principles.
>
> Part C:
>
> Students are required to analyse an unfamiliar research paper. On the basis of that analysis, they must identify a new research question, formulate a hypothesis, and design an experiment to test the hypothesis. Each year a different research study is selected. A variety of topics has been included, such as growth and development, bird migration, hormonal regulation, the social behaviour of bees, and the treatment of fruit after the harvest. For more details on the theoretical test, see Jungwirth and Dreyfus (1972).
>
> A practical test accounts for 40 per cent of the final score, and consists of three parts:
>
> Part A:
>
> Students identify an unknown plant and an unknown animal with the aid of a key. They are required not only to identify the family, genus, and species, but also to record in sequence the characteristics that warrant their conclusions.
>
> Part B:
>
> Students take an oral examination based on an ecological project which they have been performing for several months on topics of their own choice. Students bring their chosen organisms to the examination, where they must show a familiarity with the organisms and their environments. They must then

use the organisms to demonstrate biological principles. The oral format permits the examiner to design a different test for each individual student. For more information, see Tamir (1972b).

Part C:

A 2½ hour laboratory examination presents students with materials, organisms, and a problem which they must solve by performing an experiment, collecting data, making inferences, and properly discussing their findings. About ten new test problems have been designed each year. The examination can be administered to groups of 10-16 students simultaneously. Though the assessment is based mainly on the written report, some weight is also given to the students' use of materials and equipment. Thus the score is based on manipulation, experimental design, self-reliance, observation, communicative powers, and reasoning. For a fuller description of the laboratory examination, see Tamir and Glassman (1970, 1971a, 1971b) and Tamir (1974).

Student performance on examinations may assist curriculum developers to revise materials to deal with misunderstandings evident in the exams. More importantly, however, external examinations affect assessment in schools, where examinations have changed considerably to keep pace with the adoption of new curricula in the past ten years. The impact of the external matriculation examinations, as described above, has stimulated teachers to design examinations that reflect a variety of objectives (i.e. various levels of Bloom's taxonomy, or inquiry objectives such as problem identification, hypothesis formulation, experimental design, and statistical analysis of data), as well as to use several test formats including multiple-choice examinations, inferences drawn from data presented in tables and graphs, open questions, and the analysis of research papers (Tamir, 1977).

The Israel High School Biology Project has made special efforts to publish, and thereby make available to teachers, different types of test items. Test design and analysis of results have been continuously included in in-service training courses.

In addition to improved written tests, practical examinations have been emphasized in secondary schools. Here again the three types of practical tests used in the matriculation examination have been adopted by school teachers as part of their own assessment schemes.

The Involvement of Teachers. The involvement of teachers takes place in a number of ways: some teachers participate in the actual design and development of laboratory and paper-and-pencil tests. Many teachers serve as examiners for the different parts of the practical test: teachers from one school are assigned to test students in other schools. Not only do these teachers benefit from the guidance sessions which are held each year in preparation for the examinations but, significantly, they gain tremendously by interacting with students who study the same curriculum from other teachers in different settings. The grading of the different written tests is done by teachers under close supervision - another golden opportunity for the self-development of teachers. Lastly, as described above, teachers always make special efforts to participate in in-service training days devoted to the previous year's matriculation examinations. The discussions on these occasions often stimulate second thoughts among teachers as to what they have been doing and what can be done in their teaching. These occasions contribute considerably to the socialization of novice teachers. They also provide an opportunity for misunderstandings to be clarified and allow for fruitful exchanges between teachers and the project's staff.

Equipment and Learning Media. In two studies (Tamir, 1978a; Dreyfus, 1979), it was shown that, as a result of the laboratory examinations, not only are students performing laboratory investigations regularly but, almost with no exception, schools have acquired well-equipped laboratories which improve yearly in terms of materials and facilities.

Learning Materials and Experiences. It has already been mentioned that the tests themselves become valuable learning materials. However, the impact of the examinations goes beyond that. For example, the fact that the written examination contains a piece of research stimulates many teachers to direct their students to read research papers. Another example: the need to learn to use an identification key results in field trips and incidental learning about different plants in their natural habitats.

Attracting Students. Ten years ago biology was a relatively unattractive topic in high school, usually avoided by the more talented students, who elected to major in physics or chemistry. Today it is considered as a high level, highly respected, science course. About 50 per cent of candidates admitted to medical school at the university have majored in high school biology.

Impact on College. University professors have begun to realize that students majoring in high school biology are better prepared for studies in the university. First year courses are now taking into account the preparation of students in high school biology as evidenced by their matriculation examination (Tamir, 1978b).

Teacher Training Exercises. A unique feature is the teacher training exercises based on the answers of examinees in the matriculation examinations. For example, the answers of students to the inquiry-oriented laboratory investigations were collected and used for exercises, each dealing with one of the following inquiry skills:

Hypothesis formulation.
Identifying the dependent variable.
Identifying the independent variables.
Identifying measurement procedures.
Identifying controls.
Designing experiments.
Designing controls.
Performing observations.
Performing measurements.
Reporting.
Designing graphs.
Designing tables.
Interpreting data.
Concluding.
Explaining.
Applying findings in a new context.

The fact that these exercises are based on actual answers of students, correct and incorrect, routine and creative, usual and unexpected, make these unique exercises an important means of helping teachers identify the deeper level of their students' learning, achievements and understandings. Some teachers have been using these exercises with their students and have found them highly profitable and rewarding. Undoubtedly this broad and non-conventional usage of evaluation data adds a new dimension to curriculum evaluation.

Continuous Evaluation

It is suggested that a continuously operated

curriculum project, located at an institute of higher education and directed by university personnel, may be a highly supportive setting for useful and productive curriculum evaluation. We have illustrated the various aspects of evaluation which have taken place in the first five years of the IHBP. It may be appropriate to end this case study by listing a number of questions that have been identified for further study. An examination of the following list of questions which were studied in the last ten years present examples of the kind of issues that are likely to be studied under the framework of a continuous project. (Interested readers are referred to the references in brackets.)

1. To what extent are teachers aware of the programme's objectives? What are their preferences and expectations regarding these objectives? (Tamir and Jungwirth, 1972)
2. What is the relationship between the teacher's awareness of objectives, the image of the teachers in the eyes of his students, and the students' achievement? (Jungwirth and Tamir, 1973; Tamir, 1975a)
3. What is the relationship between teachers' attitudes toward the teaching of biology by inquiry and their adoption of the new curriculum? (Tamir, 1976a)
4. To what extent do student preferences for particular topics affect their achievement in these topics? (Tamir and Jungwirth, 1974)
5. What is the relationship of certain emphases in teacher training to the achievement of students in topics which have received differential emphases? (Tamir, 1976b)
6. To what extent has teaching the new curriculum changed teachers' attitudes? (Jungwirth, 1975)
7. What is the effect of the new programme, as well as that of teachers' biases regarding the programme, on the cognitive preferences of students? (Tamir, 1975)
8. What is the relationship between achievement in biology and cognitive preferences? (Tamir, 1976c)
9. What accounts for the low achievement of students in agricultural schools? (Tamir, 1972c; Dreyfus, 1975)
10. How does achievement in paper-and-pencil tests differ from achievement in practical laboratory tests? (Tamir, 1972d)

11. How do students and teachers regard various parts of the new matriculation examinations? (Tamir, 1973)
12. How has the new curriculum affected the number of laboratories, the equipment of laboratories, and the availability of assistance by laboratory technicians? (Tamir, 1978a)
13. What kinds of teacher-training practices help prepare teachers to teach biology by inquiry? (in progress)
14. What are the concerns of teachers who follow the IHBP programme and what are the implications of these concerns for the future? (Dreyfus, Jungwirth and Tamir, 1982)
15. What are the long-term effects of studying the IHBP programme on students' attitudes and achievement? (Tamir and Amir, 1981)

As may be seen, the unique role of the evaluator in a continuous project is to be alert to problems and issues as they emerge, to select those which are suitable for study and to feed into the system information which can help in decision making. The continuous nature of the project is advantageous in several ways:

1. It offers the necessary conditions for long-term studies.
2. It gives an opportunity for carrying out series of studies in which one study builds on the results and experiences of previous ones.
3. It provides for cumulative evidence from a variety of sources which gives information much more reliable than that of one-shot studies.
4. It leads to research studies involving basic variables related to teaching and learning.

REFERENCES

Ben-Gal (Glassman), S. (1973) 'A Good Word for the Anathemic Doctrine: Teach for the Test!' *Science Teacher*, 40(8), 5-6

Biological Sciences Curriculum Study (1963a) *Biological Science: Molecules to Man*. Houghton Mifflin, Boston

Biological Sciences Curriculum Study (1963b) High School Biology, *BSCS Green Version*, Rand McNally, Chicago

Biological Sciences Curriculum Study (1963c) _Biological Sciences: An Inquiry into Life, Harcourt, Brace and World, New York_

Dreyfus, A. (1975) 'Information Processing Within and Outside the School Curriculum by Students in Agricultural Schools as a Starting Point for Instruction'. PhD Thesis, Hebrew University of Jerusalem, (in Hebrew)

Dreyfus, A. (1979) 'Evaluation of the Impact of the BSCS on the Laboratory Facilities in Schools', Unpublished paper, The Israel Science Teaching Center

Dreyfus, A., Jungwirth, E. and Tamir, P. (1982) 'Biology Education in Israel as Viewed by the Teachers', _Studies in Educational Evaluation_, in press

Grobman, A.B. (1969) _The Changing Classroom, Doubleday, Garden City, NY_

Grobman, H.G. (1970) _Developmental Curriculum Projects: Decision Points and Processes_, F.E. _Peacock, Itasca, Ill_

Jungwirth, E. (1969) 'Active Understanding of the Processes of Science', _Journal of Biological Education_, _3_, 45-55

Jungwirth, E. (1970) 'An Evaluation of the Attained Development of the Intellectual Skills Needed for "Understanding of the Nature of Scientific Enquiry" by BSCS pupils in Israel', _Journal of Research in Science Teaching_, _7_, 141-51

Jungwirth, E. (1971) 'Content-learning in a Process-Oriented Curriculum: Some Aspects of BSCS Biology in Israel', _Science Education_, _55_, 85-96

Jungwirth, E. (1972) 'TOUS Revisited: A Longitudinal Study of the Development of Understanding of Science', _Journal of Biological Education_, _6_, 187-96

Jungwirth, E. (1975) 'A Study of the Stability of Biology Teachers' Priorities and Expectations', _Journal of Curriculum Studies_, _7_, 69-77

Jungwirth, E. and Dreyfus, A. (1972) 'The Israeli "Bagrut" Examination in BSCS Biology', _Journal of Research in Science Teaching_, _9_, 361-8

Jungwirth, E. and Tamir, P. (1973) 'The Teacher's Image as a Predictor of Students' Achievement', _Journal of Biological Education_, _7_, 40-4

Nuffield Foundation Science Teaching Project (1965a) _Synopsis of the Nuffield O-Level Biology Course_, _Nuffield Foundation, London_

Nuffield Foundation Science Teaching Project (1965b) _A-Level Biology: Aims and Outline Scheme_,

Nuffield Foundation, London

Tamir, P. (1972a) 'Understanding the Processes of Science by Students Exposed to Different Science Curricula in Israel', Journal of Research in Science Teaching, 9, 239-45

Tamir, P. (1972b) 'The Role of the Oral Examination in Biology', School Science Review, 54, 162-5

Tamir, P. (1972c) 'Biology and Agriculture: A Problem in Education', Journal of College Science Teaching, 1, 48-50

Tamir, P. (1972d) 'The Practical Mode - A Distinct Mode of Performance in Biology', Journal of Biological Education, 6, 175-82

Tamir, P. (1973) 'Attitudes of Students and Teachers Toward the Practical Examination in Biology', BSCS Newsletter, 53, 2-5

Tamir, P. (1974) 'An Inquiry Oriented Laboratory Examination', Journal of Educational Measurement, 11, 25-33

Tamir, P. (1975) 'The Relationship Between Cognitive Preferences, School Environment, Curriculum, Teachers' Curricular Bias and Subject Matter', American Educational Research Journal, 12, 263-80

Tamir, P. (1976a) 'Attitudes of High School Biology Teachers to the BSCS Program in Israel', Studies in Educational Evaluation, 2, 123-9

Tamir, P. (1976b) 'The Teaching and Achievement in Botany and Zoology as Affected by the Teachers' Background', Science Education, 60, 291-8

Tamir, P. (1976c) 'The Relationship Between Achievement in Biology and Cognitive Preference Styles of Highschool Biology Students', British Journal of Educational Psychology, 46, 57-67

Tamir, P. (1977) 'Questioning Practices in the Teaching of High School Biology in Israel', Journal of Curriculum Studies, 9, 145-56

Tamir, P. (1978a) 'The Impact of the BSCS on Laboratory Facilities for Biology Students in Israeli High Schools', International Evaluation Newsletter, 19, 20-3

Tamir, P. (1978b) 'The Potential Role of Examinations in Innovative Curricula', The American Biology Teacher, 40, 353-7

Tamir, P. (1980) 'Retrospective Curriculum Evaluation - An Approach to Longterm Curriculum Evaluation', Paper presented at the annual meeting of the American Educational Research Association, Boston

Tamir, P. and Glassman, F. (1970) 'A Practical Examination for BSCS Students', Journal of

Research in Science Teaching, *7*, 107-12

Tamir, P. and Glassman, F. (1971a) 'A Practical Examination for BSCS Students: A Progress Report', *Journal of Research in Science Teaching*, *8*, 307-15

Tamir, P. and Glassman, F. 1971b) 'Laboratory Test for BSCS Students', *BSCS Newsletter*, *42*, 9-13

Tamir, P. and Jungwirth, E. (1972) 'Teaching Objectives in Biology, Priorities and Expectations', *Science Education*, *56*, 31-9

Tamir, P. and Jungwirth, E. (1974) 'Botany and Zoology - A Curriculum Problem', *Journal of Research in Science Teaching*, *11*, 5-16

Tamir, P. and Jungwirth, E. (1975) 'Students' Growth Developed as a Result of Studying BSCS Biology for Several Years', *Journal of Research in Science Teaching*, *12*, 263-80

Tamir, P. and Amir, R. (1981) 'Retrospective Curriculum Evaluation: An Approach to Evaluation of Long Term Effects', *Curriculum Inquiry*, *11*, 259-74

Welch, W.W. (1968) 'The Impact of the National Curriculum Projects: The Need for Accurate Assessment', *School Science and Mathematics*, *68*, 225-34

9. THE AUTONOMOUS UNIT OF EVALUATION: COMBINING THE STRENGTHS OF IN-HOUSE AND EXTERNAL EVALUATIONS

A. Lewy

Despite the growth of in-house evaluation services attached to large-scale action projects, the general public still has less confidence in an in-house evaluation than in external evaluation. In line with the Talmudic saying, 'The baker is not relied upon to testify about the quality of his own dough', both users and grant-giving agencies tend to prefer external evaluation. This tendency was intensified through recurrent complaints of consumers' organizations that producers often deliberately conceal evidence about the shortcomings of their products, and only make publicly available selected portions of in-house evaluation reports.

In the field of curriculum evaluation, the constructive role of both in-house and external evaluation activities has been widely recognized by experts. It has been suggested that formative evaluation activities can be best done by in-house evaluation, while summative evaluation should be delegated to external evaluation agencies.

The preoccupation of experts with comparing in-house and external evaluation activities created the erroneous conception that these two organizational patterns constitute distinctly separate categories of evaluation activities. According to this view, a particular evaluation study is either an in-house activity or an external one. In reality, however, one may discern a variety of organizational patterns, located on a continuum, the two poles of which are the in-house and external modalities. At one end of the continuum are those evaluation studies which are carried out by the development team itself. This team may carry out both the production and the evaluation activities simultaneously; alternatively it may operate according to some sequential pattern, working for a while on production, then switching to evaluation, and vice versa. At the other end of the continuum are those evaluation activities which are carried out by an external team fully detached from development activities.

Curriculum evaluation employs a variety of organizational patterns, and some of these occupy in-between positions on this continuum. Some traits resemble the in-house pattern, while others are close to the pattern of external evaluation. An example of such a pattern is the activity of the Evaluation Unit established within the framework of the Israel Curriculum Center (ICC) in the Ministry of Education and Culture.

The ICC was established in 1966 with the aim of producing new curricula and innovative instructional materials for the whole educational system. To cope with this task, ten teams started to work, each of them preparing curriculum and learning materials for a certain grade level in a particular subject field. Gradually the number of the teams increased, and in 1981 30 curriculum project teams operated within the center. At the very outset of its operation, the ICC also established a single Evaluation Unit, which assumed the role of providing services to all the curriculum projects. One may say that during the first few months of the existence of the ICC, the whole staff, including members of the Evaluation Unit, was engaged in discussions and deliberations which led towards specifying a commonly agreed upon set of working principles. The search for such principles was justified by the fact that within the framework of the ICC several production teams provide services for a single group of consumers While separate teams prepare the curricula for subjects such as the mother tongue, mathematics, science, etc., the learning materials which they produce will all reach the hands of the same students and teachers.

Beyond the commonly agreed upon principles and working procedures, each curriculum project was given a high level of autonomy in its work. Within the framework of the common principles, the Evaluation Unit, too, was given full autonomy in preparing its working schedule, in determining preferences, in establishing contact with production units, etc. In this respect the Evaluation Unit operates as an external agency, because its activity has been fully independent of the curriculum teams, the products of which constitute the target of evaluation. On the other hand, since both the Evaluation Unit and the curriculum projects operate within the same institute, and both are subordinated to the Director and Directory Board of the center, the activity of the Evaluation Unit is partly that of an in-house study.

The successful combination of the advantages of in-house and external evaluation activities had a beneficial effect on the work of the Evaluation Unit. The full autonomy of the Evaluation Unit contributed to the credibility of its reports, and the close relationship with the production units increased the relevance of the evaluation findings to actual needs. Nonetheless it would be presumptuous to claim that the institutional proximity between the Evaluation Unit and the curriculum teams was enough to guarantee the relevance of the evaluation activities. It was mainly the common pattern of working procedures which was followed by every team, which enabled the Evaluation Unit to meet the increasing demand of the projects for information. As a result of the common production pattern of the teams, it turned out that studying the problems of one project had transfer value for understanding the problems of another as well. Also, whenever the Evaluation Unit successfully completed a certain evaluation study, demands emerged on behalf of other projects, requesting that the study be replicated in <u>their</u> project. Thus the Evaluation Unit faced the demand of conducting a series of studies following the same pattern of data collection, analysis and summary.

As the Evaluation Unit was engaged in such activities, a pattern of study emerged, which became known as Serial Evaluation Activities (SEA). Conducting SEA increased the capability of the Evaluation Unit to cope with the information demands of a great number of curriculum projects. Being able to use the same study design recurrently, and operating in a setting in which there is no need to develop a conceptual framework for each evaluation activity separately, had a decisive role in shaping the work of the Evaluation Unit. Additionally, the fact that a study of a particular type was frequently carried simultaneously for several curriculum projects, increased the detachment of the Evaluation Unit from the individual project, and gave it the status of a quasi-external evaluation activity.

The purpose of this chapter is to describe the work of the Evaluation Unit within the framework of the ICC, and to specify those aspects of its operation which enabled it to keep its autonomy and detachment from the individual projects, and at the same time to remain close to those whose work served as the target of the evaluation. It will deal with the following issues: (1) the organizational structure of the Evaluation Unit; (2) the conceptual framework of the Evaluation Studies; (3) the working strategies; and (4) the clientele. Using colloquial words, the chapter deals with the 'who, what, how and for whom' questions.

THE ORGANIZATIONAL STRUCTURE OF THE EVALUATION UNIT

The formal structure of institutes may be an outgrowth of historical developments, but, in the case of new institutes, it usually reflects a certain conception of roles and of hierarchical role division. This does not mean that the formal structure fully describes the relative importance of each unit within an institute. It is well known that units having equal formal status within an institute frequently differ from each other with regard to their actual power, their access to resources, and their impact on decision-making processes. Nevertheless, given the fact that the Israel Curriculum Center is a relatively new institute, it is of interest to study the formal status of the Evaluation Unit within its framework. Such a study, even if it does not reveal all the relevant facts about the actual status of the unit within the center, nevertheless may reveal the conception of those who established the center as to the role evaluation should play in its framework.

Since the ICC was set up with the aim of introducing a curriculum reform in the school system, its major domain of activity has been the production of innovative educational programmes and instructional materials. Evaluation was meant to aid the process of production and was not considered as an aim in itself. Its purpose was to serve the needs of those who prepared the new curricula. This conception of role division and role hierarchy was reflected in the formal structure of the institute. The major units operating within the institute were the curriculum projects. A curriculum project was defined as the production of a new programme (including textbooks, teacher's guide, instructional aids, etc.) in a single subject area for a group of classes in schools of a certain type, for example: Biology for the disadvantaged learners in the middle school, or Bible for the upper section of the religious high school. Each project constituted an organizational sub-unit within the centre, having its own team and its own director. In addition to these production units, several service units were established in the center, such as the Graphics and Printing Unit, the Library and the Evaluation Unit.

The Evaluation Unit, from the very outset, has been considered as a service unit, and was supposed to serve all production units. The fact that the Evaluation Unit was similar in its formal status and staff size to the majority of the 30 ongoing curriculum projects, determined the parameters of its activity. Due respect was given to evaluation within the framework of the center; provision was made to guarantee its autonomy. At the same time, however, the formal organizational structure manifestly conveyed the message that by no means should the Evaluation Unit have claims to privileges which were not granted to other units of the center. The formal structure reflected the manifest goals of the center, but at the same time also gave expression to the basic philosophy underlying its operation, according to which empirical support should be sought for improving the quality of the new programmes and for increasing their success in the school system.

By establishing an Evaluation Unit, the stage was set for starting the evaluation activities. It was clearly evident that a small evaluation team could not provide all necessary services for all teams operating within the center. It was important to find a way to ensure the conducting of evaluation studies for all the projects without increasing the size of the Evaluation Unit. This was achieved by dividing the responsibility for the evaluation activities related to each project into two parts. One part of the evaluation activities was assigned to the project team itself, while the other part remained the responsibility of the Evaluation Unit. This latter guided the evaluation activities and provided some technical services, but the role of carrying out these activities became the responsibility of each project team. Each team nominated one of its members to serve as the coordinator of evaluation and this person also served as a liaison with the Evaluation Unit. The liaison person took part in the team conferences and contributed to the development work of the project, while at the same time carrying out and coordinating evaluative activities. Apart from the evaluation activities coordinated by the project liaison person, the Evaluation Unit itself sometimes initiated and carried out small-scale evaluation studies related to a particular project or cutting across several projects facing similar problems. Thus it turned out that, in practice, both internal and external evaluation activities were carried out. The internal evaluation was done by the team itself, and the external evaluation by the Evaluation Unit. Clearly, the evaluation done by the Evaluation Unit cannot be fully considered as an external evaluation, since it is performed by a team which has continuous and prolonged contact with the production team. It is nevertheless somewhat detached from the production activity, and is consequently less affected by the bias of the development team than are the evaluation activities initiated by the liaison person.

This organizational arrangement permitted very intensive evaluation activities without altering the original balance between the relative magnitude and power of the Evaluation Unit and the individual projects. Given the fact that most projects faced similar evaluation problems, and that the nature of evaluation activities assumed the form of serial evaluation activities, it became relatively easy to provide guidelines common to all projects. A weekly seminar for the liaison persons of all the projects served a double purpose: firstly to guide the projects in whatever evaluation they were involved in at the time; and secondly to provide systematic knowledge about basic topics in the field of evaluation. Additionally, conferences were scheduled in which the Evaluation Unit team, and the team of a particular project including the liaison person participated, to discuss unique problems related to the evaluation of that particular project. If needed, the liaison person could recruit help for carrying out evaluative activities from his team. For example, in many cases, auxiliary workers affiliated to a project performed observations in classes or administered tests. Moreover, in certain cases, at some critical stages of the programme development, the liaison person succeeded in recruiting the whole project team for carrying out evaluative activities for a short period of time. The cooperation between the Evaluation Unit and any single project in carrying out a study is schematically outlined in Figure 9.1. This presents sequential steps in carrying out a study. The activities appearing in rectangular frames are joint decisions of the two teams. It can be seen that both the determination of the study parameters and the formulation of the recommendations are performed jointly by the two teams, while the implementation of the recommendations is the responsibility of the project team. The major responsibilities of the Evaluation Unit consist of guiding the work of sampling, instrument development, providing training for people doing the work of data collection, carrying out data analysis, publishing the evaluation results, and filing the data and the instruments used in the studies. But beyond the specific test-orientated activities, the existence of the Evaluation Unit constitutes a permanent reminder of the necessity for empirical examination

Figure 9.1: Sequential Steps in an Evaluation Study

Curriculum Project Team	Liaison Person	Evaluation Unit
-Identifies problem		-Suggests topic for study
Agree about parameters of the study		
		-Determines technical features of the study (sampling, instruments, etc.)
	-Performs technical preparations	
		-Controls, edits
	-Performs field work	
		-Carries out statistical analysis
	-Interprets results	
Formulate conclusions, suggestions, reccommendations		
-Implements recommendations		-Publishes, files data and reports

of the quality of new curricula. Of course, a reminder does not in itself initiate action. It is up to the Evaluation Unit to create cooperation with the project teams and to motivate them to carry out evaluative activities. Without the Evaluation Unit's vigorous intervention, the effect of a reminder may be no more than that of creating a remorseful feeling by the curriculum project team for not doing what one is expected to do.

The description of the formal structure should be complemented by details of some of the informal features of cooperation between the teams. Despite the uniformity of the pattern of the cooperation between the team, some differences emerged regarding the role of the liaison person. Three different patterns emerged.

1. The liaison person had had his basic training in evaluation. He had limited knowledge in the subject area of the project, and was delegated to the project by the Evaluation Unit.
2. The liaison person had had his basic training in the subject area of the project. He was nominated as a liaison person by the project.
3. The director of the project himself served as liaison person. This usually happened whenever the director had some basic training in evaluation and wanted to participate in all decisions related to evaluation. In most cases this reflected sincere interest in evaluation, but sometimes it was the result of fear or suspicion that evaluation might jeopardize his freedom of action.

While each of the three patterns had certain advantages, the second proved to be most fruitful. It turned out that being immersed in the project was extremely important for establishing a good working relationship with the Evaluation Team, and facilitated the implementation of the evaluation recommendations.

Contrary to expectations, the directors of the curriculum projects did not function well as liaison persons. Their commitment to the project and the continuous pressure exerted upon them to increase the quantity of instructional materials produced by their teams, left them very little time to act in the roles of liaison persons. Given their dual alliances, their commitments as directors were usually dominant, frequently at the cost of their neglecting their duties toward the Evaluation Unit.

Summarizing the experiences derived from the organizational structure of the curriculum center one may suggest the following principles as general guidelines for serial evaluation activities operating within the framework of institutes.

THE AUTONOMOUS UNIT OF EVALUATION

1. An autonomous Evaluation Unit, even if it is a small one, may serve as a catalyst for initiating evaluation activities, the limits of which exceed the working capacity of the unit itself. It may create awareness of the work of evaluation and emphasize its role in the course of the daily activities.
2. Fruitful cooperation and mutual trust between the Evaluation Unit and units being evaluated can be successfully established when the Evaluation Unit keeps a low profile within the institute and does not receive privileges, such as access to resources, which are not granted to other units.
3. A realistic assessment of actual needs in terms of manpower and other resources and their satisfactory provision constitute prerequisites for the successful operation of the Evaluation Unit. It is not the absolute size of the budget which determines the successful operation of the Evaluation Unit, but rather the match between the resources available and the appropriate definition of the evaluation tasks.
4. Within each production subunit of an institute, separation of the responsibility for evaluation from the responsibility for running the production unit is desirable. A liaison person who is not himself responsible for the production may create better cooperation between the two units than would a relationship which is built solely on personal contacts between the directors of the units.

A CONCEPTUAL FRAMEWORK FOR EVALUATIVE STUDIES

As a working definition of evaluation, the Evaluation Unit adapted the statement that 'evaluation is a systematic data collection and data summary process which comes to increase the rationality of decision making'. Operating with this working definition of evaluation, three principles are presented in this section. They reflect characteristics of evaluation activities within the Israel Curriculum Center, but in a broader sense, they may apply to serial evaluation studies of any type carried out in institutes which are responsible for both the evaluation and the target being evaluated. The three principles are:

1. Since most projects face more decision situations than can be realistically examined by empirical studies, the Evaluation Unit has to determine priorities and to select topics for study.
2. Since a project team may encounter various decision points spread over time, the evaluation activities should consist of a series of small-scale focused studies, rather than a single complex one.
3. Though the evaluation of one project may be quite different to that of another one, within the framework of serial evaluation activities, it is recommended that a subset of minimum evaluation requirements, to be incorporated in the evaluation design of each project, be defined.

SELECTING TOPICS FOR STUDY

The need to keep a proper balance between investments in evaluation and in the project being evaluated has already been emphasized. The process of evaluation as specified by Alkin (1970) implies the task of 'ascertaining the decision areas of concern' and we would like to add to Alkin's statement the qualification 'which most require support and clarification, based on empirical data collection'. Indeed, the team frequently will have to satisfy itself in handling 'decision areas of concern' by consulting experts or even by sharing experiences accumulated during the time. It is impossible to conduct an empirical study whenever one comes across 'decision areas of concern'. The evaluation team, together with the project team, have to identify those junctions which can be crossed without stopping by utilizing intuitive knowledge based on past experience, and those junctions where a full stop is required and where data should be systematically collected before any decisive step is taken.

The selection of topics should be done on the basis of consent between or at least a compromise among the two teams. The suggestion of any topic may nevertheless come from either of the teams. It is true that it is usually the project team which feels confused when arriving at a junction, and that it is accordingly more likely to ask for help in identifying the best road to follow. It may be, however, that the project team is in a hurry, and, reaching a junction, may deliberately close its eyes and act as if only one way is open before it. On the other hand, it may concentrate on a certain direction without noticing the existence of alternative ones. In such cases, it is the responsibility of the evaluation team to sketch the road-map exactly and to call attention to the existence of such alternatives. This should be a cooperative task in which each of the partners has their own well-defined role. The project team has to move forward, and the evaluation team has to put up the road signs at the crucial junctions.

The cooperation between the two teams has to take the form of cooperation between equals, where the nature of the expertise of the two teams lies in different fields. It would be wrong to claim that the evaluation team operates at a higher scientific level than does the project team. The truth is that there are some junctions where the project team's judgement provides valid guidelines for selecting the way to be continued, and other junctions where the evaluator's expertise can provide the most valid guidelines. The evaluator needs to master not only the methodological techniques of producing satisfactory evidence, but also how to acquire insight in locating those junctions where his evidence is most relevant and valid.

A Series of Focused Studies

The development and implementation of a new programme are processes which require a relatively long period of time. Institutes tend to operate according to work plans which extend over years rather than months or weeks. The work plan cannot, and should not, nevertheless, constitute a detailed blueprint, which is meant to specify all steps to be taken. Consequently, during the process of carrying out a plan, institutes must continuously make decisions. Accordingly, evaluation units have to conduct studies focusing on a particular decision problem faced by the institute in whose service they operate. One of the most important traits of such studies is the timeliness of the evaluation results. Indeed, one of the major distinctions made between research and evaluation activities is the time dimension of the study.

The traditional conception of scientific inquiry links science to the notion of 'timelessness'. On the other hand, evaluative information should be available at the time when the development team faces a decision. The pace of the development imposes the criterion of timeliness upon the evaluation and sets its deadlines.

To meet the requirement of timeliness within the framework of serial evaluation activities, one should preferably focus on a single decision situation and design short duration studies.

Within the framework of the Curriculum Center it was found convenient to utilize a classification scheme of decision situations based on a mapping sentence of three facets: the stage of the curriculum development; the component of the programme or the entity being evaluated; and the type of decision. A brief description of these facets is given below.

The stages. In the development of a curriculum project six consecutive stages have been distinguished. The focus of development and evaluation activities is described in Table 9.1.

The entity. Essentially, evaluation is concerned with the effectiveness of a programme as a whole. Thus the basic concern of evaluation is the success of the entire programme including all its components. Quite frequently, however, evaluation may deal solely with specific components. The focus of a small-scale evaluation study may be a particular chapter of the programme; a particular activity associated with its use, such as the organization of the dissemination network; or a particular t pe of instructional material included in it, such as the textbook, the teacher's guide, audiovisual aids, enrichment supplements, experimental equipment, or the teacher-training programme. Moreover, an evaluation study may be concerned only with specific features of these components. For example, evaluation may deal with some unique aspect of the textbook such as the quality of the illustrations, the clarity of the explanation, the readability of the text, the sequence of learning experiences, or the adequacy of the exercises. Some unique aspect of the programme as a whole may be investigated, such as the effectiveness of the type of classroom management prescribed by the programme, or the effectiveness of a unique learning strategy employed in it.

The type of decision. Three major types of decision are made during the process of developing a programme and implementing it: (1) selecting programme components; (2) modifying programme elements; and (3) qualifying the use of the programme.

Table 9.1: Six Stages of Curriculum Development and Evaluation (Lewy, 1977)

Stage	Development Activities	Evaluation Activities
Determination of general aims	Decisions about: general aims school structure	Studies on: expected changes cultural values social forces present level of achievement feasibility of programmes
Planning	Writing outlines Preparing instructional material	Examining adequacy of objectives, contents, strategies Judgement of material
Testing	Monitoring teaching in test classes Modifying material	Collecting evidence through observation, judgement, discussion with teachers, students Student products
Field-trial	Slightly modifying the programme Determining optimal conditions of programme use	Selecting sample Collecting evidence about the efficiency of programme under various conditions
Implementation	Links with supervisors, the examination system, teacher training	Examining final form Evidence on efficiency of system links Evidence of efficiency of teacher training
Quality control	Implementing recommendations Planning 'second generation' programmes	Examining quality of implementation Studying reasons for changes in efficiency Suggesting remedies if needed

1. Selecting programme components
At the early stages of programme development, questions arise as to what should be included, what should be taught, what strategies should be employed, and so on. Frequently, several alternatives are presented to the programme developer, and he has to select the most appropriate one.
2. Modifying programme elements
At the test stage of the programme it may turn out that some element (e.g. an exercise, illustration, or explanation) contains certain flaws. Perhaps it does not adequately help the students achieve certain desired goals, or perhaps it is producing undesired effects. Evaluation results may call attention to such problems, and may help programme developers improve their programme by eliminating the flaws.
3. Qualifying the use of the programme
A third type of decision may be that of qualifying programme usage. In other words, evaluation may aid in the specification of the optimal or minimal conditions for usage. Unlike the other two types of decisions, which deal with issues related to the development of the programme, the third focuses on how and under what conditions a programme should be used. Conditions may be specified for various aspects of a programme, such as teacher training; availability of equipment, space, time, or professional prerequisites; the consent and support of the community; existence of a skilled supervisory or monitoring staff, and so on. For any particular school, the specification of conditions may constitute a basis for the adoption or rejection of a particular programme.

A Classification Scheme. The three facets described above, combined in a mapping sentence, may serve as a classification scheme of decision situations which should be dealt with in evaluation studies.

The mapping sentence in its totality constitutes an overall inventory of decision situations which one may encounter during the process of curriculum development. Each such decision situation may require the conducting of a short-duration focused evaluation study, in which the summary of empirical data may contribute to the rationality of the decision. The mapping sentence containing the three facets is presented in Figure 9.2.

Figure 9.2: Mapping Sentence Classification Scheme of Curriculum Evaluation Studies

	A: Stages	
Evaluation is the provision of information at the	determination of aims planning tryout field trial implementation quality control	stage of programme development

	B: Entity	
concerning the	teacher's guide study material equipment whole package	for the

	C: Decision Situations	
sake of making decisions about	selecting elements of modifying qualifying the use of	the programme

One may define a particular type of focused evaluation study by selecting a single line from each of the three facets appearing in the mapping sentence. Thus, for example, a focused evaluation study may aim to provide information at the test stage of the programme development concerning the teacher's guide for the sake of making decisions about modifying the original version.

Minimum Evaluation Requirements

It has been emphasized that it is the evaluator's task to identify the crucial decision situations and the critical junctions where evaluation may yield the most useful information. These junctions may differ from one programme to another. Nevertheless, whenever an evaluation unit assumes responsibility for carrying out serial evaluation activities, one may determine within the evaluation space several junctions where the evaluator is requested to place 'road signs' on the basis of systematically collected empirical data.

Within the framework of the Israel Curriculum Center, three such junctions have been identified, and at each of these, empirical evidence of a specific type is requested in order to determine which direction to follow. These junctions are:

1. Obtaining expert judgement about the scientific quality of the instructional materials as soon as the first version of the programme has been prepared.
2. Observing the teaching and learning process during the first testing of the materials in the class in order to determine the feasibility of using these materials and to specify teacher-training needs.
3. To examine the cognitive achievements of the learners at the end of the first test of the materials in the experimental classes and to compare the actual level of the achievement with the expected level, as specified by the programme objectives or implied by the contents taught.

These three evaluation activities have been considered as minimum requirements by the Evaluation Unit, with the first two performed mainly by the project team under the leadership of the liaison person and under the supervision of the Evaluation Unit, while the third was mainly performed by the evaluation team.

THE MANAGEMENT OF EVALUATION STUDIES

It has already been mentioned that evaluative information can serve as input for decision making only if it meets the requirement of timeliness. Stufflebeam (1969) listed the trait of 'timeliness' as one of the most important of the traits which determine the merits of an evaluation study, and he attributes to the 'timeliness' a significance matching that of reliability and validity. Timeliness in evaluation studies is to a large extent a function of realistic planning and good management. Fortunately, evaluation units operating within the framework of institutes and carrying out serial evaluation activities can more easily meet the requirement of timeliness than can ad hoc freelance contractors. The former may take advantage of the fact that they are dealing with events or targets which repeat themselves according to a recurrent pattern.

The Evaluation Unit of the Israel Curriculum Center established an infrastructure geared especially toward the needs of the serial evaluation studies carried out in the Center, and which facilitated the quick completion of focused studies. In this respect the ICC tried to capitalize on experiences accumulated in various institutes of survey research, such as those predicting voting trends, examining public opinion about dominant political and social issues, carrying out market research, exploring exposure to mass communications, etc. The ICC applied some techniques developed in the domain of surveys for enhancing timeliness. One has to admit that there are differences between the task of carrying out surveys of the above mentioned types and evaluation studies in the field of education. There are, nevertheless, procedures employed in surveys which are transferable to educational evaluation. Additionally there are developments in the field of evaluation which, when combined with the routines of the survey techniques, can enhance timeliness.

Comprehensive Conceptual Framework

Conducting short duration, focused studies does not imply that one may disregard the need for establishing an adequate conceptual framework as a basis of formulating questions, selecting variables, determining the mode of data analysis, etc. By no means should evaluation be degraded into a series of data collection and data analysis routines. Without a conceptual framework, data summaries remain disjointed sets of facts, which do not contribute to our understanding of the dynamics of various phenomena. But in a serial evaluation study the establishment of the conceptual framework should be done in a comprehensive way and commonly for the entire series of studies, rather than separately for each one. One may identify several basic concerns, concepts or variables, etc. which play a crucial role in the whole series of the studies and then in each particular study, focus on those which are uniquely relevant. Thus, two studies of a single series, though founded on a common comprehensive conceptual framework, may differ from each other with regard to their actual design.

Permanent Institutional Setting

Surveys are conducted by professional people who are permanently employed in institutes carrying out such work. Although surveys are less complicated professionally than are evaluation or research studies, survey institutes are often staffed by more highly qualified and competent professional people than are evaluation studies. No doubt the permanent nature of their job is a crucial factor in attracting highly qualified people to those institutes. Experts are not hired to perform a particular survey, but rather are asked to perform a series of studies, which have several recurrent components in common. Thus the experts may develop a high level of familiarity with the working procedures relevant to their job.

Pre-arranged Sample Plan

One of the time-consuming procedures in the process of carrying out an evaluation study is drawing a sample and ensuring the cooperation of the sampled subjects. In studies which deal with whole populations, the question of sampling does not exist. But the majority of evaluation studies in education will restrict data collection to a sample of the target population. Drawing a sample requires a series of sequential steps, each of them quite time consuming: the exact definition of the target population, the identification of those stratifying variables which are the most effective in reducing the magnitude of sampling errors, etc. Sampling in educational studies is especially complicated because it usually requires multi-stage sampling procedures, e.g. the selection of schools, classes within the schools and individuals within the classes. Furthermore, some variables describe individual behaviour, such as the learner's scores on certain cognitive or affective measures, while other behaviours relate to larger units, such as the class or the whole school. Examples of such variables are the training of the teacher, the utilization of a certain curriculum in the school, the availability of equipment of a certain type, etc.

In serial evaluation activities the sample plan should be prepared in advance, before the actual start of a particular inquiry.

Advance Planning of Computer Analysis

With the advent of standardized computer programmes, one would expect that the time needed for performing analysis of data would be largely reduced. No information is available on whether or not this has indeed occurred, but first impressions of a variety of data summary projects seem to indicate that the time necessary for data analysis was not shortened. The availability of easily manageable computer programs decreased the amount of thoughtful planning of data analysis and increased the appetite for a greater range of data analysis modes. In most studies, only a small portion of obtained data summaries are reported. Frequently, such a selection of 'results' not only causes prolongation of the time needed to complete a project, but actually causes a bias, resulting from the selection procedures.

In serial evaluation activities, careful planning should prescribe the major data analysis procedures, and the forms and the patterns of presenting results. By doing this, one may develop computer outputs in a photo-proof form for immediate inclusion in the research report. One example of an output set is a test-scoring program produced for the University of Illinois Medical Center (Lewy and Crawford, 1966), which contained tables and histograms in a form which was considered useful for the evaluation reports. To ensure timely data summary, it proved advantageous to perform a 'dry run' analysis, in which a small set of simulated data were analysed, in the exact form in which they were to appear in the final report. In general, inspection of the 'dry run' results permits the early detection of errors in the control card prepared for the summary of a particular set of data.

THE CLIENTELE

Evaluation experts suggested that each evaluation activity should be geared toward the needs of a specific clientele (Stake, 1972; Stake and Craig, 1974). Evaluation methods and reports should not only be relevant but should also appear credible to the decision maker. The results should be presented in a way which yields easily and unambiguously derivable decision rules. Moreover it has been recommended that the decision rules should be determined on the basis of an agreement between the evaluator and his client before the study design has been finalized. Some experts claim that if agreement about the decision rules cannot be obtained before starting the study, there is little chance that the evaluation results will affect decision making. One should, nevertheless, be aware that while agreement in itself may be a necessary condition, it is certainly not a sufficient one. In science, no agreement has validity unless it is based on publicly defensible principles. In any scientific endeavours, the parties are not only permitted but are supposed to cancel agreements, if one of the parties realizes that the agreement was based on erroneous or non-valid principles. The notion of 'publicly defensible' implies that it is not enough for an evaluation study to be an internal affair among contracting parties, but it should be made accessible to a non-homogeneous type of clientele. This leads to the formulation of two principles:

1. Evaluation results should be presented to a multiple clientele.
2. Evaluation results should be presented in a form which enables access of the clientele not only to the recommendations but also to the data on which the recommendations are based.

Multiple Clientele

The organizational setting of the evaluation unit and the definition of evaluation as a series of short-duration focused studies, clearly suggest that the direct clientele of the serial evaluation activities carried out at the Israel Curriculum Center is the Curriculum Project team, which is responsible for producing new curriculum materials. It is supposed to utilize the evaluation results for the purpose of decision making. The reports produced by the evaluation unit should nevertheless be valid for clienteles of different types too. Firstly, they should contain valuable information for the superiors in the office hierarchy of both the project team and the evaluation teams. This constitutes a safeguard that the project team is not in a position to disregard evaluation results. It is not that one fears a sinister attitude of the project team toward evaluation results. But in an institutional setting one cannot build a system in which the execution of a certain task is left entirely to the discretion and benevolence of those who have to carry out that particular extra work. There is a need for a certain control mechanism. This may be achieved by broadening the clientele of the evaluation report. It may well be that the form of the report presented to one's superiors should be different from that presented to the project team, but it is important that the two parties should be informed about the results. Of course this can be done only if mutual trust exists among all parties interested in the project, so that the report does not constitute a threat for those whose work is evaluated. This is especially important in a situation where an evaluation team maintains a continuous working relationship with the project team during a period of several years.

Additionally, evaluation results should be communicated to the community of evaluation experts. Gaining their approval and their acceptance of the decision recommendations serves as support for the demand that the recommendations should be implemented. Finally, teachers, parents, etc. should also be informed about the merits and shortcomings of programmes suggested to them.

Access to Data and to Written Reports

Evaluation experts tend to denigrate the importance of preparing formal evaluation reports, let alone reports which are written in a scholarly style and which contain detailed analysis of all the data collected within the framework of a study. They often consider it quite satisfactory if, in certain cases, evaluation results are transmitted orally. Indeed, the decision maker can often better absorb an oral communication than a written report. The preparation of a written report is a time-consuming process and, from the point of view of the decision maker, may be a waste of time and money. In practice it may be almost impossible both to prepare scholarly evaluation reports and to complete evaluation studies within a reasonable time.

While one may agree that, in the process of curriculum evaluation, constant contact should be maintained between evaluators and decision makers, and that research findings should be conveyed as soon as possible, there are several reasons which support the contention that formal evaluation reports should be prepared as well.

First of all, an orally or informally communicated series of findings may not have a high level of public credibility. It will be treated as a series of remarks made by colleagues on the basis of in-house examination of the situation, but by no means will the general public and even the producers of the programme pay them due respect. The decision maker may more easily disregard or 'explain' an informally conveyed message than a research report. This is likely to happen when following evaluation recommendations requires extensive work on the part of the curriculum worker. Secondly, the standard of curriculum evaluation may deteriorate if no demand is imposed upon the evaluator to prepare scholarly and defensible reports. Finally, one has to consider the fact that curriculum evaluation is an emerging field of scientific endeavour. A sound theory of curriculum evaluation can be developed only on the basis of the critical analysis of well-written published empirical studies. The lack of empirical studies in this field may create a situation in which theory and practice are not related to one another at all.

REFERENCES

Alkin, M.C. (1970) 'Products for Improving Educational Evaluation', Evaluation Comments, 2(3), 1-15

Bauer, M., Kempf, W.F. Postlethwaite, N. and Lewy, A. (1977) 'Collecting and Analyzing Evaluation Data', in M.A. Lewy (ed.), Handbook of Curriculum Evaluation, Longman, New York

Choppin, B. (1978) 'Item Banking and the Monitoring of Achievement', National Foundation for Educational Research in England and Wales, Slough

Kempf, W.F. (1976) 'A Dynamic Text Model and its Use in Microevaluation of Instruction Materials', in M.H. Spada and W.F. Kempf (eds.), Structural Models of Thinking and Learning, Haber, Beru

Lewy, A. (ed.),(1977) Handbook of Curriculum Evaluation, Longman, New York

Lewy, A. and Crawford, R. (1966) 'Scoring Text Battery', Educational and Psychological Measurement, 26, 185-8

Postlethwaite, N. (1978) 'The IEA Item Banking Project Proposal', University of Hamburg

Rasch, G. (1960) Probabilistic Models for Some Intelligence and Attainment Tests, Danish Institute for Educational Research, Copenhagen

Stake, R. (1972) 'Responsive Evaluation', University of Illinois, Urbana

Stake, R. and Craig, G. (1974) 'An Evaluation of

TCITY, The Turin City Institute for Talented Youth', in R. Stake (ed.), Four Evaluation Examples, Rank MacNally, Chicago
Stufflebeam, D. (1969) 'Evaluation as Enlightenment for Decision Making', in M.W.H. Beatty (ed.), Improving Educational Assessment, Association for Supervision and Curriculum Development, Washington DC

10. CONCLUDING COMMENTS

P. Tamir

The purpose of this book is to identify and describe the variety of roles played by curriculum evaluators. Some of the roles are common to many studies, others are unique to a particular study. Based on the case studies presented, it may be seen that curriculum evaluators can play a number of important roles in addition to their obvious formal role, namely the collection and collation of feedback data at the formative and summative stages of curriculum development and implementation. In this summary chapter an attempt has been made to summarize the case studies and extract from each a list of the roles which evaluators have played in them. While this overview does not intend to provide a cohesive theoretical framework for curriculum evaluation, it does provide an account of the potential contributions of curriculum evaluators to the process of curriculum development and implementation.

With the exception of Lewy's chapter which provides a description of an evaluation unit which deals with curriculum development projects in many disciplines, the remaining chapters focus on science projects. Even so, there is great variation among the chapters. It is reasonable to assume that curriculum evaluators in other disciplines such as the arts may operate somewhat differently. Yet the impressive variety displayed in this book, as well as the general principles which have emerged, apply by and large, to the whole field of curriculum evaluation.

Hulda Grobman reflects back on her experiences as the first in-house evaluator of the BSCS. Her article is of special interest for several reasons:

1. The BSCS, being one of the major NSF supported curriculum development projects in the

late 1950s and early 1960s, was a pioneering enterprise not only in curriculum development but also in shaping up the role of evaluation in this context. Grobman's paper illustrates many aspects pertaining to the evolution of curriculum evaluation as an important and indispensable field of study.

2. Grobman was the only educational researcher on the Biological Science Curriculum Study (BSCS) staff and as the wife of the BSCS director held a unique and delicate position. She had to stand up to the standards of the scientists, on the one hand, and at the same time to maintain and defend the standards of educational measurement and research. At one point, for example, she had to overcome the potential criticism of measurement specialists in her decision to take over the externally designed and executed evaluation and substitute it with internally controlled evaluation - quite a daring decision in those days.

3. The BSCS addressed a great variety of evaluation problems and utilized a number of different approaches to evaluation, including: an historical study of biology education in the US from 1890 to 1960, an exploration of operational options of other curriculum projects, a study of the characteristics of successful biology teachers, an invited review of the materials by a prominent educational psychologist and involvement of field consultants in formal and informal evaluation activities.

4. The BSCS evaluation suffered from a number of constraints which illustrate the kinds of constraints likely to be encountered by any curriculum evaluators. These include matters such as:

- when money is scarce the first item to cut is evaluation;
- scientists and curriculum developers tend to distrust evaluation results;
- curriculum developers often consider evaluation as a threat. Even when this is not the case, evaluation is often regarded as an unnecessary burden which slows down the really important work of curriculum development;
- in-house evaluators often have competing tasks leading to an inability to cope on time with the evaluation demands;
- testing and measurement specialists may be unprepared for the special demands of curriculum evaluation;
- difficulty in obtaining unbiased samples of

teachers and/or students as controls for the new experimental subjects;
inability of consumers to make sense of evaluation data;
reluctance of teachers to spend time on testing;
pressures from funding agencies as to the kind of data which should be collected and/or the kind of results that may be released to the general public;
hostility of the research community towards evaluation which is often looked upon as a step-sister.

5. Many of the potential roles of evaluators have been identified by Grobman. These include:

providing timely feedback to the writing teams;
providing feedback on the needs and effects of teacher training;
maintaining contact with external testing agencies;
identifying implementation techniques as well as factors which affect implementation;
helping in the design of tests to be part of the curriculum package;
finding out whether the use of the new materials becomes easier as teachers gain experience, with time;
commissioning external evaluation studies;
translating evaluation data to users.

It is doubtful whether this wide experience of the BSCS evaluation has made the impact it could have made on future evaluation studies because much of what is included in Grobman's paper has never been published, certainly not in a form which makes it readily useful to evaluators.

Fraser makes a sharp distinction between the roles of in-house and external evaluators. He deals with an innovative course, the Australian Science Education Project (ASEP) which had planned to integrate formative evaluation within the development process. Special members of the project staff were assigned to evaluation, but they had to divide their time between evaluation activities on the one hand, and the development of diagnostic tests which were part of the individualized learning process featured by the ASEP curriculum package on the other hand. Thus, the internal evaluators played the following roles:

1. Developing curriculum materials, i.e. designing the diagnostic tests as well as the teacher guide on how to use these tests in the instructional process.
2. Selecting a variety of experts and procuring their comments on the curriculum materials.
3. Designing assessment instruments both structured and unstructured which would provide the kind of information which would be effective and highly usable in revising trial materials.
4. Collating evaluation data in a way and a at a time which makes them easily accessible and usable to the units' writers.
5. Evaluating the way feedback data were actually used in rewriting the curriculum materials.
6. Determining and selecting cost effective evaluation procedures.

It may be concluded that the best way to fulfil such roles is by including the evaluators as full members of the project staff. In this way formative evaluation has the best chance of actually contributing to course improvement in the sense advocated by Cronbach (1963). Since the mandate of the ASEP project was essentially to develop curriculum materials and make them available to potential users, no summative evaluation has been undertaken under the auspices of the project. Nevertheless, as indicated by Fraser, a variety of external evaluation studies of ASEP were carried out and many of them have been published. Although a variety of procedures have been employed in these summative studies, with special emphasis on classroom transactions, no discussion of the roles of these external evaluators is presented in the chapter.

Boud, Dynan, Parker and Ryan describe how they utilize the illuminative model of evaluation (Parlett and Hamilton, 1972) in the evaluation of the Physical Science course in Western Australia. According to the retrospective view of the evaluators, who enjoyed a high level of support from the Office of Education as well as from their target populations, they have served in their capacity as evaluators at one time or another, the following roles:

- describing and providing data on environmental and societal contexts;
- demonstrating credibility of the project to teachers and non-academics;
- providing feedback for refining and revision of the materials;
- providing feedback for improving implementation (e.g. informing teachers on students' perceptions);
- assessing the effectiveness of induction courses and support for teachers;
- providing information to future adapters;
- recording the evolution of the project especially for the benefit of future projects);
- assisting various interest groups to clarify their own perspective and to be aware of that of others so as to give a sound basis for decision making;
- identifying unforeseen issues *in situ*; ensuring that the *silent majority* is not forgotten;
- providing antidote to mis-information.

Since the evaluation was commissioned by the Department of Education the presence of evaluators conveyed the message of its serious commitment to the project. It also stressed the increasing acceptance of systematic evaluation as a necessary component of curriculum development.

Some interesting constraints and conflicts of interest are also described. For example, while evaluators want freedom to investigate and report, the sponsor does not agree to *carte blanch* . Evaluators are pressed to *first* satisfy the needs of the sponsor, *second* that of the developers and only *then* follow their own interests. In a way this is a clash between fidelity feedback and the illuminative approach.

Two chapters in this book deal with the Scottish Integrated Science course. The first, by *Kellington and Mitchell*, represents a rather traditional approach which seeks to find out to what extent the course objectives have been attained. There are, however, two important features of the study which are less common. First, since the course has been designed to be taught in mixed ability classes, there is an attempt to assess separately the achievement of students of different abilities. The second feature relates to the evolving roles of the evaluators who started as team members with no specific brief and gradually shaped up their functions to meet the emerging needs of the project. Eventually the evaluators:

served as advisers to the team on various issues;
provided suggestions for revision of materials;
developed assessment procedures and instruments to be used by the teachers;
helped in formulating expected outcomes;
helped in the promotion and dissemination of the course;
provided feedback on the achievement of the course objectives.

The advantages of being in-house evaluators (e.g. all evaluation procedures were agreed upon by the development team; results of evaluation were actually considered in decision making by the team), as well as disadvantages (e.g. the difficulty of ramaining unbiased; the pressure on the evaluators to promote dissemination; the limited time allocated to evaluation; the danger that the team makes decisions in order to satisfy the evaluator rather than for reasons that are valued by other team members) are indicated.

The major implications of this study are:

1. Evaluation has become an integral component of curriculum development in Scotland. Evaluation should commence at the beginning of course development.
2. Many of the procedures developed in this study have become a standard practice in the evaluation of other curriculum projects in Scotland.
3. It has been realized that evaluation and dissemination should not be confused. A relatively small selected sample of schools, conveniently located and willing to cooperate should be preferred for the first trials.

The study has also raised questions for further research such as the value of specifying objectives for teaching or the value of the guidelines for allocating different activities to individual students. Problems such as those just outlined have been recognized but not studied. Brown's chapter, on the other hand, presents a research approach to the evaluation of the same Scottish Integrated Science course. Rather than dealing with the extent to which specific expected students' outcomes have been attained, her approach emphasizes issues that are relevant to curriculum innovation in general. The study focuses on implementation and follows three stages. In the first stage evidence was collected on issues such as understanding of the course rationale and objectives by the teachers, their willingness to adapt the course, how they actually implemented the materials and what was the achievement. At the second stage hypotheses were formulated on factors which had influenced effectiveness. Lastly an explanatory system was developed which helped in the identification of issues salient to the operation of the course. A central role of the evaluator under this framework is to clarify the meaning of the innovation (e.g. integrated), identifying ambiguities (e.g. objectives selected _after_ selection of contents) and describing the events and processes as they actually take place. Typical issues highlighted in Brown's study are lack of congruence between teachers' concerns and those of the curriculum planners or the effect of subject departments on the success of innovations in schools.

A major constraint on the work of research-oriented evaluators is the pressure exerted by the sponsors who want to know how teachers can be persuaded to use the programme rather than to develop understanding of the processes and interactions associated with the use of the materials by the teachers. An important follow-up of research-oriented evaluation is a planned intervention which attempts to test directly specific hypotheses about the effectiveness of alternative approaches, based on the results of previous evaluation. This action-research may become one of the new and more promising roles of curriculum evaluators who have tended to leave the 'dirty work' of carrying out their recommendations to others.

The importance of conceptualizing evaluation findings under an explanatory system is illustrated also by _Elliott_. His focus is on some key concepts underlying teachers' evaluations of innovations. His chapter deals with an unusual curriculum package, the Progress of Learning Science (PLS), which attempts to train teachers to become better diagnosticians of their students' difficulties and needs. He finds that the key to success of such projects is understanding how teachers make decisions about change proposals. Three characteristics of most teachers in this regard are individualism, immediacy and concreteness. The PLS has apparently failed to present the materials in a way which would be conceived as practical by teachers.

Following are some of the problems identified in the implementation of PLS: teachers became frustrated as they found out that they were not able to cope with the recommended procedures of PLS, although they valued the purpose of these procedures; this inability hurt their self-image; teachers expressed disbelief in the freedom offered by PLS. The role of the evaluator which evolves under these circumstances is:

to identify problems and difficulties encountered by the programme (including negative effects);
to identify and/or develop an explanatory system which helps to conceptualize the findings;
to present the practical teacher points of view to the developers;
to cooperate with the developer in seeking solutions;
to try the solution (e.g. using the 'practical ethic' rather than a more theory-oriented approach) and evaluate the results.

The last two case studies are taken from the Israeli educational arena. Israel has projected a massive curriculum development in the last 20 years. As in many other countries, national curriculum development activities began with mathematics and the sciences at the senior high school level, gradually moving down to the junior high and to the elementary school levels. Because of historical reasons curriculum development for senior high and for elementary schools has been performed under the auspices of the Israel Science Teaching Center (ISTC), located in different universities; while the junior high materials for all school subjects has become the responsibility of the Israel Curriculum Center (ICC), administered directly by the Ministry of Education and Culture. The unique feature of both organizations is their permanent existence which allows for continuous activities. This is in sharp contrast to the more common curriculum and evaluation projects which are funded for a limited time, usually between three and five years at the most. The existence of a permanent organization such as the ICC or the ISTC has significant implications for curriculum development, implementation and evaluation. Tamir describes the evaluation of the Israel High School Biology Project (IHBP). Due respect was given to evaluation within the framework of the IHBP, and provision was made to guarantee its autonomy within the project. This was achieved by nominating an evaluator who had no responsibility in curriculum development but who occupied himself solely with designing and carrying out evaluation. Evaluation has made increasingly more and more contributions during the years. Here are some of the roles played by evaluators of IHBP during the years:

aid in decisions concerning the production of materials;
design assessment instruments for use by teachers and students in schools;
provide data to help in matching study materials to different types of students;
invent innovative evaluation measures and procedures (e.g. inquiry laboratory tests);
design matriculation examinations to reflect the aims, spirit and experiences of the IHBP;
provide information on perceptions and attitudes of teachers and students regarding various components of the programme;
help to qualify the use of the programme for various clients;
develop and maintain an item bank;
file, document and publish evaluation data;
develop standardized means of marking non-routine tests (e.g. plant identification tests, or inquiry-oriented laboratory examinations);
carry out follow-up evaluation to identify long-term effects;
design materials to train pre-service and in-service teachers in evaluation of student achievement and in interpretation of test data;
replicate studies in order to identify changes and trends;
identify relevant research topics and carry out research studies (e.g. cognitive preferences, or the concept of life held by different students);
provide assistance to the national educational system in various evaluation issues based on the cumulative experience of IHBP;

provide to university professors who teach the first year biology courses information about the level of knowledge and skills of their entering students so that they have a sound basis for planning and teaching.

Arieh Lewy describes the evaluation activities of ICC. Some of the characteristics of the ICC evaluation follow.

1. Since the ICC was set up with the aim of introducing curriculum reform in the schools, its major activity has been the production of innovative programmes and instructional materials; hence, evaluation was designed to aid and serve this process of production and to help in improving the quality of the products.
2. The establishment of a separate Evaluation Unit helped to maintain its autonomy and independence. Yet, its location within the ICC enhanced close cooperation with the different curriculum development units, and helped the evaluators in locating critical junctions where evaluation evidence would be most useful.
3. Evaluation studies were initiated either by the members of the curriculum development projects or by the Evaluation Unit. Contacts between the two were maintained by project members who acted as liaison persons. The actual selection of topics for study was made by the mutual consent of both groups.
4. Since most curriculum projects faced similar evaluation problems, a standard procedure of serial evaluation activities aimed at six stages (Lewy, 1977) was developed and implemented. It resulted in small, limited, focused studies which provided specific information to help in making decisions at critical stages. A set of minimum evaluation requirements was also established. These requirements included expert judgement of the quality of the instructional materials, observing test classes and assessing students' cognitive achievement at the end of the first trial against stated programme objectives.
5. The major responsibility of the Evaluation Unit was in guiding the procedures

of sampling, in instrument development and in training people in the collection, analysis and reporting of data, which facilitated the quick completion of focused studies.

6. The existence of the Evaluation Unit constituted a permanent reminder to project teams of the need for conducting evaluations and for examining the quality of the new curricula.

7. Fruitful cooperation and mutual trust between the Evaluation Unit and development projects has been successfully established, presumably due to the low profile kept by the members of the Evaluation Unit.

8. The serial evaluation activities of the ICC were geared mainly to the curriculum development teams who were to use the evaluation results for decision-making, and to a lesser extent to their superiors. Timeliness required that many reports be made informally, either orally or in draft form, yet the need for systematic formal reporting to a multiple clientele has been recognized.

It may be worthwhile to list the roles played by evaluators in a system such as the ICC and compare them with those listed in previous chapters in which evaluation accompanied a single curriculum project. The evaluators working within the ICC framework have played during the years the following roles:

- aid in decisions concerning the production of materials;
- alert development teams to potential difficulties;
- point to alternatives in design and development;
- create a pattern of evaluation procedures, establish minimum evaluation requirements, develop techniques to enhance timeliness;
- serve as a reminder for the necessity of evaluation;
- provide technical facilities for evaluation;
- meet the needs of several projects simultaneously;
- help to qualify the use of programmes for various clients;
- motivate development teams to carry out

evaluation;
assist and guide projects initiated evaluation (e.g. sampling; design of instruments; data analysis);
select topics most appropriate for study;
file evaluation data;
replicate studies in different projects.

The brief overview of the case studies shows the enormous development of curriculum evaluation in the last 20 years as well as the variety of approaches and patterns that have evolved. The potential roles of evaluators in curriculum development are well recognized. It is up to curriculum sponsors, developers, users and evaluators to choose the kinds of evaluation activities which would best meet their needs and preferences. The interests of each of these groups are equally legitimate in making the choices. Hence, a process of deliberation and negotiation among these four interest groups is to be maintained continuously during the process of curriculum development. In this context curriculum development does not terminate when the first commercial edition of materials is published but continues as long as the programme is used in schools and is periodically being revised.

REFERENCES

Cronbach, L.J. (1963) 'Evaluation for Course Improvement', *Teachers College Record*, *64*, 672-83

Lewy, A. (ed.) (1977) *Handbook of Curriculum Evaluation*, Longman, New York

Parlett, M. and Hamilton, D. (1972) 'Evaluation as Illumination: A New Approach to the Study of Innovatory Programs', Occasional Paper No. 9, Centre for Research in Educational Sciences, University of Edinburgh

CONTRIBUTORS

DAVID BOUD is currently Senior Lecturer in the Tertiary Education Research Centre at the University of New South Wales. Formerly he was a Visiting Fellow in the School of Applied Science at the Western Australian Institute of Technology.

SALLY BROWN is Senior Research Fellow at Stirling University (Scotland). Her research and publications have been broadly concerned with science education, curriculum innovation and assessment. Until recently she was seconded to the Scottish Education Department as Research Adviser with responsibility for a programme of 25 research projects.

MUREDACH DYNAN is currently Senior Lecturer in Curriculum Studies, Faculty of Education, WAIT. He is involved in a major study of the implementation of the Physical Science course in Western Australia.

JOHN ELLIOTT is Tutor in Curriculum Studies at the Cambridge Institute of Education. He has written extensively about the theory and practice of curriculum evaluation and educational action-research. He directed the Ford teaching Project (1972-5), the SSRC Cambridge Accountability Project (1978-80), and the Schools Council Project on Teacher-Pupil Interaction and the Quality of Learning (1981-3). From 1976 to 1978 he was Evaluator of the Schools Council Progress in Learning Science Project and is currently assisting with a major review of police training in the United Kingdom.

BARRY J. FRASER is Head of the School of Curriculum Studies and Director of the Science and Mathematics Education Centre at the Western Australian Institute of Technology in Perth. He is author of *Learning Environment in Curriculum Evaluation* and *Annotated Bibliography of Curriculum Evaluation Literature*.

HULDA GROBMAN, Ed.D., currently Professor of Health Education at St Louis University Medical Center, served as Staff Consultant on Evaluation for the BSCS from 1960 to 1965, the period during which the experimental editions of High School Biology were being developed. She has written extensively on developmental curriculum projects and their evaluation.

STEUART H. KELLINGTON has been an evaluator for the new materials for Scottish Integrated Science and was then involved in the development of assessment procedures for science in the secondary school. He is now Vice Principal of Burnley College of Arts and Technology, Burnley, Lancashire, UK, and maintains a strong interest in science education and educational management.

ARIEH LEWY is an Associate Professor at Tel-Aviv University and Head of the Evaluation Unit, Israel Curriculum Center, Ministry of Education. He is Editor of the international review journal *Studies of Educational Evaluation* and of the Curriculum Section of the *International Encyclopedia of Education* (Pergamon Press, Oxford). His main publications are *Handbook of Curriculum Evaluation* (Longmans 1977) and *Evaluation Roles* (Gordon & Breach 1981). His fields of interest encompass school assessment, curriculum evaluation and cross-national comparative studies.

ALISON C. MITCHELL was an Evaluator for the new materials for Scottish Integrated Science. She is now Director of the project 'School based assessment using item banking', based in Jordan Hill College of Education, Glasgow, UK. The project is concerned with the use of microcomputers in schools for various forms of assessment including criterion-referenced assessment.

LESLEY PARKER is currently Lecturer in Education at The University of Western Australia. Her research focuses on the education of girls, especially in the physical sciences.

ANTHONY S. RYAN is Head of the School of Foundation Studies in Education at the Western Australian

Institute of Technology. His research and development interests include school and programme evaluation and the evaluation of teachers.

PINCHAS TAMIR is a Professor at the School of Education and the Israel Science Teaching Center, Hebrew University, Jerusalem. He received his Ph.D. at Cornell University in 1968. Since 1969 he has been the Director of the Israel High School Biology Project. He has published numerous chapters in books and more than 100 research papers in science education, curriculum and educational psychology journals, mainly in the USA, Canada and the UK. In addition he has published numerous papers in Hebrew, in Israel, and edited several books.

His research deals with topics such as curriculum development, evaluation, teacher education, instruction, cognitive preferences and various aspects of science education. He is the recipient of the 1977 Palmer O. Johnson Award of the American Educational Research Association for the best research paper. He has presented papers at numerous professional and international conferences and served as visiting professor in Australia, Mexico, Canada and Norway, as well as a number of universities in the USA.

INDEX

INDEX

INDEX

For Product Safety Concerns and Information please contact our EU
representative GPSR@taylorandfrancis.com
Taylor & Francis Verlag GmbH, Kaufingerstraße 24, 80331 München, Germany

www.ingramcontent.com/pod-product-compliance
Lightning Source LLC
LaVergne TN
LVHW020710110826
845149LV00012B/2191
* 9 7 8 1 1 3 8 3 2 2 0 2 8 *